CISTERCIAN STUDIES SERIES: NUMBER FORTY-SIX

D1559996

pachomian koinonia

Volume Two

Pachomian Chronicles and Rules

pachomian koinonia

the lives, Rules, and Other Writings of
Saint pachomius and his Disciples

CISTERCIAN STUDIES SERIES: NUMBER FORTY-SIX

pachomian koinonia

Volume Two

pachomian Chronicles and Rules

Translated, with an introduction,

by

Armand Veilleux
Monk of Mistassini

Cistercian Publications Inc.
Kalamazoo, Michigan
1981

© Cistercian Publications, Inc., 1981
Kalamazoo, Michigan 49008

Translation of the works contained in this volume
was made possible in part by a translator's grant from the
National Endowment for the Humanities,
Washington, D.C.

Typeset by the Carmelites of Indianapolis

Available in Britain and Europe
through A. R. Mowbray & Co Ltd.
St. Thomas House   Becket Street
Oxford OX1   1SJ

Library of Congress Cataloging in Publication Data

Pachomian chronicles and rules.

(Pachomian koinonia; v. 2)   (Cistercian studies series; 46)
1. Monasticism and religious orders—Early church, ca. 30–600.   2. Monasticism and
religious orders—Egypt.   3. Monasticism and religious orders—Rules.
I. Veilleux, Armand.   II. Series.   III. Series: Cistercian studies series; 46.

BR1720.P23P3 vol. 2   [BX2460]   281'.3s   [271'.8]   80-21802
ISBN   (hardcover)   0-87907-846-4 (v. 2)
       (paperback)   0-87907-946-0

Typeset and printed in the United States of America

CONTENTS

ıntroduction

paralıpomena

A LONG WITH THE LIVES of Pachomius, there is in Greek a series of anecdotes known as the *Paralipomena* (the 'leftovers' or the 'things omitted'). This name was assigned them by Papebroch who published them in his *Acta Sanctorum* along with the First Greek Life (G¹) from the Florence Manuscript.[1] For his edition in the *Sancti Pachomii Vitae Graecae*[2] F. Halkin was able to use the Ambrosian fragments as well, but unfortunately not the Athenian manuscript.

We have many indirect witnesses to this text. The first are the various Greek Lives that have either completely or partly integrated them.[3] But most importantly, we have a very valuable Syriac translation from the sixth century that we find in various ascetical collections in Syriac, chiefly in the *Paradise of the Fathers* of the Nestorian monk Anân Isho, composed at the request of Patriarch George (661–680).[4]

The various witnesses to the text of the *Paralipomena* can be divided into two groups. Or, more exactly, the Florence manuscript — used by Papebroch and Halkin as the basis of their editions — is distinct from all the others in the order of the narratives and in the textual tradition. Of the other witnesses, the Syriac translation is undoubtedly the best. Our translation, however, is based on Halkin's critical edition of the Greek text.

All the Greek Lives, except G¹ and G⁴, have incorporated the *Paralipomena* in different ways and to various extents. Yet the re-

1

lationship of the *Paralipomena* to G[1] is difficult to ascertain. G[1], in fact, does not use them, but has a few parallel narratives. According to the early Bollandists, the author of G[1] wanted to complement his work by the addition of the *Paralipomena*. The Bollandists of 1932 considered that the *Paralipomena* were composed in order to complement a form of G[1] more primitive than the one we know, and that some of these anecdotes were later added to G[1] under a revised version.[5] According to Lefort, the authors of the Lives made use of collections of *Ascetica* from which our *Paralipomena* depend directly and consequently he takes the *Paralipomena* as the point of departure for his study of all the Lives.[6] But P. Peeters rightly argues that compilations 'of such an enigmatic quality' are too fragile a basis for the genealogical classification of the Lives.[7]

The author of the *Paralipomena*, like the last redactor of G[1], at times uses a terminology alien to pachomian usage. It remains all the same an important source for the knowledge of early pachomian monasticism.

lettER of Bishop ammon

Bishop Ammon's letter to Theophilos and Theophilos' answer to Ammon are found in the two most important manuscripts that have transmitted G[1] and the *Paralipomena* to us: the *Florentinus* and the *Atheniensis*. Papebroch published the Letter in the *Acta Sanctorum* according to the *Florentinus* text.[8] He says that he saw it also in the *Ambrosianus*, but it cannot be found there at present and it is unlikely to have been there at Papebroch's time. The text of Theophilos' answer was reproduced by Migne in his *Patrologia Graeca* among the *Theophili Alexandrini episcopi epistolae ad diversos*.[9] Halkin published a critical edition of Ammon's letter and of Theophilos' answer in his *Sancti Pachomii Vitae Graecae*, according to the *Florentinus*.[10]

Who were Ammon and Theophilos? Although Lefort expresses some doubt,[11] it is very probable that Theophilos was the Patriarch of Alexandria (385–412). As for Ammon, we can gather from the details given in his letter that he spent three years as a pachomian monk at Phbow, where he arrived in 352, six years after Pachomius' death. In 355 he left for Nitria, where he lived many years before becoming bishop.

The authenticity and the historical value of Ammon's Letter, generally acknowledged by the historians,[12] were radically questioned by L.-T. Lefort,[13] whose conclusions were in turn refuted by P. Peeters[14] and especially by D.J. Chitty.[15] A. Favale, in his study on Theophilos of Alexandria, also defends the authenticity of Ammon's Letter which was presumably addressed to the Patriarch around 399-400.[16]

Ammon lived in Phbow under Theodore, for whom he developed a great admiration, and his letter is something of a panegyric. What he remembered of Theodore and of Pachomius was not the important events of their lives or their outstanding virtues but rather their spirit of prophecy and their miracles. Ammon, who lived many years in Nitria after his three years at Phbow, used a terminology and evinced preoccupations that are not particularly pachomian, but he had a good memory for dates. Chitty has shown that his chronological indications are accurate and often more reliable than those of the Lives.[17]

ÐRAGUET FRAGMENTS

R. Draguet published two pachomian fragments that are probably only two samples of many similar narratives existing in unpublished manuscripts.

The first fragment[18] is a pachomian anecdote interpolated in a Greek manuscript of the Lausiac History (Vatican Gr. 2091). This manuscript, of Italo-Greek origin, is from the end of the eleventh century, and therefore only a little posterior to the *Florentinus* transcribed in Northern Italy in 1020-1021.

Draguet considers the text of the story full of copticisms, from the linguistic as well as the stylistic point of view, and thinks it takes its biblical quotations from the Coptic translation.

The context of the anecdote, according to Draguet, fits in well with what the most ancient Coptic fragments tell us about the difficult beginnings of the pachomian *Koinonia* and has the same tone of authenticity. There is a great similarity between one element of this anecdote and the apophthegm Besarion 7. In a recent study Adalbert de Vogüé found also some points of contact with another apophthegm — Macarios the Egyptian 21 — and with a story from chapter 18 of the Lausiac History.[19] And he concludes that our anecdote was a composition, without any real pachomian character, elaborated from those three sources. The argument has some weight but does not seem utterly convincing.

The second fragment[20] comes from the very valuable manuscript Karakallou 251, from which Draguet published a text that was the source of two apophthegmata of John Kolobos[21] and an 'Isaian' section of nine apophthegmata.[22] Zanos, the main character of the adventure narrated in this text, introduces himself as a monk from 'the monastery of the Tabennesiots', or 'the monastery of Pachomius'. Although this story has no parallel in the Lives, its *realia* can easily be harmonized with the historical setting they describe.

the histoRy of the monks in Egypt

The *History of the Monks in Egypt* describes the life of the monks of Lower Egypt.[23] The author, however, tells us something also about a monk called Ammon who was the father of a monastery of pachomian monks. We do not know which one of the pachomian monasteries the author of the *History* visited. As he wrote in 394, his visit there must have been during the time Horsiesios was still the father of the pachomian *Koinonia* or very shortly after his death at an unknown date after 387. From the *History of the Monks in Egypt* we have translated only the pertinent chapter eighteen.

the lausiac history of palladius[24]

The chronicle about the Tabennesiots which we read in chapters 32-34 of the *Lausiac History* of Palladius is without doubt the most popular piece of pachomian hagiography. The historical value of that chronicle does not, however, justify that popularity.

Modern criticism has been less than indulgent to Palladius. The historical value of the *Lausiac History* was first attacked by H. Weingarten a century ago.[25] In spite of the efforts of O. Zöckler to 'defend' Palladius,[26] R. Reitzenstein went still further than Weingarten, claiming that, in a large part of the *Lausiac History*, Palladius reproduced already existing documents among which he interpolated some '*Wir-Stücke*' in order to give to the whole the appearance of a travel diary.[27] Without going so far, and in spite of the defence of Palladius by Dom Cuthbert Butler, the learned editor of the *Lausiac History*, more recent critics have continued to be very severe.

W. Bousset applied Reitzenstein's theory to Chapters 32-34 and tried to rediscover the source used by Palladius by suppressing all the '*Wir-Stücke*' of that chronicle. He thought he could arrive in this way at the text preserved in the Greek Lives ($G^{2\cdot3\cdot5\cdot6}$) and the Latin Life of Pachomius.[28] But Halkin showed that these chapters of the Greek Lives depend, in fact, on the text of the *Lausiac History*, through a common source,[29] and H. van Cranenburgh has recently showed that the Rule of the Angel in the Latin Life also comes from the *Lausiac History*, although from a source distinct from that of the Greek Lives.[30]

In a long study of chapter 32 of the *Lausiac History*, R. Draguet arrived at the conclusion that the style of that chapter is different from Palladius' usual style and that Palladius was using a written source.[31] This conclusion is firmly established. Draguet proposes a few other secondary conclusions which are less certain: Palladius' source was Coptic, as the quantity and the nature of the copticisms seem to prove.[32] Palladius may have used the Coptic text, but more probably he had access to a Greek translation. The document was composed in the semi-anchoritic milieu of Lower Egypt. Finally, it is probable that the same conclusions could apply also to chapters 33 and 34.

De Vogüé has called attention to a few possible points of contact between chapter 32 of the *Lausiac History* and some texts of Horsiesios.[33] Interesting as these points of contact are, they are certainly not important enough to demonstrate the pachomian authenticity of the Rule of the Angel, the main element of this palladian chronicle.

Our pachomian sources are not lacking in miracles and even numerous apparitions of angels. But the legend of Pachomius receiving from an angel a rule ready made and written on a brazen tablet is completely foreign to the tradition of pachomian origins. The beginning of pachomian cenobitism was difficult and painful, and it is in the light of his experience and his failures that Pachomius gradually drew his regulations from the Scriptures.

A study of the contents of the Rule of the Angel brings us to the same conclusion. Although Tillemond[34] and Ladeuze[35] had demonstrated the unlikeliness of some prescriptions of the angel and showed some of the elements of the palladian chronicle that were in formal contradiction with the most reliable sources of the pachomian *corpus*, Butler considered the Rule of the Angel as the most authentic summary of the earliest Christian rule,[36] and Leipoldt spoke of it as a more recent 'Bearbeitung' of the regulations of Pachomius.[37]

Now that we have excellent critical editions of the authentic rules of Pachomius and that the authenticity of Jerome's version is confirmed by the Coptic fragments that have been found, no hesitation is possible. The famous Rule of the Angel is a document composed in Lower Egypt by someone who had only a very superficial knowledge of the pachomian *Koinonia*.[38]

Δpophthegmata

The number of pachomian *apophthegmata* found in the collections of the Sayings of the Desert Fathers is very small. These collections come mostly from Lower Egypt, and the monastic centers of Lower and Upper Egypt were separated not only by geographical distance and dialectal differences, but also by a different form of spirituality and divergent ascetical practices. In this volume we have translated the only three *apophthegmata* not taken from the *Coptic* or *First Greek Lives.* Two of them were later integrated in the *Third Greek Life.*

The Rules of Pachomius and His Disciples

When Pachomius wanted to transform into a community the group of men who had come to live with him and whom he had served for a few years, he drew up for them a series of rules he took from the Scriptures.[39] Later on, when his sister also decided to live the monastic life and was joined by other women, he sent them the rules he had written for the brothers.[40] When he founded new monasteries or adopted existing communities into the *Koinonia,* he established in the new foundations the same rules as in the monastery of Tabennesi.[41]

These rules were certainly not a set text. They constantly evolved with the evolution of the *Koinonia,* during Pachomius' lifetime as well as under his successors. We have four series of regulations attributed to Pachomius and one to Horsiesios. This last exists only in Coptic while the former, known for centuries only in a Latin translation made in the fifth century by Saint Jerome, and through some Greek *Excerpta,* are now also partially known in Coptic.

THE PACHOMIANA LATINA. In 404 Jerome translated into Latin a series of documents attributed to Pachomius and his disciples Theodore and Horsiesios. All these documents came from the monastery of Metanoia (Canopos) near Alexandria, where pachomian monks had been introduced by the Patriarch Theophilos. The books were in Coptic, but Jerome translated them from a Greek translation made for him.[42]

The *Pachomiana Latina*, as they are called, include not only the Rule of Pachomius, but also his Letters, one Letter from Theodore, and Horsiesios' Testament, called in Latin the *Liber Orsiesii.*

Now that we have the Coptic text of part of the documents translated by Jerome, we are able to evaluate his fidelity as a translator. The comparison reveals that the Coptic original of the text translated by him corresponded substantially to the Coptic fragments we have, and that he followed it faithfully on the whole. But we realize also that Jerome was not a very scrupulous translator: he often introduced a few words of explanation, corrected his original, or paraphrased.[43]

THE COPTIC FRAGMENTS. The Rule of Pachomius (like all the pachomian legislative texts) was evidently written in Sahidic, the language of Upper Egypt, and the only idiom known to most of the pachomian monks and to Pachomius himself. Of the several copies of those regulations that must have circulated in the various monasteries only a few fragments have survived.

Lefort in 1919 announced his first discovery of a Coptic fragment, which he published in *Le Muséon* of 1927[44] with two folios from the Egyptian Museum identified in 1916 by H. Munier.[45] It was reprinted in 1932 as an *appendix* to the *Pachomiana Latina* of Boon.[46] Another fragment, identified later (the Michigan fragment) was presented by Lefort in *Le Muséon* of 1935.[47] Finally he published all these fragments again, with a French translation, in 1956, in the *Corpus Scriptorum Christianorum Orientalium.*[48] In 1962 H. Bacht identified the *Proemium* of the *Praecepta et Instituta* in a fragment Lefort had misplaced among the works of Horsiesios.[49]

All in all, we have in Coptic ¶¶ 88-130 of the *Praecepta* and all the *Praecepta et Instituta*, although ¶ 130 of the *Praecepta* and ¶ 18 of the *Praecepta et Instituta* are incomplete.

THE GREEK EXCERPTA. A Greek translation of the Rule of Pachomius probably existed at a very early period for the use of the Greek-speaking monks who did not know Coptic and whose first housemaster was Theodore the Alexandrian. Saint Jerome had a copy in his hands in 404, when he made the Latin version. Unfortunately no manuscript of that Greek translation has survived. But we have a collection of Greek *Excerpta* which, just like the short recension of the Latin text of Jerome, represents an adaptation of the pachomian rule to a monastic organization different from that of the pachomian monasteries.

The *Excerpta* have been preserved in several manuscripts that can be divided into two families. Lefort gave a critical edition of both series in *Le Muséon* of 1924.[50] It has been reprinted along with the Coptic fragments in the *Appendix* to A. Boon's *Pachomiana Latina*.[51]

THE ETHIOPIAN TRANSLATIONS. The Rule of Pachomius can be found in several Ethiopian munuscripts. But we should not lose sight of the fact that these manuscripts usually give three distinct documents under the name of the 'Rule' of Pachomius. The first is a translation of Palladius' 'Rule of the Angel' and the third is a late Ethiopian compilation devoid of real value. The second document is a translation of the Greek *Excerpta* made from a manuscript of the second family (F.M.N.). Since the Greek text is well preserved and the Ethiopian version is not always faithful, its interest is very limited.

The Ethiopian text was published by A. Dillmann in his *Chrestomatia aethiopica* from only one manuscript.[52] O. Löfgren, after publishing a critical apparatus of the first two of these three rules, based on five other manuscripts,[53] also published a Swedish translation.[54] A few other translations existed already in English,[55] German,[56] and French,[57] all based on Dillmann's text. Another edition of the Ethiopian text, with a Latin translation, was published by V. Arras in 1963.[58]

THE 'STRUCTURE' OF THE PACHOMIAN RULE. In the complete text

that we find in Jerome's translation, the Rule of Pachomius is composed of four distinct books called in Latin: *Praecepta, Praecepta et Instituta, Praecepta atque Judicia, Praecepta ac Leges.*

The *Praecepta atque Judicia* are a kind of 'Penitential' measuring out the penances for various types of offences. The *Praecepta ac Leges* regulate the *synaxis* in the individual houses every evening and deal with the responsibilities of the housemaster. The *Praecepta et Instituta* are addressed to the housemaster who, with his house, was in charge of the weekly service in the general assembly of all the brothers. The *Praecepta* were probably, at least originally, the book of the superior of the monastery, dealing first of all with everything that concerned the morning assembly of all the brothers.

The *Praecepta* are by far the longest of these texts and the most composite in character. The repetitions and the various conclusions indicating different blocks of rules show that the series of precepts was periodically complemented and expanded according to the new needs of the *Koinonia.*

Attempts have been made at establishing a chronological order for the four sections of the Rule, and it has been claimed that the *Praecepta et Instituta* were the most ancient collection and the *Praecepta* the latest one.[59] The whole argument starts from the postulate that one of these four series must have been composed before the others and that each one of them should represent the state of pachomian legislation at some specific point in history. Since they have different purposes, it seems to us much more natural to assume that they were parallel texts which evolved at the same time in different contexts, along with the development of the *Koinonia.* Against the theory that the *Praecepta et Instituta* were the first series of texts is the very strong argument that they refer very explicitly to existing sets of rules, one of them being in all probability the *Praecepta* themselves—although perhaps an earlier and shorter version of the *Praecepta.*[60]

AUTHENTICITY. Pachomius and Horsiesios wrote some series of rules, and Theodore did probably the same. In 404, about sixty years after Pachomius' death and probably more than ten to fif-

teen years after Horsiesios', Jerome received the text of a pachomian Rule to be translated into Latin. The text came from a monastery near Alexandria where some Tabennesiots (i.e. pachomian
monks) had lived since c. 390.[61] These texts are therefore pachomian in at least the broad sense of the word. How much of them and
what part of them can claim Pachomius himself as their author, we
do not know for certain, and none of the recent studies have
brought any decisive light to the problem. We can assume that a
small group of precepts were composed by Pachomius himself and
that this core had been added to over the years. But we have no
means of knowing for sure which precepts are the most original.
And we cannot rule out the possibility that the text transmitted to
Jerome from the monastery of Metanoia had undergone some
modifications under the influence of the surrounding monastic
communities of Lower Egypt.

If we compare the Rules, as a whole, and the Lives, we find some
points of contact, but we are mostly surprised by the difference of
atmosphere. Granted that an hagiographical text does not have
the same style as a legislative one, it remains obvious all the same
that there is no trace in the Lives of a great number of detailed
legislations described in the Rules. For example, there is no mention in the Life of the Office of the Six Prayers, so important in the
Rules (if we except one mention in G¹ 58-59, which is an addition
borrowed from the Rule by a late redactor).[62] One could argue
that such an Office was a primitive custom, witnessed to in the
Praecepta et Instituta, that had disappeared at the time the Lives
were written. But the first primitive Lives were written shortly after
Pachomius' death, and the same mention of the Six Prayers is still
found in the Regulations attributed to Horsiesios.

Unfortunately we do not have the beginning of the *Praecepta* in
Coptic; and the Prologue of the *Praecepta et Instituta,* which we
have in Coptic, does not mention the author.

THE REGULATIONS OF HORSIESIOS. E. Amélineau published in
1888, with a French translation, a series of precepts which, follow-

ing Révillout, he attributed to Schenoute.[63] J. Leipoldt included them in his *Sinuthii Vita et opera* in 1913,[64] although he had some doubts about the attribution. He found the style of this document very different from Schenoute's style, and he concluded that although the document could have been elaborated in a schenoutian monastery, it must have been written in a period posterior to Schenoute.

Lefort published again the same document under the title 'Regulations of Horsiesios'.[65] He argued from the vocabulary that the text came from a pachomian rather than a schenoutian milieu, and this first conclusion seems well grounded. Then, on the basis of the fact that the Life mentions Horsiesios making new regulations and does not say anything similar about Theodore, he concluded that the author must be Horsiesios. This second conclusion is much less certain than the first. There is at least one passage of these regulations that leads us to believe that the author may be one of Horsiesios' successors at the head of the *Koinonia*. The author mentions indeed that various superiors of the *Koinonia* after Pachomius made new regulations.[66] If the author were Horsiesios, he could refer only to Theodore, since Petronios, who was superior only for a few days cannot have written new regulations during his illness. Since the author is speaking of various successors of Pachomius, we tend to think that he wrote at least after Horsiesios' death. Leaving the question of the authorship of this document open, we have kept the traditional name 'Regulations of Horsiesios.'

These observations about the Regulations of Horsiesios are not without serious consequences, because they may oblige us to revise our conceptions about the date of the pachomian rules as a whole. Although these Regulations are more of a commentary than a code of law, their terminology and their style have much in common with some parts of the Rule of Pachomius, especially the *Praecepta et Instituta*[67] and they correspond to the same stage in the development of the pachomian legislation.

CONCLUSION. It seems to us that the pachomian legislation is a living reality that grew from a few precepts written by Pachomius himself and that it was adapted periodically to the needs of new situations. The four series of Precepts known as the Rule of Pachomius and the other series known as the Regulations of Horsiesios, taken as a whole, are witnesses to the state of that legislation at the end of the fourth century.

Notes to the Introduction

[1]*Acta Sanctorum*, May, III, 1686[3], pp.44*-53*; Latin translation, ibid. pp. 333-345.

[2]Pp. 122-165.

[3]G[2], G[3] and Den. We could add G[5] and G[6], but both follow G[3] in this section.

[4]The text was first published by P. Bedjan in Vol. V of his *Acta Martyrum et Sanctorum* (Paris-Leipzig, 1895) pp. 122-176 and 701-704. F. Nau gave a French translation of the Syriac text facing the parallel Greek text of G[6], in PO IV,5 (J. Bousquet and F. Nau, *Histoire de saint Pacôme. Une rédaction grecque inédite des Ascetica publiée avec la traduction de la version syriaque* (Paris, 1907) pp 430-480 and 494-498. The Syriac text was published again with an English translation by E.A.W. Budge in *The Book of Paradise* (London, 1904). Budge published a revised translation in *The Paradise or Garden of the Holy Fathers* (London, 1907) I:283-316; he reproduced again the same translation in *Stories of the Holy Fathers* (Oxford, 1934) pp. 373-416. Anân Isho was an outstanding translator; and Thomas of Margâ dedicated a full chapter to him and another to his *Paradise of the Fathers* in his 'Monastic History'. See E.A.W. Budge, *The Book of Governors, The Historia Monastica of Thomas of Margâ a.d. 840* (London, 1893); the Syriac text of these two chapters is in Budge, Vol. I, pp. 78-80 and 86-88, and the translation in Vol. II, pp. 174-179 and 189-192.

[5]See F. Halkin, *Sancti Pachomii Vitae Graecae*, pp. 88*-105*.

[6]See L.-T. Lefort, *Les Vies coptes*, pp. XIX-XXVII.

[7]See P. Peeters, 'Le dossier copte de s. Pacôme...' in *AnBoll* 64 (1946) 263-267.

[8]*Acta Sanctorum*, May, III, 1686[3], pp. 54*-61*; Latin translation, pp. 346-355.

[9]PG 65:61.

[10]F. Halkin, *Sancti Pachomii Vitae Graecae*, pp. 97-121.

[11]See L.-T. Lefort, *Les Vies coptes...*, p. LII.

[12]See for example the importance given to this document by A. Ehrhard, 'Zur literarhistorischen und theologischen Würdigung der Texte', in W.E. Crum, *Der Papyruscodex*, pp. 132-145.

[13]See L.-T. Lefort, *Les Vies coptes*, pp. L-LXII.

[14]See P. Peeters, 'Le dossier copte de s. Pacôme', in *AnBoll* 64 (1946) 276.

[15]See D.J. Chitty, 'Pachomian Sources Reconsidered', in *JEH* 5 (1954) 43.

[16]See A. Favale, 'Teofilo d'Alessandria', in *Sal* 18 (1956) 223-224.

[17]See D.J. Chitty, 'A Note on the Chronology of Pachomian Foundations', in *Studia Patristica*, Vol. II (*TU* - 80) (Berlin, 1962) pp. 266-269.

[18]R. Draguet, 'Un morceau grec inédit des Vies de Pachôme apparié à un texte d'Evagre en partie inconnu', in *Muséon* 70 (1957):267-306.

[19]A. de Vogüé, 'L'anecdote pachômienne du "Vaticanus graecus" 2091. Son origine et ses sources', in *RSH* 49 (1973): 401-419.

[20]R. Draguet, 'Un Paralipomenon pachômien inconnu dans le Karakallou 251', in *Mélanges Tisserant* II, (*ST* - 232), Vatican 1964, pp. 55-61.

[21] See R. Draguet, 'A la source de deux apophtegmes grecs, P.G. LXV, Jean Colobos 24 et 32', in *Byzantion* 32 (*Mélanges P. van den Ven*, 1962), pp. 53–61.

[22] See R. Draguet, 'Une section "isaïenne" d'apophtegmes dans le Karakallou 251', in *Byzantion* 35 (1965): 44–61.

[23] A.J. Festugière, *Historia Monachorum in Aegypto. Edition critique du texte grec*, (*Subsidia hagiographica* - 34), Brussels 1961.

[24] C. Butler, *The Lausiac History of Palladius*, 2 Vol. (*Texts and Studies* — VI, 1-2), Cambridge 1898-1904.

[25] See H. Weingarten, 'Der Ursprung des Mönchtums in nachconstantinischen Zeitalter', in *Zeitschrift für Kirchengeschichte* 1 (1876):1-35 (especially 24-30) and 545-574. These articles were published the following year in the form of a book: *Der Ursprung des Mönchtums*, Gotha 1877. The author defended his position again in his article *Mönchtum* in Herzog-Plitt, *Encyclopädie für protestantische Theologie* 10 (1882), pp. 758 ff.

[26] See O. Zöckler, article *Palladius* in Herzog-Plitt, *Encyclopädie* (see note 25) 11 (1883):173-175. *Idem, Askese und Mönchtum*, Frankfort 1897², Vol. I, pp. 217-220.

[27] See R. Reitzenstein, *Historia Monachorum und Historia Lausiaca*, (*Forschungen zur Religion und Literatur des Alten und Neuen Testaments* - 24), Göttingen 1916.

[28] See W. Bousset, 'Komposition und Charakter der Historia Lausiaca' in NGG 1917, pp. 191-192; *Idem*, 'Zur Komposition der Historia Lausiaca', in *Zeitschrift für die neutestamentliche Wissenschaft und die Kunde der älteren Kirche* 21 (1922):81-98. Bousset was less explicit about this in another posthumous study published in his *Apophthegmata. Studien zur Geschichte des ältesten Mönchtums*, Tübingen 1923, pp. 209-224.

[29] F. Halkin, 'L'Histoire Lausiaque et les Vies grecques de S. Pachôme', in *AnBoll* 48 (1930):257-301.

[30] H. Van Cranenburgh, 'La "Regula Angeli" dans la Vie latine de saint Pachôme', in *Muséon* 76 (1963):165-194, especially 189.

[31] R. Draguet, 'Le Chapitre de HL sur les Tabennésiotes dérive-t-il d'une source copte?' in *Muséon* 57 (1944):53-145 and 58 (1945):15-95.

[32] R. Draguet found a Coptic source to another chapter of the Lausiac History. See: 'Une nouvelle source copte de Pallade, le ch. 8 (Amoun)', in *Muséon* 60 (1947):227-255.

[33] A. de Vogüé, 'Points de contact du chapitre XXXII de l'Histoire Lausiaque avec les écrits d'Horsièse', in *StMon* 13 (1971):291-294.

[34] See Tillemond, *Mémoires pour servir à l'histoire ecclésiastique des six premiers siècles*, Vol. VII. First edition of Venice, revised and corrected. Venice 1732, pp. 679-682.

[35] See P. Ladeuze, *Etude sur le cénobitisme pakhômien*, pp. 256-266.

[36] In *Cambridge Medieval History* I (1911), p. 524.

[37] J. Leipoldt, *Schenute von Atripe und die Entstehung des national ägyptischen Christentums*, (*TU* - 25), Leipzig 1903, p. 98, n. 4.

[38] The 'Rule of the Angel' has been translated in several oriental languages; see Ph. Gobillot, in *Recherches de science religieuse*, 12 (1927), p. 60, n. 2. Many Greek and Latin recensions can be found in M.P.B. Albers, *Sancti Pacomii Regulae monasticae*, pp. 60-75 and 87-90.

[39] See SBo 23; G¹ 25; S¹ 17.

[40] See SBo 27; G¹ 32.

[41] See SBo 49, 50, 51, etc. (= G¹ 54, etc.).

[42] For a critical edition of the *corpus* translated by Jerome, see A. Boon, *Pachomiana latina. Règle et épîtres de s. Pachôme, épître de s. Théodore et "Liber" de s.*

Orsiesius. Texte latin de s. Jérôme. (Bibliothèque de la Revue d'histoire ecclésiastique - 7), Louvain 1932.
[43]We gave a few examples of this in *La liturgie*, pp. 120-122.
[44]L.-T. Lefort, 'Un texte original de la règle de saint Pachôme', in *Comptes Rendus de l'Académie* [1919], pp. 341-348; *Idem*, 'La Règle de s. Pachôme (Nouveaux documents)', in *Muséon* 40 (1927):31-64 (text and Latin translation).
[45]See *Manuscrits coptes (Catalogue général du Musée Egyptien)*, Cairo 1916.
[46]Pp. 155-162 (Coptic text) and 163-168 (Latin translation).
[47]L.-T. Lefort, 'La Règle de s. Pachôme (nouveaux fragments coptes), in *Muséon* 48 (1935):75-80.
[48]L.-T. Lefort, *Oeuvres de s. Pachôme et de ses disciples*, (CSCO - 159), Louvain 1956, pp. 30-36; French translation (CSCO - 160), Louvain 1956, pp. 30-37.
[49]See H. Bacht, 'Ein verkanntes Fragment der koptischen Pachomius-Regel', in *Muséon* 75 (1962):5-18. The fragment in question was published by L.-T. Lefort in *Oeuvres de s. Pachôme*: p. 80, translation: p. 80.
[50]See L.-T. Lefort, 'La Règle de s. Pachôme (étude d'approche)', in *Muséon* 34 (1921):61-70; *idem*, 'La règle de s. Pachôme (2e étude d'approche)', in *Muséon* 37 (1924):1-28.
[51]Pp. 169-182. In the articles quoted above (note 50) Lefort gave a full list of the preceding editions. Among others, an edition of the Greek text was published in the *Acta Sanctorum* of May, III, 1866[3], pp. 53*-54* (Greek) and 345-346 (Latin translation). It was reproduced in the *Patrologia Graeca* of Migne, Vol. 40, col. 947-952.
[52]A. Dillman, *Chrestomatia Aethiopica*, Leipzig 1866, pp. 57-69. The second Rule, corresponding to the translation of the Greek *Excerpta* is found in pages 60-63.
[53]O. Löfgren, 'Zur Textkritik der äthiopischen Pachomiusregeln I, II', in *Le Monde Oriental* 30 (1936):171-187.
[54]O. Löfgren, 'Pakomius' etiopiska klosterregler. I svensk tokning', in *Kyrkohistorisk Årsskrift* 48 (1948):163-184.
[55]G.H. Schoode, 'The Rules of Pachomius translated from the Ethiopic', in *Presbyterian Review* 6 (1885):678-689.
[56]E. König, 'Die Regeln des Pachomius', in *TSK* 51 (1878):328-332.
[57]R. Basset, *Les apocryphes éthiopiens traduits en francais*, fasc. 8, Paris 1896, pp. 28-40.
[58]Another Ethiopian translation of the Greek *Excerpta* was published by V. Arras in his *Collectio Monastica*, (CSCO - 238); Latin translation, (CSCO - 239), Louvain 1963; text, pp. 141-143; translation, pp. 104-105.
[59]See the four articles by M.M. Van Molle mentioned in our Pachomian bibliography and our review of these articles in the *Bulletin of Monastic Spirituality (Cistercian Studies)*, 1972, n. 487, pp. [216]-[220].
[60]See Inst. 1, note 3.
[61]See Jer. Pref. 1, note 2.
[62]See G[1] 58, note 2 and G[1] 59, note 1.
[63]E. Amélineau, *Monuments pour servir à l'histoire de l'Egypte chrétienne aux IVe, Ve, VIe et VIIe siècles, (Mémoires publiés par les membres de la Mission archéologique française au Caire* - 4), Paris 1895, pp. 248-277.
[64]J. Leipoldt and W.E. Crum, *Sinuthii archimandritae Vita et Opera omnia*, Vol. IV, (CSCO - 73) Louvain 1913, pp. 129-153; Latin translation by H. Wiesmann, (CSCO - 108), Louvain 1936, pp. 77-91.
[65]L.-T. Lefort, *Oeuvres de s. Pachôme*, text (CSCO - 160) pp. 82-99; translation (CSCO - 160) pp. 81-99.
[66]See Hors. Reg. 48, note 1.
[67]We have given some examples in *La liturgie*, pp. 128-129.

CRITICAL EDITIONS

of the texts translated in this volume

Paralipomena:
F. Halkin, *Sancti Pachomii Vitae Graecae, Subsidia hagio-graphica* 19. Brussels, 1932. Pp. 122–165.

Letter of Bishop Ammon:
F. Halkin, *Sancti Pachomii Vitae Graecae*..., pp. 97–121.

Draguet Fragment I:
R. Draguet, 'Un morceau grec inédit des Vies de Pachôme apparié à un texte d'Evagre en partie inconnu', in *Muséon* 70 (1957) 267–306.

Draguet Fragment II:
R. Draguet, 'Un Paralipomenon pachômien inconnu dans le Karakallou 251', in *Mélanges Eugène Tisserant*, Vol. II, *ST* 232. Vatican, 1964. Pp. 55–61.

Extract from the *History of the Monks in Egypt:*
A.-J. Festugière, *Historia Monachorum in Aegypto. Edition critique du texte grec, Subsidia hagiographica* 34. Brussels, 1961. Pp. 39–40.

Extracts from the *Lausiac History* of Palladius:
C. Butler, *The Lausiac History of Palladius*, Vol. II, Texts and Studies VI, 2. Cambridge, 1904. Pp. 26; 48; 52–53; 87–100.

Apophthegmata:
a) F. Halkin, *Sancti Pachomii Vitae Graecae*..., pp. 364–365.
b) *Patrologia Graeca* 65: 189 and 304.

The Rules of Saint Pachomius:

L.-T. Lefort, *Oeuvres de s. Pachôme et de ses disciples,* *CSCO* 159. Louvain, 1956. Pp. 30-36; 80. (Coptic text).

A. Boon, *Pachomiana latina. Règle et épîtres de s. Pachôme, épître de s. Théodore et 'Liber' de s. Orsiesius. Texte latin de s. Jérôme, Bibliothèque de la Revue d'histoire ecclésiastique* 7. Louvain, 1932. Pp. 3-74. (Latin text).

The Regulations of Horsiesios:

L.-T. Lefort, *Oeuvres de s. Pachôme...,* 82-99.

pachomian chronicles

paralipomena

from the Life of holy pachomius
(paral.)

PROLOGUE

IN MY OPINION, what has been written about
the Holy Man can be of great profit. And to
continue on the same subject does not cause any
harm, for to hark back to these things leads the
hearer more firmly toward the contemplation of
what was said. On the other hand, to decline
through negligence to write these things brings
danger upon him who so declines. Therefore, let
us hark back on what was said and recount a few
things akin to what was written before.

Chapter 1: About holy Theodore

1. It was a custom with the brothers of our
God-loving and holy father Pachomius, to assemble every evening in an appointed place in
the monastery to hear his teaching. Once, as
they were assembled as usual to hear the Great
Man, he commanded a certain Theodore, who
had been in the monastery twenty years, to speak
to the brothers. Straightaway, without any disobedience, he spoke to them about things profitable to them. Some of the eldest [brothers], when
they saw what was happening, did not want to
listen to him. They said within themselves, 'He

Some old
brothers refuse
to listen to
an instruction
given by young
Theodore

19

is a beginner and he is teaching us! We will not
hear him.' They left the *synaxis* of the brothers
and withdrew to their cells.

When the brothers were dismissed from the instruction, the Great Man sent for and called those
who had withdrawn. They came to the Holy Man
and he asked them, 'Why did you leave us and
withdraw to your cells?' They said, 'Because you
have made a boy teacher of us, a large group of
old men and of other brothers'. When the Great
Man heard this, he groaned and said, 'Do you
know where the beginning of evil came into the
world from?' As they said, 'From where?', he replied and told them, 'From pride, for which *the
bright star dawning in the morning was dashed in
pieces upon the ground,* and for which also Ne-
buchadnezzar, the king of Babylon, *dwelt among
the wild beasts.* Or, have you not heard what is
written, *The man with an arrogant heart is ab-
horrent to the Lord? For everyone who exalts
himself will be humbled.* Now you have been de-
spoiled by the devil of all your virtue, not knowing that pride is the mother of all evils. For it was
not Theodore whom you left when you went
away, but you fled from the word of God and you
fell away from the Holy Spirit. Truly wretched
are you, and worthy of all pity. How is it that you
did not understand that it was Satan who was
causing this in you, and because of this you have
been separated from God? O what a great wonder! *God humbled Himself and became obedient
even unto death* for our sake; and yet we, who are
by nature lowly, puff ourselves up. The order is
overthrown by us: He who is above all things and

**They are
rebuked by
Pachomius**

Cf. Si 10:12-13.

Is 14:12.

Dt 5:21.

Pr 15:9; 16:5.

Lk 14:11.

Ph 2:8.

exceedingly great brought the world to himself through his humility, when he could have burned it up by a mere glance! And we who are nothing make ourselves proud, not knowing that by this we are pushing ourselves into the depths of the earth. Did you not see that I was standing and listening to his teaching? In truth I tell you, I profited greatly from listening to him. For it was not to test him that I enjoined him to speak to you, but because I expected to draw profit for myself. How much more then ought you to have heard his word with great eagerness and humility? Verily I, your father in the Lord, was listening to him with all my soul as one who *does not know his right hand from his left.*[1] Therefore, before God, I tell you that if you do not show great repentance for this error, and if you do not weep and mourn for yourselves so that what happened may be forgiven you, *you will go to perdition.*[2]

Jon 4:11.

Dn 2:5.

Chapter 2: About Silvanos

2. Once there was a brother called Silvanos, who had been wearing the monastic habit for twenty years. He was originally an actor. In the beginning of his [life of] renunciation he was extremely vigilant about his soul, spending all his time in fasting and frequent prayers and in all humililty. But after a long time had elapsed, he began so to disregard his own salvation that he wanted to live softly and enjoy himself, and even fearlessly declaimed among the brothers improper quips from the theater.

Our holy father Pachomius called him in and

After twenty years of monastic life, Silvanos becomes negligent

Pachomius
orders him
expelled from
the monastery

in the presence of the brothers ordered him to be
stripped of the monastic habit, to be given secular clothes, and to be expelled from the monastery by the brothers. He fell at [Pachomius'] feet
and entreated him saying, 'Father, if you forgive
me this once, and do not expel me, you will cause
me to do penance for the things in which I have
showed negligence, so that you shall rejoice at the
change of my soul'. The Holy Man answered him,
'You know how much I have borne with you, and
how much I have admonished you, even beating
you many times. I am a man who does not want
to stretch out his hand with this intent, and when
I was obliged to do this in your case, I suffered
more in my soul through sympathy than did [you]
who were being beaten. I thought to beat you for
the sake of your salvation in God, so that by this
means we might be able to correct you from your
error. Now if you did not change when I admonished you, and did not improve when I exhorted
you, and did not fear when I beat you, how is it
possible for me to forgive you any more?'

After Silvanos'
supplications
and promises,
Pachomius
forgives him

Silvanos multiplied his entreaties and promised to amend in the future. Then the Great Man
asked sureties from him, that after he was forgiven he would no more continue the same behavior. And when a certain Petronios made himself a surety for him for the things he had promised, the Great Man forgave him.[1] Silvanos, having received remission, so struggled with all his
soul that he became a pattern of every virtue of
religion to all the brothers, small and great.

He becomes
an example of
virtues

3. The outstanding achievement among his
virtues was his absolute humility and the tears
that flowed from his eyes unceasingly. When he

was eating with the brothers he was unable to control his weeping, and *his tears were mingled with his food.* And when the brothers told him that he should not behave like that in the sight of strangers, he would affirm strongly, 'I have often wanted to control my tears for this reason, and I was not able'. Then the brothers said, 'It is possible for him who is pricked by compunction to weep by himself and to do likewise when he is at prayer with the brothers. But when someone eats at table with the brothers, it is possible for his soul to weep continually without those visible tears. Therefore we want to know what thought keeps you so ceaselessly soaked with tears that many of us seeing you are turned from eating to satiety.'

Cf. Ps 102(101):9.

He answered those who were questioning him, 'Do you not want me to weep when I see holy men waiting upon me, the very dust of whose feet I am not worthy? Ought I not then to mourn for myself, when I, a man from the theatre, am being waited on by such holy men? I weep therefore, brothers, fearing to be swallowed up like Dathan and Abiram,[1] especially because when I had come from ignorance to knowledge I did not care for my soul's salvation, so that I fell into the danger of being expelled by the brothers and I had to give sureties with awful oaths that I would not longer disregard my life. For this reason I am not ashamed to continue this behavior. *I know my sins, indeed,* for which, even if I could give my soul, there is no grace for me.'

He mourns for his past negligence

Nb 16:32;
Dt 11:6;
Ps 106(105):17.

Ps 51(50):3.

4. As he was struggling in this manner, the Great Man bore testimony about him before all the brothers, saying, 'Behold, brothers, *I bear testimony before God* that from the time this

Pachomius bears testimony about him

1 Tm 5:21.

Community came into existence,[1] among all the
brothers who have been with me, there has been
no one who has completely copied my example,
save only one'. When the brothers heard this,
some of them thought that the one man of whom
he spoke was Theodore, others Petronios or Horsiesios.[2] And when Theodore asked the Holy Man
about whom he had said this, the Great Man did
not want to say. But as he persisted, along with
the other great brothers, entreating him to let
them know who it was, the Great Man answered,
'If I knew that he about whom I am going to
speak would become vainglorious for being
praised, I would not have commended such a
man. But since I know that when he is praised he
rather humbles himself and thinks scorn of himself all the more, I will, before you all, call him
blessed, so that you may imitate his example.[3]
You, Theodore, and all those like you who are
striving in the monastery, have bound the devil
Jb 40:29. *like a sparrow* placing him under your feet, and
daily you trample him down like dust. But if you
neglect yourselves, the devil under your feet will
rise up and flee, and he will again make war
against you. As for the young Silvanos, who but a
short time ago was about to be expelled by me
from the monastery for his negligence, he has so
completely subjugated the devil and slain him,
that the devil will never be able to approach him,
for he has utterly vanquished him by his very great
humility. When you humble yourselves, you do so
as men who have [to their credit] works of righteousness and are augmenting their virtue, relying
on what you have already done. As for this man,
the more he struggles, the more he declares that he

is unworthy, thinking from his whole soul and
mind that he is useless and contemptible. This indeed is why he is always on the verge of tears, be-
littling himself utterly and saying that he is unworthy even of the visible things. You outdo him
in your knowledge and your endurance and in
your contests against Satan that are beyond
measure; but he has surpassed you in humility.
And nothing so weakens the demon as humility
coming with active power from the whole soul.'

When he had struggled in this manner for
eight whole years, he completed his contest, lay-
ing down his life. The servant of God testified of
his departure that an endless throng of holy angels took his soul with great rejoicing and psalmody, and brought it to God as a choice sacrifice,[4]
and as a marvellous incense offering to God
found among men.[5]

His departure
from this world

Chapter 3: About the brother buried without
psalms.

5. It happenend once that our holy father Pachomius went to another monastery to visit the
brothers dwelling there. As he was on his journey,
he met the funeral procession of a certain brother
of that monastery who had died. All the brothers
of the monastery followed the procession singing
psalms. With them also were the parents and relatives of the dead [brother]. From a distance the
brothers saw the Holy Man coming toward them,
and they set the bier down on the ground so that
the Holy Man might come and pray over him. So
the brothers stood there singing psalms with the

Pachomius or-
ders a brother
buried without
psalmody

secular folk. When the Blessed Man had come
and had prayed, he ordered the brothers not to
sing psalms any more in front of [the dead
brother]. He had the dead brother's clothes
brought [to him] and ordered them burned in
front of everyone. Then, when they had been
burned, he commanded [the brothers] to take up
the body and to bury it without psalmody. And
when the brothers and the parents of the dead
brother threw themselves at his feet and entreated him to let them sing psalms over him, he
would not endure it.

The parents [of the dead brother] said, 'Father, what are you doing, inflicting on our son
this new and unjust treatment? It befits not your
holiness to display toward this corpse a heartlessness that could lead even the rude barbarians to
pity and sympathy. Even an enemy, when he sees
the body of his adversary lying immobile and
voiceless, knows many times how to show pity.
We have seen now, among you Christians, a new
spectacle that has never been seen even among
barbarians. By such heartlessness you have inflicted an ineffaceable disgrace on our family.
Would that we had not seen you today, that our
house had not inherited an eternal taunt through
you! Would that our miserable son had never followed this savage life! For then he would not have
bequeathed us this eternal sorrow. We beseech
you, even though you have caused his clothes to
be burned, allow the psalm to be said.'

6. He answered and said to them, 'Truly,
brothers, I have more compassion for the one
who lies here than you have; and I showed more
care for him, as a father, when I commanded this

to be done. You care for this visible body; I struggle for his soul. Indeed, if you sing psalms for him, he will receive more punishments to account for the psalm, for he departed without having with him the power of the psalms. If you want to add to his eternal sorrows, sing psalms for him; but he will suffer more pain then because of the psalm and he will curse you. Because I know what is expedient for his soul, I take no care of his dead body. If I allow you to sing psalms, I will be found, in the sight of God, someone who pleases men, because for the sake of human satisfaction I have disregarded what was expedient for the soul which is going to be punished in judgement. God, who is a fountain of goodness, seeks pretexts which he can seize to pour forth on us the streams of his grace. If then we, who have been found worthy by God of being skilled in the art of his divine healing, do not apply the appropriate aid for each suffering, we are rightly called despisers, as it is written, *Behold, you despisers, and wonder marvellously, and perish.* For this reason I entreat you: that his punishment may be lightened. Take him away without psalms. For God who is good knows how to give him release because of this dishonor inflicted upon him, and to call him again to life. Had he listened to me on the several occasions on which I admonished him, he would not have come to this.' After these words of the Blessed Man, he was taken away to the mountain without psalms, and buried.[1]

6a. Our holy father spent a few days in that monastery admonishing and teaching each of the brothers the fear of God and how we must struggle against the demon and how we may with sharp

Hab 1:5.

sight apprehend his arts and his wiles and, by the power of the Lord, bring to nothing his machinations against us.

Chapter 4: About unorthodox anchorites coming to the Holy Man.

Some great anchorites come to Pachomius' monastery

7. Another time, while the Great Man was conversing with the brothers about things useful to their souls, the porter came and told him, 'Some great anchorites have come and they want to meet you'. He said, 'Call them here'. They entered the monastery therefore and with the brothers he embraced them. After they had seen all the community and had gone round all the cells of the brothers, they wanted to converse with him privately.

When they talk with him, he perceives a stench from them

As they sat in a secluded cell, the Old Man perceived a strong stench from them. He did not know the cause of such a stench, because he was conversing with them face to face and could not learn the cause by a supplication to God. Seeing their eloquence and their familiarity with the Scriptures, he could not understand their sickening stench. After the Great Man had conversed long with them about the holy Scriptures, and the ninth hour was come, they rose up to go away to their own place. The Holy Man entreated them to eat there, but they did not accept, for they were in haste to reach their place before sunset. So they prayed and made their farewell, and then they departed.

The Great Man, in order to know the cause of their stench, went into his cell and prayed God to make it known to him. An angel of the Lord came and told him, 'It was some doctrines of impiety from Origen that, in their souls, produced such a stench. But send quickly and call these men back and warn them not to be caught again by such harmful and destructive doctrines, for they lead to perdition.' Straightway therefore, he came out of his cell. He sent a brother after these men and when they had returned he said to them, 'I want to ask you a question'. They answered, 'Speak.' He said to them, 'The writings of the man called Origen, do you read them?' When they heard this, they denied it and said, 'No.' The Holy Man told them, 'Behold, *I bear testimony to you before God* that every man reading Origen and accepting his writings is going to reach the *bottom of hell,* and his inheritance shall be *the outer darkness, where there will be weeping and grinding of teeth.*[1] Now, what I learned from God I have testified to you; *I am innocent therefore before God on this account. It is your concern.*[2] Behold, you have heard the truth. If you believe me, and if you wish truly to satisfy God, take all of Origen's books you have and cast them into the river, and never want to read them again, and especially the blasphemous ones.' After saying these things, he dismissed them.

It is revealed to him that they read Origen

1 Tm 5:21.

Pr 14:12.

Mt 8:12.

Mt 27:24; cf. Dn 13:46.

Chapter 5: About the brother who wanted to become a martyr.

8. There was one of the very outstanding brothers who was practising *ascesis* by himself. He heard of the godly life of the great Pachomius

A brother strongly desires to become a martyr

and begged him to receive him into the Community. The Great Man received him; and after he had spent a short time with the brothers, he greatly desired to become a martyr, at a time when the world was at peace and the Church was flourishing and also at peace, by the grace of God—the blessed and Christ-bearing Constantine was reigning at that time.[1] That [brother] continually entreated the Blessed Man saying, 'Pray for me, Abba, that I may become a martyr'. The Great Man admonished him saying, 'Do not allow this thought to enter your heart again'. And he would say to him, 'Brother, endure the monk's contest nobly and blamelessly, directing your life according to what is pleasing to the Lord, and you will have the fellowship[2] with the martyrs in heaven'.

As he desired this thing more and more every day, and as he was pestering the Holy Man to pray for him, the Great Man, shaking off his importunity, told him, 'Be it so. I will pray; but if you want it, you shall have it. Be on your guard lest, when the hour comes, instead of becoming a martyr you shall be found denying Christ. Truly you commit an offence in desiring to put yourself into temptation when our Lord Jesus Christ commands us to *pray not to fall into temptation'*. And having said these things to him, he admonished him to take good heed of himself and not to think of this any more.

9. It happened two years later that some of the brothers were sent by the Great Man to a village upstream to collect rushes to make mats for the monastery. Now, the village was near the barbarians who are called Blemmyes. And while the

Pachomius warns him against such a desire

Lk 22:40.

The brother is sent on an errand

brothers were there, on an island where there were many rushes, the Blessed Man sent to them the brother who desired to become a martyr, to carry some small things to them. He admonished him to take good heed of himself, quoting enigmatically these words of the Scripture, *Behold, now is the favorable time; this is the day of salvation;*[1] *giving no offence in anything, so as not to bring discredit on our ministry.* So, he took the donkey loaded with the things and went to the brothers.

2 Co 6:2-3.

When he had come near the desert, the barbarians, coming down to draw water, came upon him. They took him down from the donkey and bound his hands. Then, taking the donkey with the baggage, they led him up to the mountain to the other barbarians. The barbarians seeing him coming with the donkey, began to mock him saying, 'Monk, come and worship our gods'. They slew some animals and made libations to their idols. Then they brought the monk and urged him to make libations with them. As he did not want to do it, they approached him with anger, holding their naked swords and threatening to kill him at once if he refused to sacrifice to their gods and to pour out libations to them. Seeing their naked swords and frightened at their savagery, he took the wine at once and poured it in libation to their idols and ate with them of the meat sacrificed to the idols. Fearing the death of the body, he slew his immortal soul, denying God, the master of all. Then, when he had done this, the Blemmyes let him go.

He is captured by some barbarians and he pours a libation to their idols

Cf. Jude 4.

10. When he had come down from the mountain and come to himself, he *knew his iniquity*, or

Ps 51(50):5.

He comes back to Pachomius to confess his sin

*Is 37:1.

Lk 15:21.

Cf. Lk 18:13.

Pachomius rebukes him

Mi 7:18-19.

rather the impiety which he had done. *He rent his garments,** struck his face[1] repeatedly and came to his monastery. The Blessed Man, knowing what had happened to him, came out to meet him with great affliction. When the brother saw him coming to him, he threw himself on his face on the ground, weeping and crying, 'Father, I have sinned against God and against you,* because I did not listen to your good advice or to your admonition.[2] For had I listened to you, I would not have experienced this.' Hearing this, the Great Man told him, 'Rise up, wretched man. You have shut yourself out from such goods, O miserable one. Truly a crown was laid up for you, and you have cast it from you. You were ready to be numbered among the holy martyrs and you have banished yourself from their holy fellowship. Christ, the Master, was there with his holy angels, willing to set his diadem upon your head, and you have denied him for the sake of an hour. Through fear of the death — which you are going to endure [in any case] though unwillingly — you have fallen away from God and lost eternal life. Where are the words you used to say before this? Where is your craving?' Then he said, 'I have sinned in all things, O Father. *I cannot lift up my face to heaven.*[3] I am lost, O Father. I did not expect it would happen this way.' As he said this with tears, the Great Man said to him:

11. 'O wretched man, you have estranged yourself completely from the Lord. But the Lord is good and he never *kept his anger for a testimony, for he delights in mercy* and he is able *to sink our sins in the depths of the sea,* for *as heavens are from the earth, so far away does he*

set our sins from us. * For he desires not the death of the sinner but his repentance,^{†1} and that the man who has fallen should not remain in his fallen condition, but should rise up, and that he who has turned away should not go far off, but return quickly to Him. Therefore, despair not of yourself; *there is hope* of salvation. For, as it is said, *if every tree is cut down, it will sprout again.* Then, if you will even now listen to me in everything I say to you, you shall have forgiveness from God.' He answered with tears, 'In all things I will listen to you from now on, O father!'

The Great Man ordered him to withdraw to a quiet place, to shut himself off and to hold converse with no one until his death; to eat every other day, salt and bread, and to drink only water for the rest of his life; to make two mats every day, and to keep vigil as much as possible; to pray as much as he could and not to cease at all from weeping. He withdrew, as the Blessed Man had commanded him, and he doubled all he had told him to do. He held converse with no man except the Great Man and Theodore and a few of the other great old men. After he had spent ten years struggling in this manner, he died, having, by the Lord's grace, borne a good witness.[2]

Chapter 6: About temptations and the active life.

12. The great Pachomius was asked once by a brother, 'Why is it that before the demon comes to trouble us, we possess our mind's understanding in a healthy state and we philosophize about temperance, humility, and the other virtues, but

*Ps 103(102): 11-12.
†Ez 33:11.

Jb 14:7.
Ibid.

He does penance the rest of his life and he dies in the Lord

Importance of the fear of God against temptations

when the hour comes to display in deed what we
have been philosophizing about, such as long
suffering in the time of anger, absence of vainglory when subjected to praise, and many other
similar things, we are often defeated?' In answer
to this the Great Man said, 'Because we do not
pursue the active life perfectly—this is why we do
not understand all the demons' mind and versa-
tility well enough to be able, when the troubler
manifests his presence, to repel swiftly the confusion of such thoughts which surrounds us by the
contemplative power of the soul. Therefore,' he
said, 'let us pour the fear of God like oil upon the
contemplative part of the soul, every day and
every hour.[1] That fear, which accomplishes
works and is a lamp for the contemplation of the
things that concern us, makes our mind unshak-
able, not carried away by anger, wrath, rancor,
and any of the other passions which lead us to
wickedness. It makes it contemplative and raises
it to that incorporeal region; it forces it to hold in
contempt the things which are wrought by devils
and prepares it to *tread underfoot serpents and
scorpions and all the whole strength of the
enemy.*'[2]

Lk 10:19.

Chapter 7: About the contemplation of the soul.

13. Once some brothers from the monastery of
Chenoboskion came and told the Holy Man, 'A
brother is sick and he wants to see you and to be
blessed before he dies'. When the Man of God
heard this, he rose up and followed them. When
he was about two miles from that monastery, the

**Pachomius
contemplates the
soul of a brother
being carried to
heaven by angels**

Holy Man heard a holy voice in the air. He lifted
up his eyes and saw the soul of the sick brother
with the holy angels, singing psalms and being
taken to the blessed life of God. Now the brothers
who were following him neither heard nor saw
anything. As he stood and gazed a long time to
the east, they said to him, 'Why are you standing,
O Father? Let us go quickly, that we may find
him alive.' He answered them, 'We shall not find
him, for I am right now seeing him being taken
up to eternal life. Return, then, to your monastery, children.' As the brothers entreated him to
tell them how he saw the soul of the dead brother,
he told them the manner. After they had heard
it, they departed to their monastery. They veri-
fied very exactly from the brothers in the monastery the hour which the Great Man had told
them, and then they knew that what the Holy
Man had told about the dead brother was true.[1]

Chapter 8: About the demons who said, 'Behold
the blessed man of God'.

14. As the holy old man Pachomius was journeying to his own monastery,* and had come
near the desert called Amnon, legions of demons
rose both on his right hand and on his left, some
following him and others running in front of him,
saying, 'Behold the blessed man of God'.[1] They
were doing this, wishing to sow vainglory in him.
But he knew their cunning, and the more they
shouted, the more he cried out to God, *confessing
his sins*. And undoing the demons' cunning, he
spoke out to them saying, 'O wicked ones! you

**Demons try to
sow vainglory
in Pachomius'
heart**

*Phbow

Mt 3:6.

Ps 51(50):3.

cannot carry me away with you into vainglory, *for I know my failures,* for which I ought to weep constantly over eternal punishment. I have therefore no need of your false speech and guileful deceit, for your work is the destruction of the soul. And I am not carried away by your praises, for I know the cunning of your unholy minds.' And although holy Pachomius said these things to them, they did not stop their shamelessness; they followed alongside the Blessed Man until he drew near his monastery.

About the boy's petition and the cooked food.

A boy complains that no cooked dishes are served to the brothers

15. When the brothers came out to meet him and embraced him, a boy from the monastery who had come out with the brothers to embrace the Holy Man began to entreat him, saying, 'Truly, Father, from the time you left to visit the brothers until now they have not cooked either vegetables or porridge for us'. To this the holy Old Man answered kindly, saying, 'Do not be afflicted, my son, I will have these things cooked for you from now on'.

The cook explains to Pachomius why he stopped preparing cooked dishes

Going round the monastery, he came to the kitchen. As he found the cook working mats, he asked him, 'How long have you gone without cooking vegetables for the brothers?' He answered, 'Two months'. The Great Man told him, 'Why have you done this, when the commandments and the holy fathers order cooked vegetables for the brothers every Saturday and Sunday?'[1] The cook answered him, 'Truly, O father, I was willing to cook for them every day; but I saw

that the cooked vegetables were not eaten, for almost all the brothers practise abstinence and do
not eat cooked food. Therefore, seeing that they
were not eating them I did not cook them, so that
the expense which had required such great labor
should not be thrown outside because no one eats
it. For we put forty measures of oil a month into
the ordinary cooked food of the brothers; and I
thought it was not right to throw out so great an
expenditure. Thus, so that I should not sit idle, I
work mats with the brothers. For I thought that
one man is sufficient in the kitchen to prepare the
small dishes for the brothers, that is, charlock
with vinegar and oil, garlic and fine greens.'

16. When the Holy Man heard this, he said to
him, 'How many mats have you made, leaving
the kitchen to give yourselves to this work?' He
said, 'Five hundred'. He said to him, 'Bring them
to me here that I may measure them'. When the
mats were brought, he ordered them cast into the
fire. When they were burned he said to the
cooks,[1] 'Just as you have, by a satanic thought,
forsaken the rule given you concerning the care of
the brothers, so I too have mercilessly burned the
work of your hands, that you may learn what it is
to disregard the fathers' ordinances which were
given for the salvation of souls. How great is the
profit of which you have robbed the brothers by
not cooking! Do you not know that when a man
has the possibility of looking for something and
he abstains from it for God's sake, he will receive
a great reward from God; but if he has not such
power over a thing and is forced by necessity to
abstain from it because he does not have it, he
will seek a reward for this in vain? Do you not

He is severely
rebuked by
Pachomius

know that if something is set on the table and the
brothers do not taste it because they practise abstinence for God's sake, they shall have a great reward; but if no cooked food is given them, the abstinence from what they do not see shall not be
credited to them? For the sake of eighty measures
of oil you have cut off so great a harvest of virtues!
May the whole substance of the world be destroyed rather than one small virtue be cut off
from the soul. Truly, I want food cooked every
day and set before the brothers in abundance, so
that practising abstinence daily and refraining
from the things given them, they may add to their
virtue every day. And if someone who is ill does
not want to go to the infirmary and, coming to
the table to receive some of the vegetables given
to the brothers according to the custom, does not
find any, what happens? Will he not be scandalized at not finding his need on the common table? Or do you not know that boys especially are
not able to continue in virtue unless they are
granted some relaxation or small comfort?'

Chapter 9: About the revelation.

**The future
dejection of the
brothers is
revealed to
Pachomius**

17. As the brothers were going to prayers, he
also joined them and completed the prayers.
When they went out to the meal, he remained
alone in the house in which he was accustomed to
perform the prayers of the *synaxis.* He shut the
door and prayed to God to make known to him
what would subsequently be the condition of the
brothers and what was going to happen to them
in later times. He went on praying from the tenth

hour until the time they gave the signal to call the brothers to the night service.[1] About midnight an apparition suddenly came from heaven and made known to him the end of the subsequent condition of the brothers, and that they would live in the same way with *devotion according to Christ,*[2] and the future expansion of the monas- teries. But he saw also a numberless multitude of brothers journeying along a deep, parched val- ley. Many of them wanted to come up out of the valley, but were unable. Many came face to face with each other because of the great darkness that shrouded them, but did not recognize each other. Many fell down through exhaustion, and others cried out with a pitiful voice. A few of them were able with much labor to force their way out of that valley; as soon as they came up they were met by light, and coming to the light they gave thanks to God heartily. Then did the Blessed Man know what was going to happen to the brothers in the end, what negligence there would be in those times, the great hardening and error, and the failing of the shepherds which was going to affect them. Those who are the most negligent today shall rule over the good, van- quishing them by their number. These things—the beginnings of which we, who are writing, have gone through—are only an ex- ample; for bad men shall rule the brothers and those without knowledge shall have control of the monasteries and shall fight for rank. The just shall be persecuted by the wicked, and the good shall not live in the monasteries with confidence, and as it is said, divine things shall be changed to human.

2 Tm 3:12.

Pachomius
intercedes to
the Lord

18. Now when the Blessed Man knew these
things, he cried out to God with tears, saying, 'O
Lord Almighty, if this must happen, why did you
allow these communities to come into being.[1] If
those who are going to rule over the brothers in
those days are bad, what will those be like who
are shepherded by them? *For if one blind man*

Mt 15:14.

leads another blind man, both will fall into a pit.
Have I toiled in vain? Remember my labors,
Lord, and those of all the brothers who are pres-
ently practising *ascesis* with all their soul.
Remember that you made a covenant with me
that this spiritual seed of mine would last *until*

Mt 28:20.

the end of time.[2] You know, O Master, that since
I put on the monastic habit I have never taken my
fill of anything on earth, not even of water.'

*Cf. Ac 10:13.

As he said this, a voice came to him* saying,
'Are you boasting, Pachomius, you who are a

Christ appears
to him

man? Ask mercy for yourself, for it is by my mercy
that everything stands.' When he heard this, the
Blessed Man straightway threw himself on the
ground and asked God for mercy, saying, 'Lord
Almighty, send your mercy upon me and never
take it away from me, for I too know that without
your mercy nothing can exist'. As he said this,
two angels of God immediately stood by his side.
And with them was a young man whose face was
ineffable and whose aspect was inexpressible. He
had a crown of thorns upon his head. Then the
angels made Pachomius stand and said to him,
'Since you have asked God to send you his mercy,

1 Co 2:8.

behold, this is his mercy, *the Lord of Glory,* Jesus
Christ *his Only-begotten Son whom he sent into*

1 Jn 4:9.
Mt 27:29.

the world; but you have crucified him and have
put a crown of thorns upon his head.'[3]

Pachomius said to the Young Man, 'I pray your immaculate nature, Master, I did not crucify you'. Then the Young Man, relaxing his face a little in a smile, said to him, 'I too know that it is not you but your fathers who crucified me. Take courage, for the root of your seed shall not fail for ever, and your seed shall be preserved upon the earth *until the end of time.* And the few who are going to be saved from the abundant darkness in these times shall be found above those who practise a very great *ascesis* now. For they have you as a lamp before their eyes and they practice *ascesis,* counting on your light; but if those who shall come after them and shall dwell in a parched place run out of the darkness and pursue righteousness in good mind and on their own accord, with no one to guide them to the truth, verily I say to you that they shall be found with those who now practice *ascesis* greatly and blamelessly, enjoying the same salvation.' After he had said these things, he went up to heaven at once.

19. As the Great Man was marvelling at these things, the signal was given at once to call the brothers to the night *synaxis.* And when the night service was completed, the brothers sat down to listen to his word. *He opened his mouth and said to them:*

Pachomius is assured by Christ of the salvation of a remnant

Mt 28:20.

He exhorts the brothers

Mt 5:2.

Importance of striving for salvation

A very profitable instruction of the Great Pachomius

'Brothers, as long as you have breath in your bodies, strive for your salvation. Before the hour comes in which we shall weep for ourselves, let us practise virtue eagerly. For I tell you that if you

knew what good things are in heaven, what promise is laid up for the saints and how those who
have fallen away from God are punished and also
what torments are laid up for those who have
been negligent—especially *those who have known*

1 Tm 4:3.

the truth and have not led a way of life worthy of
it so as to inherit that blessedness which is reserved for the saints and to flee the punishments
of these torments—then you would endure every
pain in order to be made perfect in the virtue
which is according to Christ.

'Go to the tombs and see that the assurance of

The vanity of
mortal life
*Cf. Ps 103(102):
14; Si 10:9.
Ga 6:10.

men is nothing. Why then does man who is dust
indulge in vainglory?* Why does he who is all
stench exalt himself? Let us therefore weep for
ourselves *while we have time,* lest, at the hour of
our departure, we be found asking God for extra
time to repent.

'Truly wretched and three times miserable is
the soul that has left the world and dedicated itself to God but has not lived in a manner worthy
of its promise. Then, brothers, let us not allow
this age, which is short and contemptible and

Ws 5:9.

passes like a shadow, to steal that blessed and
immortal life away from us.

'Truly, I fear that our fathers according to the

Our parents who
live in the world
will condemn us

flesh, who live in the world and are absorbed in
cares and vexations and who think of us (who are,
of course, men dedicated to God and already in
possession of a pledge of entering into the blessed
life!) expecting to receive succour from us in the
age to come, will be found to condemn us and to
quote the words of Scripture, *How have you be-*

Jr 9:18.

*come wretched, greatly put to shame? Great is
your affliction; a fire is kindled upon you; your*

branches have become useless. For this cause they   Jr 11:16.
have become a prey. The lions have roared at it
and have given out their voice against it. For this   Jr 2:14-15.
reason, *the beloved are like the abhorred* and *the*   Ho 9:10.
crown of your head is taken away. Cities that face
the south, how are you shut off? There is nobody
to give access to you. Let indeed the wicked be re-   Jr 13:18-19.
moved, that he may not see the glory of the Lord.   Is 26:10.
You have heard.

20. 'Therefore, brothers, let us strive with all
our heart, bearing death before our eyes every   **The need to**
hour, and every moment imagining the fearful   **meditate con-**
punishment. By these things the mind comes to   **stantly on death**
perception and the soul is weighed down weeping,
but it is also made contemplative and prepared to
be turned toward God, undistracted by earthly
things. And not only this, but once humility is
worked out by these, the soul is persuaded to become compassionate and without vainglory, lowly
and made a stranger to all worldly mentality.

'Let the soul then, brothers, teach wisdom to
this thick body every day when we come to our
bed at evening, and say to each member of the   **Let the soul**
body, "O feet, while you have power to stand and   **teach the body**
to move before you are laid out and become mo-
tionless, stand eagerly for your Lord". To the
hands, let it say, "The hour comes when you will
be loosened and motionless, bound to each other
and having no motion whatever; then, before you
fall into that hour, do not cease stretching yourselves out to the Lord". And to the whole body let
the soul say, "O body, before we are separated
and removed far away from each other, and before I am taken down to Hades to receive *ever-*
lasting fetters under darkness, and you are   Jude 6.

changed into the primal matter and dissolved into earth, consumed in stench and corruption,
stand boldly, worship the Lord. Make my perception made known by tears; make known to the
Master your good service. Bear me as I eagerly
confess God, before you are borne by others; do
not condemn me *to eternal punishment* in your
desire to sleep and to take your rest. For there will
be a time when that most heavy sleep is going to
overtake you. If you listen to me, we shall together enjoy the blessed inheritance. If you do
not listen to me, then woe to me that you have
been bound to me; because of you I also, wretched as I am, am condemned."

'If you train yourselves daily in this manner,
truly you will be a true *temple of God.** And since
God is dwelling in you,† what satanic wile is able
to deceive you? For instead of having a myriad of
teachers, *the word of God is dwelling in you,*
teaching you more and making you yet wiser by
his own knowledge. And whatever human speech
cannot say, the all-holy Spirit teaches. For as it is
said, *we know not how to pray as we ought; but
the Spirit himself expresses our plea for us with
groanings that cannot be put into words.*

'There are many other profitable things that
we could say to you by God's grace. But so we do
not stay too long on the same subject, let us direct
our word to something else.'

About the hundred coins of wheat

21. A famine once took place in the time of our
blessed father Pachomius and the brothers had

Mt 25:46.

**Be a real
temple of God**
*2 Co 6:16.
†*Ibid.*
Col 3:16.

Cf. Lk 12:12.

Rm 8:26.

no wheat. Moreover, wheat could not be found in almost the whole of Egypt. The holy Old Man sent one of the brothers to go round the cities and villages seeking wheat to buy. He had given him one hundred coins[1] to buy wheat. Having gone around many places, the man who had been entrusted with this errand came to a city called Hermonthis. And by a disposition of God, he found there a councillor, a very religious, God-fearing man, who had heard about the life of the holy Pachomius and the brothers. Now this councillor was in charge of the public wheat. The brother came to him and entreated him to sell him one hundred coins' worth of wheat. He answered him, 'Truly, brother, if I had wheat of my own, I would take it from my children and give it to you, for I have heard about your godly and virtuous way of life. Listen to what I am going to tell you. I have some public wheat in store and for the time being it is not required by the commander. If you wish to take it, I can do without the public goods until threshing time. Therefore, if you know you can return the wheat at that time, then take as much as you want.'

The brother answered, 'I do not want it like that, but if you want to give me wheat for one hundred coins,[2] at whatever rate you want, you do well'. The other said, 'Yes, I can, and not only for one hundred coins; if you want to take wheat for another hundred coins, you will do me a favor.[3] Only pray for me.' The brother said, 'We have only this [money]'. And the councillor answered, 'Do not worry about that. Take the wheat and when you find the money, bring it to me.' Under these conditions, the brother loaded the

A brother is given one hundred coins to buy wheat

He buys at a very low price

boat with wheat, at thirteen bushels[4] a coin—
when one could not find wheat in the whole of
Egypt at five bushels a coin—and sailed down to
the monastery with great joy.

22. When the Great Man heard that the boat
had moored, loaded with wheat, and when he
learned how the wheat had been purchased, he
sent straightway to the boat, saying, 'Do not bring
one grain of that wheat to this monastery. And do
not let the one who made the purchase come into
my presence,[1] because what he has done is very
unlawful. And not only that, but he has taken
another hundred coins worth of wheat, which I
had not ordered him to do. Obeying his own
mind, he loved to have more; and fired by the
passion of the love of gain, he enslaved all of us,
putting us in debt; he used the giver's kindness in-
satiably and he acted in a greedy manner, bringing us wheat beyond our need. He has borrowed
on his own initiative what we have no means of re-
paying. Moreover, suppose that from some human cause the boat had sunk on its way here,
what could we have done? Would we not have
been slaves forever? Therefore, let him sell all the
wheat which he has brought to the seculars of this
area, as he has received it from the man who
trusted him, at the price of thirteen bushels a
coin. Then let him take the gold and carry it to
the one who trusted him. And with our hundred
coins, let him buy wheat at the price it is sold
everywhere, and let him bring it.'

He did as the Great Man had said, and he
brought the wheat, which he bought at the price
of five bushels and a half a coin. From that time,
he appointed another in his place and he did not

*He is rebuked
by Pachomius
who orders the
wheat sold*

*The brother is
replaced in his
charge*

let him go out of the monastery for the service of the brothers.

23. Another time, this brother[1] received from the shoemaker many sandals and some other articles to sell. He received for them a higher price than the shoemaker had mentioned and he brought the money to him. When the shoemaker took the thing and found that the money was three times the value, he went off at once to the Great Man and told him, 'Really, father, you have done wrong in appointing that brother to the ministry of those errands of your monastery, because he has a worldly mind in him. I gave him sandals and some other articles to sell, telling him the price. He sold them for a higher price and brought me three times what I had told him.' When he heard this, the Great Man called the brother and told him, 'Why have you done this?' He answered, 'Father, the price the brother said, I told it to the men who were buying, and they told me, "Brother, unless these are stolen articles, they are worth a higher price". In confusion I told them, "They are not stolen articles; this is the price I have been ordered to sell them for; but give what you want to give". They gave what pleased them and I did not count the money they gave me.'

When the Great Man heard this, he said to him, 'You have greatly sinned, loving to have more. But run quickly and give back the excess over the price to those who gave it to you. Then come and repent of your offence; and sit in the monastery, doing your own work. It is not good for you to do this work any more.' Then the Great Man appointed the Blessed Zacchaeus for the ministry of all the errands of the monastery. He was a good man who

Another brother sells sandals at a higher price than he was told

He is also rebuked and discharged, and he is replaced by Zacchaeus surpassed all human praises in the performance of good works.[2]

Chapter 10: About the nightly apparition

24. It happened once, that the great Pachomius and Theodore, his beloved [disciple], walking in the monastery at night, suddenly saw from afar a great apparition[1] full of great deceit. What appeared was the form of a woman of an unutterable beauty. When Theodore saw the apparition, he was greatly perturbed and his face changed. The Blessed Man saw that he was perturbed and afraid, and he told him, 'Have courage in the Lord, Theodore, and do not be worried'.

After saying this, the Holy Man began to pray with him, that the frightful apparition might be driven away from them. But as they prayed, she moved shamelessly closer to them. She came nearer and nearer, with a throng of demons running before her, and the prayer did not drive her back. Coming to them she said, 'You labor in vain; you cannot presently do anything whatever against me. I have received from Almighty God the power to tempt those whom I want. Indeed, I have been asking him for this for a long time.' The Holy Man asked her, 'And you, where are you from, and who are you, and whom have you come to tempt?' She answered, 'I am the devil's daughter and I am called "all his power", for every phalanx of demons serves me. It was I who brought down the holy luminaries to earth. It was I who snatched Judas from the apostolic company. Now, Pachomius, I have received the power to make war against you.

I could not endure the demons' reproach; nobody has made me as weak as you have. You have reduced me to being trampled underfoot by boys and old men and young men. And you have assembled against me such a crowd — setting around them the fear of God as a wall most unbreakable — that our ministers can no longer draw near any of you with confidence. Now all this happened to me because of the Word of God made man; it is he who *gave you the power to tread underfoot all our strength* and to hold us in derision.'

Lk 10:19.

25. Then holy Pachomius asked her, 'Have you come to tempt only me or others as well?' And she said, 'Both you and all those like you'. Pachomius said again to her, 'Therefore, Theodore too?' She answered, 'I have received power over you and over Theodore; but I cannot draw near you at all'. They said, 'Why?' and she answered, 'If I were to make war against you, you would have an occasion for profit rather than for injury, because you have been made worthy to see the glory of God. But you will not live forever for those for whom at present you make a wall through your prayers and whom you help. A time will come, after your death, when I will dance among them whom now you protect against me. For you have made me to be trodden underfoot by such a multitude of monks!'

They will tempt the brothers after Pachomius' death

Cf. Jn 1:14.

The Great Man said to her, 'How do you know that those who will come after us will not be more authentic men of God than we, able to confirm in the fear of God those [who come] after us?' She said, 'I do know this'. The Great Man said to her, 'You *lie against your* ungodly *head*, for you have no foreknowledge at all.[1] Only God has fore-

How the devil knows the future.

Dn 13:55,59.

knowledge.' She answered and told him, 'By foreknowledge indeed I know nothing, as you say; foreknowledge is a property of God alone. If I know, as I told you, it is by conjecture.' The blessed Pachomius said to her, 'How do you conjecture?' And she answered, 'From what has already happened I conjecture what has not yet happened.' 'How?', he said, and she answered, 'I know that the beginning of everything finds its support in the earnest desire for things that are sought after with zeal, especially divine planting and *heavenly calling*. [That calling] is confirmed by God's will, with wonders, signs, and various powers, and gives security to those who pursue it. But when that beginning becomes older and older, it stops growing; and when it stops growing, it is either consumed by time or withered by disease or blunted by negligence.'

26. The Holy Man asked her, 'Why is it then that, as you say, you have come to tempt the great ones and not all the brothers? For as you say, your own work is the perdition of souls, and you surpass all the demons in evil, and you have the power necessary to oppose these very great men.' She answered him, 'I have already told you before that since the power of God your Saviour appeared on earth, we have been weakened and we are like *a sparrow being played with*[1] by those who want to serve the Lord and we are laughed at by these great Spirit-bearing men. But though we have become feeble we do not cease working as hard as we can, and we never rest from opposing you, sowing our own evil in the soul of the person who struggles. And if we see that he accepts it and permits us to invade him, then we inflame him

Heb 3:1.

How the devil tempts the brothers

Jb 40:29.

with fierce pleasures. But if, by his faith in God, he refuses to receive our sowing, we shall be to him like smoke which is dissipated in the air. This is the reason why we are not permitted to wage war against all, because not all have perfection. For if I were permitted to wage war against all, I would have led astray many who lean on your protection.'

The Blessed Man told her, 'O your sleepless wickedness! You will not cease from raving against mankind until the divine grace of God comes down and consumes you!' After he had said this, he bade her to go away where she was commanded, and he enjoined her never again to approach his monastery at all.

Pachomius sends
the devil away

When the morning came, he called all the great brothers and related to them everything he had seen and heard from the deadly demon. He also sent letters to the great ones who were living in the other monasteries, to confirm them in the fear of God and to inform them about the subject of the apparition.

He warns the
brothers

Chapter 11 : About the Roman [brother].

27. It happened also that the Blessed Man was visiting the brothers in their cells and correcting the thoughts of each one. He came also to a certain Roman [brother], coming from a great family, who also knew the Greek language well. The Great Man, coming to him to admonish him for his profit and to know the movements of his heart, spoke to him in Egyptian.[1] The brother did not understand what he told him; nor did the Great Man know what the Roman [brother] said,

A Roman
brother does not
want to confess
his sins to
Pachomius
through an
interpreter

because he did not know Greek. So the Great
Man was compelled to call a brother who could
interpret what they both said. But when the interpreter came, the Roman [brother] did not
want to tell the Great Man the faults of his heart
through another person. He said, 'I want only
you after God, and nobody else, to know the evils
of my heart'. Hearing this, the Great Man ordered the interpreter to withdraw and he made a
sign with his hand to the Roman [brother] to wait
until he came back to him.

The Blessed Man left him and went to pray by

himself. Stretching out his hands to heaven, he
prayed to God, saying, 'Lord Almighty, if I cannot profit the men whom you send to me from the
ends of the earth because I do not know the languages of men, what need is there for them to
come? If you want to save them here through me,
grant, O Master, that I may know their languages
for the correction of their souls.'

He prayed for three hours, entreating God
earnestly for this. Suddenly something like a letter written on a piece of papyrus was sent from
heaven into his right hand. Reading it, he learned
the speech of all the languages. Having sent up
praise to the Father, the Son, and the Holy Spirit,
he came back to that brother with great joy, and
began to converse with him faultlessly in Greek
and Latin. When that brother heard it, he said
that the Great Man surpassed all the scholars in
that language. After correcting the brother as
was required, and determining the penance corresponding to his faults, he *commended him to
the Lord* and left him.[2]

Pachomius prays to know his language

He receives the gift of tongues

Ac 20:32.

Chapter 12: About the fig tree.

28. The next day, the Blessed Man went out to
visit the other monasteries. He came to the monastery called Thmoušons and entered it. Now
there was in the middle of that monastery a large
fig tree which one of the boys was in the habit of
climbing up secretly to pluck the figs for the boys
and eat them. When the Great Man entered and
came near that fig tree, he saw an unclean spirit
sitting in it, and he knew immediately that it was
the demon of gluttony. And the Holy Man knew
that it was he who deceived the boys. Therefore
he called the gardener and told him, 'Cut down
this fig tree, because it is a stumbling block for
those who are not firm in their purpose, and also
because it is not a seemly thing that this tree
should be in the middle of the monastery'. When
the gardener heard this, he was greatly grieved.

Pachomius
orders a fig tree
cut in
Thmoušons

29. The gardener's name was Jonas. He had
spent eighty-five years in that monastery, leading
a very venerable life of *ascesis*. He cared alone for
all the fruit, and he alone had planted all the
fruit trees of that monastery. Nevertheless, never,
until his death, did he taste any fruit at all, while
all the brothers and the strangers and the people
living around ate their fill in the fruit season. Now
this brother was dressed in this fashion: he joined
three goat skins together and these were sufficient
to cover his whole body. He never wrapped himself
in another blanket either in winter or in summer.
Nor did he know what it is to give the body rest
from continuous labor, because he was always
working eagerly. He never ate anything cooked,

Virtues and
ascesis of Jonas,
the gardener

not lentils, or any other food during his whole life but only vinegar with raw fine greens. The brothers also used to affirm that he did not know which house was the infirmary nor what the sick brothers ate.

And besides all these things, according to what we have heard, until his death this blessed man never slept lying on his back. During the day he worked out in the garden, and, taking his food toward sunset, he entered his cell and sat on a stool in the middle of the cell, plaiting ropes until the night *synaxis*. And so, if it happened that the needs of nature compelled him to snatch a little sleep, he would sleep sitting and holding in his hands the ropes he was plaiting. He did not plait the ropes by the light of a lamp, but sitting in darkness, while reciting the Scriptures by heart. He had one tunic, which he put on when he was going to partake of the divine and holy mysteries of Christ; and he would take it off immediately, keeping it clean, and he kept it for those eighty-five years.[1] And that blessed old man performed many other deeds worthy of praise.

How he died

30. We found this man still alive; and he died in an unusual manner. He gave up his holy soul while sitting on his stool and plaiting the ropes according to his custom. And this holy man did not die suddenly — lest the prowess of the righteous should be diminished — but he fell ill like all men. And he would not be persuaded to go to the infirmary because he did not want to be ministered to like the other sick or to taste the foods which the sick brothers ate. And he would not lie on his back even when he was sick nor did he allow a pillow or any other thing that could give

him relief to be put under him when he was sitting.[1] No one was standing by him when he died.
He simply went to his rest holding his rope-work
and plaiting. And it is a wonder to hear how we
buried him. Since his feet could not be stretched
out because they had become stiff like wood, and
his hands could not be made to lie alongside his
body, and he could not be stripped of that hide,
we were therefore obliged to bury him that way,
like a bundle of logs.

31. It was to this man that holy Pachomius
came, asking him to cut down the fig tree. When
he heard it, he said to the Great Man, 'Oh no, father, for we are accustomed to collect a large
quantity of fruit for the brothers from this fig tree'.
When the Great Man saw that he was grieved by
this, he did not want to force him, lest he should be
excessively grieved. Indeed the Great Man knew
that his life was great and an object of wonder to
all, small and great. Now it happened that, on the
next day, that fig tree was found to have become so
completely withered that neither healthy leaf nor
fruit was found upon it. When he saw this, the
blessed Jonas was greatly grieved, not because of
the fig tree, but because of his disobedience, since
he had not cut the tree immediately when he was
told so by the Great Man.[1]

Chapter 13: About the oratory.

32. The blessed Pachomius built an oratory
and he made porticos for it and set up pillars of
bricks, and he furnished it very well. He was
pleased with the work, because he had built it

How the fig tree
that he did not
want to cut
withered

Cf. Mk 11:20.

Against com-
placency in
material beauty

well. Then he thought that it was through a dia-
bolic activity that he was marvelling at the beauty
of the house. Therefore he took ropes and tied
them to the pillars; then he made a prayer in his
heart, ordered the brothers to pull and bend all
the pillars so they remained crooked. And he said
to the brothers, 'I pray you, brothers, do not
make great efforts to adorn the work of your
hands. But whatever may enter into the work of
each one of you by the grace of Christ and from
his gift, take great care that your mind may not
stumble through the praise given to the art, and
become a prey to the devil.'[1]

Chapter 14: About the heretics who wore
hair garments.

**A heretic monk
invites
Pachomius
to walk on
the river**
Cf. 2 K 1:10.
Cf. 1 Jn 5:15.

33. Some heretic monks who wore hair garments heard about holy Pachomius. They came
to his monastery and said to some of the brothers,
'Our father has sent us to your Great Man with
this message, "If you are truly a man of God, and
if you are confident that God listens to you,
come, let us cross the river together, walking on
our feet, so that we may know which of us has
more confidence before God."' When the brothers reported this [to him], he was angry with them
and said, 'Why did you let yourselves listen at all
to people uttering such things? Do you not know
that such propositions are foreign to God and
completely alien to our way of life? They are not
fitting even for seculars who think right. And
what law of God lets us do these things? On the
contrary the Saviour commanded us in the Gos-

pels. *Let not your left hand know what your right hand is doing.* For nothing is more wretched than such foolishness, that is, that I should give up mourning for my sins and [pondering] how to avoid *eternal punishment*, and become *childish* in my outlook, turning to such propositions.'

The brothers answered, 'How is it then that this man who is a heretic and alien to God was so bold as to call on you to do this?' He answered to them, 'He was able to cross the river travelling as on dry land by God's permission, the devil working with him for his impious heresy, so that the exhibition of his undertaking should not be brought to nothing, and in order to implant the [same] faith in those he has deceived.[1] Go, then, and say to those who brought such a message, "Here is what the man of God Pachomius says, 'I put my striving and all my zeal not into crossing a river on foot but in [trying] to avoid the judgement of God and to escape, by the power of God, such satanic wiles as these.'"' With these words he enjoined the brothers not to think highly of their own achievements or to desire to have apparitions or to see demons, or to tempt the Godhead by such requests, when He has advised us in advance by the Holy Scriptures, saying, *You shall not put your God to the test.*

Mt 6:3.

Mt 25:46.
1 Co 14:20.

Pachomius explains how he can do it by the devil's action

Dt 6:16.

Chapter 15: About the man who displayed the mats he had made.

34. It happened once, as the Great Man was sitting somewhere in the monastery with some other brothers, that a certain brother of the mon-

Pachomius
rebukes a
brother who, out
of vainglory, did
more work than
was required

Jn 12:43.

astery who had made two mats during that day placed them in front of his cell, opposite the place where the brothers were sitting with the Blessed Man. He did it, uplifted by a thought of vainglory, thinking that in this he would be praised by the Great Man for displaying such zeal, since the rule was for each brother to make one mat a day. The Great Man, seeing that he had done this for display, and recognizing the thought that moved him to do it, groaned heavily and said to the brothers who were sitting with him, 'See this brother; from morning till now he has given all his toil to the devil and has left nothing whatever of his work for the comfort of his own soul, because he has *preferred the praise of men to the praise of God.* And although he has worn his body out through labor, he has made his soul empty of the fruition of the works.' Then he called the brother and rebuked him. He ordered him to stand behind the brothers at the time of prayer, holding the two mats and saying, 'I beg you, brothers, pray for my wretched soul, that the God of all compassion may forgive it and have mercy on it for having preferred these two mats to his kingdom'. And he ordered him to stand with the mats in the same manner in the middle of the place at meal time until the brothers rose from table. After this he ordered that he be confined to his cell for a period of five months, to make two mats every day, eating only bread with salt, and that no brother visit him.

Chapter 16: About the leper.

35. In addition to these, and before we bring this story to a close, we ought to mention another holy man from among the brothers who practised the life of virtues thoroughly and, for the sake of edification, to narrate a few facts of his life. This brother of blessed memory, being a leper in his body, had his cell separate from the brothers. All his life he lived on only bread and salt. He used to make one mat a day and often, when he was plaiting the ropes that go into the mats, his hands would be pierced by the rushes and covered with blood, so that the mats he was doing would be stained with his blood. Although he had such an illness, he never missed the *synaxis* of the brothers and never slept in daytime until his departure from this life. And it was his habit to recite by heart some section from the Scriptures every night before going to sleep; and then he would sleep until the signal was given for the nightly *synaxis*.

The ascesis of a brother who was a leper

One day a brother came to him and saw his hands covered with blood from plaiting mats, and he said to him, 'Brother, why do you toil and work like this when you have such a disease? Do you think that you will be charged with idleness before God if you do not work? The Lord knows you are sick, and nobody with such a disease has ever touched work; especially when nobody compels you to work. We feed others, strangers and paupers; and you who are one of us and such a holy man — ought we not to serve you from all our soul and with much joy?' The other answered, 'It is impossible for me not to work', and the brother

Another brother convinces him to anoint his bleeding hands

said to him, 'If it pleases you, then I beg you at
least to anoint your hands with oil every evening,
that you may not be weary'.[1] He listened to the
brother and anointed his hands as he had told
him. But his hands, being softened, were hurt all
the more by the rushes that pierced them.

**Pachomius
rebukes him for
not putting his
hope for health
in God**

36. The Great Man came to visit him in his cell
and told him, 'Do you think, Athenodoros, that
the oil is helping you? Who has compelled you to
work, that on pretext of work you have put your
hopes for health in the oil rather than in God?
Was God not able to heal you? But providing for
the profit of your soul, he permitted that you
should have this disease.' He answered and said to
the Great Man, 'Father, *I have sinned, and I
know my fault.* But I beg you to pray for me, that
God may forgive me this sin.' And according to
what the fathers who were with him affirmed, he
spent a full year mourning for himself over this
act, and eating every other day.

Lk 15:18,21.

**How this man
used to be
an example**

In the beginning, before this brother was too
much overcome by his suffering, the Great Man
used to send him to each monastery to provide an
example and a foundation to all the brothers by
the way he bore thankfully the grievous suffering
of his disease.

Chapter 17: About idolatry.

**The illusions of
the pagans**

37. And discoursing again, he spoke against
idolatry, saying:[1]

'It is godlessness. But some pagan will say, "I
do not worship demons but God. I do have idols,
but through them I call upon the powers of God

as gods, and through these upon God. And the Great One is not grieved; and he is attainable if he has other gods under him." It was necessary to be silent about these things until God pricked these pagans to convert to the truth, which grace I received. Now, since the Lord enjoins, *You received without charge, give without charge,* let us speak briefly.

'Since *Adam's transgression* in the beginning of the world, men have been going astray, not wanting [to obey] the law of their conscience or to recognize God the Creator of all things through the marvel, the fearfulness, and the variety of creation. So they made gods for themselves, as the evil advice of the enemy began counselling them when [they were] still in Paradise, *You will be like gods.*[2] Being envious he did not want them to be so but he wanted to be so himself. For by the fact that they do not submit to the lordship of the Word of God, he, the adversary of the Word, is surely lord over them. Indeed, where life is absent, there is death. From there came lust for women and before that fratricide* and folly of giants[†] as in the time of Nimrod[‡], and also hope in earthly things alone, although the good God had shown, even then, and in striking deeds, the hope of the heavenly things and even of the resurrection, through the translation to heaven of the most holy Enoch*,[3] and later on of Elijah[†].

38. 'Because of this came the wrath of the flood, in which a righteous man was preserved as the leaven of truth. And after these evils had come, the long-suffering Judge brought help again to man who has free-will — and free-will not for evil alone but also for good, for *All things are*

Mt 10:8.

Rm 5:14.
Idolatry began in Paradise

Gn 3:5.

Cf. 2 Th 2:4.

*Gn 4:8.
†Gn 6:4.
‡Gn 10:8.

*Gn 5:24.
†2 K 2:11.

A new law was given through Moses

permitted but all things are not expedient—by giving him a law through Moses. And it was not a law in one word like the one in Paradise, *You shall not eat of the tree of the knowledge of good and evil*, but a detailed one dealing with things like how to lead a blind man by the hand, and even how to think and how to speak, how to guard one's speech at war, and how to speak in thanksgiving at the birth of children and cattle and for the produce of the field and vineyard and similar fruits, and for the inheritance itself. He instilled fear in them by the destruction of those who dwelled there, and also in Egypt through many wonders, and moreover at the sea, so that remembering all these things they might fear God, especially since the law was written *by his finger.*

'How many fearful things accompanied that law! *A mountain burning, fire reaching to heaven*, loud sounds of trumpets†*, and the rest. And he cherished them as a father, covering them with a *cloud by day*, lighting them with *fire by night*, feeding them free from care with bread from heaven, and helping them by this not to have any desire for food—hence *the memorials of craving* for others who are intemperate. And when they found nothing to drink he often instructed them to advance like children, after Moses*—for he also was the imitator of his fathers, Abraham, Isaac, and Jacob, and of holy Joseph himself who was also truly an image of the fathers.

39. 'But someone will say, "Why is it that He did not take such interest in us from the beginning?" God always takes an interest; for he loves

Margin references:
1 Co 6:12.

Gn 2:17.

Ex 7-11,14;
Ac 7:36.

Ex 31:18.

*Dt 4:11.
†Ex 19:19.
Ex 13:21.
Ibid.
Ex 16:4-35.

Nb 11:34.

*Nb 20:8-11.

The Jews acknowledged the true God

his own creatures* and his image† in holiness and truth. Behold also the great number of witnesses of the Old Testament, especially Jews, who understand and confess its truth until now. For he says, *I who speak, here I am.* The books of Moses are truth, taking their beginning and their end from God. You then from the tribe of Judah have agreed that the first law is from Almighty God. And after this, having near you for your glory the Son of God as your own and of the same tribe, hold to God, if not out of confidence in me, yet out of confidence in all the saints and in the words of Baruch, *Do not give your glory to others* alone.[1] Do not want to have Him to yourself alone, remembering the precept, *You shall love your neighbor as yourself.*[2] You say already, with us persuading the unbelieving pagan, "*There is no other God save one*" and, "He does not want the demons to be gods over his children or servants". For in punishment he writes that he will destroy all Israel our city, and burn up the men and the vessels found there, because they made up their minds altogether to have false gods; and even our high priest—but for the holy Moses, Aaron would have been destroyed.

'Let then the pagan, hearing this, be persuaded by the Jew and believe in the only God. It is impossible for other [gods] to exist when there is only the One. So, in the case of Adam, [the demons] profited nothing, being for his sake punished by the Lord, not only by the fact that they should *crawl on their belly* and their breast and that the *righteous Lord* himself coming after this from the seed of David *shall watch your head and shall break the neck of the sinners,* but also by the fact

*Ws 11:24.
†Gn 1:27.

Is 52:6.

Ba 4:3.

Lv 19:18;
Mt 19:19.

Dt 4:35.

Cf. Dt. 9:19-20.
Cf. Dt 13:16.

Let pagans also be convinced

Gn 3:14-15.
Ps 129(128):4.

Ibid.

Gn 3:5.
Gn 2:7.

Lk 3:7.

Ac 17:27-28.

Cf. Is 40:10.

Heb 4:15.

that the one who was advised to be a God[1] (and who was *a living man*) was also expelled from Paradise. You, too, *flee from the wrath that is coming*, first of all by abandoning the alien god-making, and worship the One who is your bene-factor and ours and all men's, by recognizing him as God. *For he is not far from us, but it is in him that we live and move and exist*, as Paul, the herald of the truth, says to the Athenians. And since we see that you have from your fathers in-sensible idols, believing that the Godhead is wor-shipped through them, worship instead the One whom our master God begot, the true God be-come man for our sake, Jesus Christ, who has all the saints about him, martyrs, patriarchs, proph-ets, apostles, and most of all his own works. And just as a pearl does not need two or three witnesses to state its nature—the pearl, though silent, is an object of admiration—likewise you who are a man, guided by a man *having the same feelings and of the same stock*, will easily be brought to God and to eternal life.

40. 'As for the witness about Him, the man of **God made man was announced in the Scriptures** good understanding has the many writings of the saints, not only about His coming and His mani-festation, but also about you the pagan. For God, knowing in advance that the nations, rather than the disobedient Jews, would obey him, has pre-pared his inheritance for you. Do not reject then by disbelief the only Master of all. Although he has become like us for our sake, he remains what he was by nature, God, as was also manifested through his visible deeds.

'But you will say, "If such is the faith and glory of the Christians, how is it that it is rare to find among them so faithful a one?" Well, because man has free-will, if he does not have the faith firmly planted in his breast, and does not stand ready for *the contest that is set before him*, according to the commandments of God, he is quickly suborned by the passions of the flesh or turns coward. The noble athlete does not see the one among [the Christians] who is defeated, but he emulates those who conquer, in order to imitate them in a good manner, worthy of the same crown, being ready even to die for him. Search as much as you can and with faith, and the kindness of the Lord shall appear to you in detail.

'And we believe that the Jews themselves will return to the faith of their fathers, Abraham, Isaac, and Jacob, if they want to. And him whom they once did not know, God, son of God, Onlybegotten, become man for the sake of the human race, his creature, they will find him *present and speaking**, when they search the Scriptures,[†] old and new, which they had before us — for *He came to his own domain*. If they do not want to — which God forbid — he will say to them, *"I have been found by those who did not seek me*, but have gone astray in idolatry and ignorance; *I have revealed myself to those who did not consult me."*

41. 'And if someone says, "I do not believe [you] if you call a man God, no matter what he may do," he does nothing strange. For about Moses also, their glorious prophet, *whom they could not look in the face*, the faithless did not believe that he was a prophet of God and they wanted to stone him. But Joshua, son of Nun — who took upon himself the name and the whole figure of him who says *I am coming to gather all*

To imitate the examples of the true Christians
Heb 12:1.

The Jews shall come to the faith in Christ
Cf. Rm 11:26.

*Is 52:6.
[†]Cf. Jo 5:39.
Jn 1:11.

Rm 10:20;
Is 65:1-2.

Ibid.

Faith is difficult

2 Co 3:7.

Ex 17:4.

Is 66:18.

the nations[1] — not only believed in him as a man of God, but also gave him the name of Lord, say-

Nb 11:28.

ing, *My Lord Moses, stop them.* Because of this,

*Si 46:1.

he was also his successor.*Likewise also Caleb†

†Cf. Nb 14:6.

and many others were well-pleasing to God through him.[2]

'Now even he who is called a Christian, if he

A bad Christian crucifies Christ

does not turn again his own vision to *the inner*

*Rm 7: 22

*man** — unlike Eve who turned her vision from the inner realities to the outer to desire the visible things — and if he does not continue to see *with*

Ph 2:12.

fear and trembling[3] the power and the glory of the indwelling Christ, will not he himself also, like the Jews, crucify Christ in another way? For in every evil that a man does, especially when he rejects the second commandment, he will also reject the first one, as it is said, *Inasmuch as you have done it to one of the least of these, you did it*

Mt 25:40.

to me.[4]

'But may all, Jews, pagans, Christians, and

May all men be saved

even the barbarians be saved for the Lord through our Lord and God Jesus Christ — for *his right hand and his holy arm have made salvation for*

Ps 98(97):1.

him to the enemy's shame — and so be found in the kingdom of heaven singing with all the saints from all the ages to the highest God for ages unending.'

After he had said these things to the brothers, our father Pachomius rose up, happy that he had

Mt 25:25.

not *hidden the talent.* He prayed and dismissed the brothers, who were exulting in the goodness of God because of what they had heard. Amen.

Notes to the Paralipomena
References are given to paragraphs, not chapters

Paral. 1   [1]Various applications are made of this text. In Pach. Letter 5:4, Pachomius writes: 'I want you to be like those who did not know their right hand and their left.' But in G[1] 40, he speaks of the various kinds of people in the community, including 'boys who cannot tell their right hand from their left'.

[2]This is another version of the story found in SBo 69 (= G[1] 77). The expression 'a certain Theodore' at the beginning of the ¶ is a little surprising, if we consider the place Theodore holds in the pachomian hagiography. The indication that Theodore had been in the monastery for twenty years is absolutely erroneous. Although there is a great divergency between the sources concerning the chronology of Theodore's life and his age, there is little doubt that he came to Tabennesi in 328. From the indications given by the Lives and Am. Letter, Theodore's first instruction and his appointment as steward of Tabennesi can be dated in 336-337. See SBo 31, note 3 and SBo 69, note 1.

Paral. 2   [1]In G[1] it is to a monk called Psenamon that Pachomius entrusted Silvanos.

Paral. 3   [1]Nb 16:32 is quoted also in Inst. 18 and Pach. Letter 5:7.

Paral. 4   [1]κοινόβιον here corresponds to *Koinonia* in the Coptic documents, and it means the community or the community life rather than what we would call today a *coenobium*.

[2]In G[1] we read 'Petronios and Cornelios'. Here Cornelios has been replaced by the better known Horsiesios, just as Psenamon above has been replaced by the better known Petronios.

[3]See Pachomius' recommendation to be indifferent either to praises or to curses, in Pach. Instr. 1:22.

[4]See in SBo 82 a description of how the angels escort the souls of the righteous brothers to heaven.

[5]In G[1] 104-105 we have another version of the same story (see also S[5] 93 and Am). There, Silvanos is a young boy. As we have it here, the story is impossible: Silvanos was an actor before coming to the monastery; then, after twenty years of good religious life followed by a time of relaxation and by eight years of holy life, he died at the time when Pachomius was still alive. There is absolutely no possibility of making this fit with the chronology of Pachomius' life.

Paral. 6   [1]There is a much shorter version of this story in SBo 93 (= G[1] 103).

Paral. 7   [1]Mention of the place where there will be weeping and grinding of teeth, with reference to Mt 8:12, is frequent; see Hors. Reg. 53; Pach. Instr. 1:26 and Theod. Instr. 3:10.

[2]Pachomius uses the same expression in SBo 107.

Paral. 8   [1]Constantine, who reigned over the Western part of the Empire from

306, took control of the Eastern Empire only in 324, the year Pachomius received his first disciples at Tabennesi.

²τὴν κοινωνίαν. This and a similar case a few pages further on (Halkin, pp. 132,21; 134,22) are the only two uses of κοινωνία in Paralipomena.

Paral. 9   ¹The same text is also quoted in Hors. Test. 55.

Paral. 10   ¹A gesture of annoyance and of distress; see SBo 11, with note 2.
²The whole description is inspired by Lk 15:17ff.
³This text is quoted also in Hors. Reg. 12 and Theod. Instr. 3:18.

Paral. 11   ¹This text is also quoted in G¹ 85 and Hors. Test. 33.
²The same story is found in G¹ 85; it is absent from SBo, but we read it in Ag–Am, and fragmentarily in S¹⁰ 7.

Paral. 12   ¹This tension between active life (πρακτική) and contemplation (θεωρία) is a preoccupation alien to pachomian spirituality. The word θεωρία never occurs in G¹.
²G¹ 21 states that Pachomius very early received the power to tread serpents and scorpions underfoot. This power is acknowledged by the demons themselves below, ¶ 24. In SBo 98 Pachomius instructs the brothers not to lose confidence if they tread on snakes, scorpions, or other wild beasts. Finally, in Pach. Instr. 1:42 we hear Christ reprimanding a negligent monk: 'Did I not give you the power to tread underfoot. . .' etc.

Paral. 13   ¹See another version of this story in SBo 83 (= G¹ 93).

Paral. 14   ¹Cf. SBo 21 (= G¹ 18).

Paral. 15   ¹There is no indication in the Rules that cooked meals were restricted to Saturdays and Sundays.

Paral. 16   ¹Note the transition from the singular 'cook' to the plural 'cooks'.

Paral. 17   ¹τὴν νυκτερινὴν λειτουργίαν. Neither the terminology nor the practice is pachomian. Pachomian monks gathered in the morning for a *synaxis*; the night vigils were a private exercise. A similar expression (νυκτερινὴ σύναξις) is found also below, ¶¶ 29 and 35. We have studied these texts in *La liturgie*, pp. 302–305.
²2 Tm 3:12 is quoted also in Theod. Instr. 3:7.

Paral. 18   ¹'these communities': τὰ κοινόβια ταῦτα (ταῦτα is omitted by mss o and h). This is the only case where we find the plural τὰ κοινόβια in our Greek sources. Throughout G¹ and elsewhere in Paral. the singular τὸ κοινόβιον corresponds to the *Koinonia* of our Coptic documents and means the whole pachomian congregation or its way of life. We will find the plural *coenobia* again in the *Pachomiana latina*.
²About that 'covenant', see SBo 49. If we really have a quotation of Mt 28:20 here, the application is surprising. This text is quoted with its literal meaning in SBo 189; G¹ 135, Theod. Instr. 3:32.
³In an instruction about the Passover (Pach. Instr. 2:4), Pachomius

says: 'let the king lay down in mourning the diadem he wears and the royal crown, for *a crown of thorns* strewn with darts was prepared for the head of the king of peace'.

Paral. 21 [1]I.e. one hundred golden *solidi.* Cf. infra, ¶ 22 (Halkin, p. 149, 18): τὸ χρυσίον.
[2]The word ὁλοκοτίνα used here is the equivalent of νομίσματα used at the beginning of the ¶.
[3]The text of MS A seems to give a better sense than that of MS F followed by Halkin.
[4]Lit. 'thirteen *artabae*'; the *artaba* is a Persian measure.

Paral. 22 [1]Ms A adds: 'until he has returned the wheat to its place'.

Paral. 23 [1]ὁ αὐτὸς ἀδελφὸς, i.e. the brother appointed to replace the one who was discharged at the end of ¶ 22.
[2]G[1] 109 calls Zacchaeus a 'minister of the brothers'; SBo 96 presents him as the head of the boatmen.

Paral. 24 [1]φαντασία: the usual words are ὅραμα or ὀπτασία. On the difference between them, see D.J. Chitty, 'Pachomian Sources Reconsidered', pp. 51-52; 'Pachomian Sources Once More', pp. 57-64.

Paral. 25 [1]Cf. SBo 6 (= G[1] 3).

Paral. 26 [1]See the same use of Jb 40:29 above, ¶ 4.

Paral. 27 [1]I.e. Sahidic, the Coptic dialect of Upper Egypt.
[2]This story of Pachomius' amazing gift of tongues contrasts with the more sober and prosaic description of SBo 89 (= G[1] 95). In fact, Pachomius 'made efforts' to learn Greek, but he does not seem to have been very successful. Theodore the Alexandrian became his permanent interpreter.

Paral. 29 [1]According to the Rule (Jer. Pref. 4 and Pr. 81), the monks had two tunics, plus a third one, already worn, for sleeping and working. The present story can be related to the apophthegm of Theodore of Pherme (n. 29) who was willing to let thieves make away with all his belongings except the habit he used for the *synaxis*, his λεβίτων συνακτικός.

Paral. 30 [1]The pachomian monks slept on a type of reclining seat; see Pr. 87 with note 2.

Paral. 31 [1]It is not absolutely certain that this Jonas is the same one who was superior of the community of Thmousons and asked Pachomius to organize it according to the rules of the *Koinonia*; see SBo 51 (G[1] 54). Note the confusion between the names of Jonas and John in G[1] 54, note 10, and G[1] 79, note 2.

Paral. 32 [1]D.J. Chitty, *The Desert a City*, p. 119, is probably right in supposing that this story is 'an attempt to explain the actual crookedness of a church the writer knew, due, in fact, to inadequate foundations, faulty materials, or inexpert buidling'. The only material available was soft, sun-baked bricks.

Paral. 33 [1]Compare the story of the brother who walked on burning charcoals in front of Palamon and Pachomius, in SBo 14 (= G[1] 8).

Paral. 35 [1]About the use of oil by the sick brothers, see Pr. 92.

Paral. 37 [1]This instruction on idolatry — appended to ms F of the *Paralipomena,* but absent from all the other manuscripts, Greek or Syriac — is much more 'pachomian' in character and language than the rest of the Paral. D.J. Chitty, 'Pachomian Sources Reconsidered', p. 51, n. 1, says that the Greek of this instruction 'is allied to that of G[1] rather than of Asc. [i.e. Paral.], and would not be inconsistent with its being due to the same Greek hand as G[1]'.
[2]This text is quoted also in Pach. Instr. 1:24.
[3]Enoch's translation to heaven is mentioned also in SBo 55 (= G[1] 82) and in Pach. Instr. 1:25.

Paral. 39 [1]This text from Baruch is quoted also in Hors. Test. 50.
[2]This text, very consonant with the spirituality of the *Koinonia,* is often quoted; see SBo 48 (= G[1] 53); G[1] 38; Theod. Fragm. 4.

Paral. 41 [1]This text is quoted also in G[1] 56.
[2]Both Joshua (always called Jesus son of Nave) and Caleb are also mentioned in Pach. Letter 3:8.
[3]Ph 2:12 is used also in SBo 26 and Hors. Test. 17.
[4]G[1] quotes this text twice in combination with Mt 18:6; see G[1] 40 (cf. SBo 40) and 125.

a LetteR of
BishoP ammon
(am. LetteR)

A Letter of bishop Ammon
about the way of life of Pachomius and Theodore
and about part of their Life.

BEING A LOVER of the servants of Christ, you have been zealous to become an imitator of their purity, and you admire the holy man[1] of God Theodore, who is one of the monks called Tabennesiots among the Thebans, and [about whom] you have heard from many persons. Learning that I had spent three years in their monastery, you bade me write to Your Honor all that I have heard about him from the holy men who had lived with him and all that I was granted to see. Therefore, beseeching God to make my memory of things exact and pure, I hasten to satisfy the order of Your Holiness and I disclose these very things.[2]

Prologue

2. At the age of seventeen, having become a Christian, I heard the blessed pope Athanasius relating in church the way of life of the monks and ever-virgins and, marvelling at *the hope stored up for them in the heavens.*[1] Loving what I had heard from him, I went out and chose their blessed life for myself. After I had received *the cleansing water of rebirth,* I met with a certain theban monk in the city and I proposed to follow

Ammon is received into monastic life by Theodore

Col 1:5.

Tt 3:5.

him. Then I offered [God] what I had and I took
the advice of Paul of blessed memory, the priest
of the Church called Pereou. As he detected the
monk to be a heretic, he sent me to holy Theodore in the Thebaid, with Theophilos and Copres, men devoted to God, who happened to have
been sent by Theodore to the blessed pope
Athanasius with letters.

And when we came to the monastery where the
servant of God Theodore was — which is called
Phbow and is in the nome of Upper Diospo-
lis — the man of God Theodore deigned to meet
me at the gate. After he had told me what was necessary, he made me change my clothing and introduced me into the monastery. There I found
about six hundred monks assembled and waiting
in the middle of the monastery. Theodore sat
down under a palm tree and they all sat down
with him. Then, seeing that I was surprised at
their order and was blushing, he made me sit
down near him.

3. One of the monks rose up as if inspired and
asked Theodore to tell his faults in front of all.
Theodore loked at him and told him, *'It is good
for a man to bear the yoke in his youth. He shall
sit alone and be silent, because he had borne it
upon himself. He shall offer his cheek to the one
who strikes him, he will be filled with insults.*[1] But
you, why do you bear grievously insults [received]
for Christ's sake?' When this one sat down, another rose up and asked to hear about himself.
[Theodore] looked at him too and said, 'It is written, *A garden enclosed, my sister, my bride; a
garden enclosed, a sealed fountain.*[2] But as for
you, on the contrary, *your fruits are plucked off*

**Ammon
attends a public
correction of
the brothers
by Theodore**

Lm 3:27-28,30.

Sg 4:12.

by all those who pass by on the road.' When this one had sat down in great dejection, another rose up and asked the same question. He told him, '*I waited and waited for the Lord and he has brought me out of the pit of wretchedness and from the slough of the marsh; he has settled my feet on a rock and steadied my steps. He has put a new song in my mouth, a hymn to our God.*' And when that one had wept copiously and had sat down while many others also wept with him, another rose up and asked to learn about himself. He said, '*The patient man is great in understanding; but he who is fainthearted is very foolish.* Correct yourself.' When that one had sat down with sadness, someone called Orion, a Lybian by race and a carpenter by craft, as I learned afterwards, rose up and asked about himself. Theodore said, '*You need patience, that having done God's will you may gain the promises*'. After Orion, another one, called Patelloli, rose up and asked him to say what regarded him. He answered, '*Carry one another's burdens and so fulfill the law of Christ.*[3] Correct yourself.' When this one had gone away, he said of him to all the monks present, 'Believe me when I say he is fearful to demons'. After that another rose up and asked him. He told him, '*Blessed be the Lord who trains my hands for war and my fingers for battle.* In these things also be brave.' After this one he said to another who rose up, '*It is not against blood and flesh that we have to struggle, but against the principalities, against the powers, against those who rule this world of darkness, against the spiritual armies of wickedness.* Struggle!' After this one, another rose up and he told

Ps 80(79):12.

Ps 40(39):1-3.

Pr 14:29.

Heb 10:36.

Ga 6:2.

Ps 144(143):1.

Eph 6:12.

2 Co 7:1.

Ps 19(18):12-13.

Theodore the
Alexandrian
acts as
interpreter

*Ga 2:20.
†Cf. 2 Co 5:6.

Theodore
announces the
future perse-
cution against
the Church

Ph 1:17.

Dn 11:24.

him, '*Let us cleanse ourselves from all defile-
ment*, not only *of the flesh*, but also *of the spirit*.⁴
Give heed to your secret things.' And after this
one he said to another who rose up, 'Pray saying,
Cleanse me from my hidden [faults], *and from
aliens preserve your servant*. You have indeed a
strong warfare on both sides.'

4. We heard him saying these things in the language of the Egyptians, while a Greek interpreta-
tion was given by Theodore the Alexandrian,
who had been a reader in the Church called
Pereou.¹ He was a holy man, saying by his life as
well as by his tongue, *I have been crucified with
Christ; it is not I who live, it is Christ who lives in
me*. *² He was still *dwelling in the body*† at that
time, and well-pleasing to the Lord.³

5. I was amazed, not yet understanding the
things that had been said, because of my youth
and my great inexperience. Then the theban servant of God Theodore questioned by another rose
up, silently gazing up to heaven. He was in the
midst of the brothers, surrounded by all as by a
crown. He ordered Theodore the Alexandrian to
interpret and said, 'I know that if they hear it
again the carnal ones will be vexed; but because
the Lord has enjoined me to tell you, I say it. The
persecution which lies upon the Church of God
from her own people will develop more and will
be able to hurt many. Such indeed were those
who plotted against the holy apostle Paul, *proclaiming Christ not with purity but out of conten-
tion*. When this persecution is in its height, there
will be unexpectedly a pagan king who will *plot
his stratagems* against the mystery of Christ and
will be as zealous as he can to persecute the Chris-

tians. But Christ will put his scheme to shame, for he said about him too, *He who is haughty and contemptuous, a boastful man, shall achieve nothing at all.*[1] We must, therefore, cry out to God, that he may *extend his mercy*[2] to the churches for the salvation of many.'

6. When someone asked him who 'her own people' would be, he said, 'The evil Arians'. And saying this, he sat down again under the palm tree. And so it happened that, moving a short distance from the place I had been sitting before, I was farther from him. As the monks were conversing together in their own language, someone called Elourion, a man *clothed in Christ,*[1] told me in the language of the Greeks, 'Rise up and ask the man of God *when shall these things be?*' Seeing that I was afraid and trembling, he told me, 'Do not be afraid; he is looking at you with a cheerful look, encouraging you. Rise up then and ask him.' Respecting the man's white hair, I was all the more constrained. But when I saw the servant of God Theodore giving heed to the blessed old man Elourion and to me with a smile, and being nudged by Elourion, I stood up. Smiling, Theodore ordered Theodore the Alexandrian to interpret, and through him he said to me, 'Say what you desire, knowing that having been recently harvested, you are a new wine.' And still more constrained with fear I said, '*When shall these things be?*' He said, 'Have you not yet read the divine Scriptures? It is written, *Sound of the rushing of rain.*[2] Therefore I say to you, Sound of the rushing of the events that have been foretold. You shall see these events; and in them you shall be enduring pleasant and unpleasant things. For

Ha 2:5.

Cf. Ps 36(35):10.

The persecution will be for a time only

Rm 13:14; Ga 3:27.

Mt 24:3.

Mt 24:3.

1 K 18:41.

the Lord will bring mercy upon many souls. And first, the persecution by the pagan will be dissolved; then the persecution that lies upon the Church from her own people.'

7. While all were staring at me, the holy Theodore rose up and ordered everyone to go to prayer. Then he took me by the hand and entrusted me to teachers and guides, namely to Theodore the Alexandrian and to his second, Ausonius.[1] He said to Ausonius, 'Urge him to learn the divine Scriptures, for he will not remain in the monastery, but will be a minister of the Church of God.'

They received me and brought me to the house where lived the twenty greek monks who were under them. [The monks] sat down and required each one to say what he had remembered from the questions addressed to the holy Theodore and from his answers. And so I heard each one of the twenty, and after them Ausonius and Theodore the Alexandrian, saying what they had remem-

bered. *I pondered it in my heart*, and was able to remember what I have written. For, when I asked him, Theodore the Alexandrian immediately interpreted to me the meaning of what Theodore had said to each of those who had questioned him.

These things were said a little more than a year after Gallus was proclaimed Caesar with the title

of New Constantius.

8. Every time I heard [even] from afar the holy Theodore's voice, I was filled either with joy or grief or fear; and I wondered about what I experienced, what this might be. I inquired and learned that others also experienced the same

thing as myself. Therefore I asked both Ausonius
and Elourion, each of them separately, to tell me
the story of the man of God Theodore—for I did
not yet dare to be continually questioning
Theodore the Alexandrian—and each of them
said:

9. 'There was a certain Pachomius, leader of
these monasteries,[1] who was *well-pleasing to
God*.[2] God made known many things to him by
revelations, still more by *speaking to his heart*,[†]
and other things through angels; and he honored
him with divers gifts. Six years ago, *he absented
himself from the body and made his home with
the Lord.* Once, as he was sitting, he said to the
monks around him, "We sent the servant of God
Pecoš to Latopolis to succour the infirm there.
Now, as I sat here, an angel of the Lord brought
me the good news that he is about to arrive today,
bringing *a vessel of election*[3] for God. This is a
boy of thirteen called Theodore, *filled with the
Holy Spirit*."[4] After sunset, Pecoš, who was a true
friend of Pachomius, arrived at the monastery,
bringing as well this holy Theodore, who was
then, as I said, thirteen years old. The holy
Pachomius received him and brought him up as
his true son.[5]

10. 'When Theodore was twenty-two years old,
he was commanded [to do] something by Pachomius and accomplished it. Then, looking for the
holy Pachomius and as if guided by the Holy
Spirit, he came near the house where the monks
used to eat, near the church[1] of the monastery.
He perceived the earth shaking and he heard
Pachomius in prayer saying, "O God who are *full
of mercy and relent over our evils, spare* the race

AD 352

How Theodore came to Pachomius
*Heb 11:5; cf. Gn 5:22.
†Ho 2:16.
AD 346.

2 Co 5:8.

Ac 9:15.

Ac 7:55.

c. AD 328.

Theodore hears Pachomius praying

Jl 2:13.17.

Cf. Ps 36(35):8.

of men, and multiply still more your pity for us. Do not judge the monks and the ever-virgins, requiring the exact [observance of their] promise. Likewise, [do not judge] your people concerning the good things you have enjoined on us and planted in us. But in judging us, compare us to the world before the coming of your Only-begotten; for so you will *not enter into judgement with** us, but you will *wipe out*† our sins. If indeed you did not destroy the world then, how will you not have mercy on your people of this present time? Have mercy on us, Master, save us and acquire us [for yourself] *relenting from your wrath and anger,* for the sake of the blood of your Only-begotten by which we have been redeemed. If, indeed, for the sake of Abraham, Isaac and Jacob, you often had mercy on the Jews, how much more will you have mercy on us unceasingly for the sake of the blood of Christ! We are the servants of your Only-begotten, who has made us your sons, when we were his creatures."

*Ps 143(142):2.
†Ps 51(50):9.

Ex 32:12.14.

'Then, as Pachomius went on saying, "Have mercy", without adding anything else, the earth quaked. Theodore, with his face on the ground, prayed in great fear, until Pachomius, crying with a cheerful voice, said, *"Blessed are you, Lord,* who saved our race; *you are to be praised and glorified unto the ages.* Amen." The earthquake stopped and the light was no longer visible to bodily eyes. Then Pachomius opened the door of the house and he said to Theodore, who had risen up, "You were bold to stay; but cry out unceasingly to God, that he may *extend his mercies* upon us, without which creation cannot exist. And do not tell these things to anyone during my

Dn 3:55.

Ps 36(35):10.

life in the body." We heard this from Theodore after Pachomius' death.

11. 'Seven days after he had seen the things concerning Pachomius, and while Pachomius was visiting the other monasteries, Theodore was in the monastery called Phbow, doing what the holy Pachomius had entrusted to him. From some who had arrived from Alexandria he heard the things that the Arians said about the Only-begotten Son of God; and he prayed God that the race of men might be set free from the error. During his prayer, he saw something like three pillars of light, similar in everything, identical with each other. And he heard a voice saying to him, "Pay attention neither to the division of the visible sign, nor to its outline, but only to the identity; for there is no sign in creation that can express the Father and the Son and the Holy Spirit".

Theodore has a vision of the Trinity

12. 'When Pachomius heard this from Theodore, he told him, "It was manifested and spoken to you according to your capacity to see and to hear. I too, at the time when I chose the monastic life,[1] was urged at times by those who belonged to Meletios of Lycopolis, at other times by those who belonged to Marcion, to join them and be of one mind with them. Learning that there were also other heresies, each one of which claimed to possess the truth, I was troubled. With many tears I prayed God to reveal to me who had the truth, for I was utterly confused. As I was still praying, I went into ecstasy and saw all that is under heaven become like night. And I heard from different parts a voice saying, 'Here is the truth'. And I saw many following each voice in darkness, guiding one another. And [I saw] only

Pachomius tells Theodore about one of his own visions

in the eastern region of the universe a lamp set on high, shining like the morning star. From there I heard a voice say to me, 'Do not be deceived by those who draw [you] to the darkness, but follow this light for the truth is in it'. And at once came a voice saying to me, 'This lamp that you see shining as the morning star will shine upon you some day more brightly than the sun; it is the preaching of the Gospel of Christ, which is preached in his holy Church in which you were baptized. He

AD 312-328.

who calls is Christ in the person of Alexander the bishop of the Church of the Alexandrians.[2] The other voices, those in the darkness, are the voices of the heresies; in the leader of each one of them the demon is speaking and leading many astray.' And so I saw many in luminous garments running toward the lamp, and I blessed God.[3] Disregarding those who wanted to deceive me, I went to

c. AD 316.

live with the man of God Palamon, who was an imitator of the saints, until the time an angel of the Lord came to tell me, 'Warm those who come to you in the fire that God has kindled for you'.

c. AD 323.

Then, guided by him, I established these monasteries by God's help. But know that Athanasius, the bishop of the Church of the Alex-

Ac 7:55.

andrians is also *filled with the Holy Spirit*".[4]

13. 'Pachomius used to tell all of us, at the

Praise of
Athanasius by
Pachomius

time Athanasius was appointed bishop,[1] "Men who are not good are censuring the judgement of God that came upon him, putting forward his youth and studying to divide the Church of God. To me the Holy Spirit said, 'I have raised him as a pillar and as a lamp for the Church', and 'Many afflictions and slanders on the part of men, for the sake of devotion to Christ, await him. But overcoming every trial, he will preach the truth of the Gospel to the Churches until the end, being strengthened by Christ.'"

Cf. Ga 2:14.

14. 'After this, Theodore was together with Pachomius in the above-mentioned monastery of the Tabennesiots, which is in the nome of Niten-tori.[1] [One night] he was occupied with nightly prayers by himself, and as he was weighed down with sleep he began to walk through the monastery. Unseen by man, since it was night, he prayed a little at a time. Deciding to rest his body with equal measure,[2] he sat down by the door of the monastery church, and slept, satisfying only the needs of nature.

Another vision of Theodore

'An angel of the Lord came and woke him up saying, "Follow me".[3] He rose up and, following him, he entered the church. He saw it all filled with light and a throng of angels gathered together at the place where the priests offer up worship to God. He was afraid; but called by one of those who were assembled, he came near. Then someone who was in much glory fed him with a strange food and, strengthening him, ordered him to consume what was given into his mouth. When he had eaten that food at the commandment of the one who had given it to him and experienced a strange taste, he saw the light and the assembled angels going out. Inspired, he hastened to be with Pachomius, filled with joy and gladness. As he told him these things, he, seeing his secrets by revelation, smiled as he spoke. Pachomius said, "*The man who had received the two talents brought four and the one who had received five talents brought ten.*[4] Therefore, *gird up your loins* and bear fruit to him who has given

Cf. Ac 12:7-8.

Mt 25:22.20.
1 P 1:13.

you grace." Theodore groaned and asked him to intercede for him to God. From that day on he was granted continual revelations from the Lord.[5] Pecos̆, who had heard these things from Pachomius, handed them down to us after his death.'

15. When I had learned these things from Ausonius and Elourion, I hastened to get the servant of God Pecos̆ as my father. Learning what great power against the demons he had received from Christ, I asked him to recount to me what Pachomius had told him about Theodore. And I marvelled when he told me the same things.

16. I asked Ausonius to demonstrate to me from the Holy Scriptures if it is at all possible for a man to see the secrets of men's hearts. He said, 'I will give you the chance to know by experience if God will reveal your secrets to Theodore;[1] for without a revelation from God, no creature can know what is in the hearts of men. But in order that you may be convinced also from the divine Scriptures, listen to the prophet Samuel saying to Saul, *Come and I will tell you all that is in your heart; and as for your asses which were lost three days ago, do not worry about them, for they have been found.* Read also what was said by the Lord to Samuel about the sons of Jesse, so that you may know that when the Lord gives a revelation to his servants, they see; but when he does not, they see within themselves the common measure of men.[2] Indeed, if you read the whole book of the stories of the kings, you will also hear the prophet Elisha saying to his own minister about a god-fearing woman, *There is bitterness in her soul, and the Lord has not revealed it to me,* giving to under-

Ammon hears the same stories from Pecos̆

Biblical examples of men knowing the secrets of other men's hearts

1 S 9:19-20.
1 S 16:7-13.

2 K 4:27.

stand that God had revealed to him the hearts of
many.³ And [you will know this] especially from
what you will hear him saying, when he says to his
own minister, *From where are you coming, Gehazi?* and as he answered *Your servant has not
been anywhere,* he spoke to him again, *Was my
heart not with you when* Naaman the Syrian
leapt down *from his chariot to meet you? Now
you have the money* and the garments, *and you
will get yourself gardens, olive groves, and vine-
yards, flocks and herds, male and female slaves;
and Naaman's leprosy will cling to you and to
your descendants for ever.*⁴ It is also written in the
Proverbs of Solomon, *You shall know well the
souls of your flocks and you shall set your eyes on
your herds*; and again, *The righteous man will
understand the hearts of the ungodly and he de-
spises the ungodly in evils.* It is also written in the
Acts of the Apostles, *A man sat at Lystra, a crip-
ple from his mother's womb who had never
walked. He listened to Paul preaching. Looking
at him and seeing that he had the faith to be
saved, Paul said in a loud voice, "Get to your feet,
stand upright."* And he jumped and walked.
Now faith is seen in the heart and not bodily in
the face. Likewise Peter, seeing the wickedness of
Simon the magician not in his bodily face but in
his heart, said to him, *I see that you are in the gall
of bitterness and the bond of iniquity.*' Having
heard these things from Ausonius, I received the
Books and read them.

17. Some time later, necessity pressing me, I
went out of the house at midnight, when it was
dark. I heard the voice of Theodore and I was so
frightened that I sweated although I was clad on-

2 K 5:25-27.

Pr 27:23.

Pr 21:12.

Ac 14:8-10.

Ac 8:23.

**Example of
Theodore know-
ing the secrets of
the hearts**

ly in a linen sack and it was winter, during the
month the Egyptians called Tobi. Since I knew
the theban language by that time, he called me
by name and set me near him. And he said to a
theban monk called Amaeis, 'Why have you *no*

Ps 36(35):1.
fear of God before your eyes? Do you not know
Ps 7:9.
that God *tries the hearts and the loins?* Why is it
that sometimes in your heart you see harlots and
embrace them and sometimes you think you sleep
with a lawful wife and you pollute your whole
body? Then you become a soldier and in your
thoughts you see yourself as a victor in battles;
you please the generals and you receive gold from
them. And thinking about all the things contrary
to the monks' profession, you have decided to do
also in body what you are thinking about. Know
therefore that if you do not repent and if you do
1 Jn 3:3.
not propitiate the Lord, *purifying yourself* with
tears in the fear of God, but instead persist in this
Dt 28:29.
project, the Lord *will not prosper your way* but
will condemn you to eternal fire.'

The monk, falling at Theodore's feet, and confessing that he was in such a state, promised to repent and asked him to pray for him. Theodore
said, 'May the Lord grant that you truly condemn
yourself, repent, and be saved. For, as I see, *your*
Jr 17:5.
heart has gone away from God. But if you want
to, you can return, for God receives those who
truly return to him.' After weeping much, he dismissed him.

Amaeis left the monastery after four months
and gave himself to the military service. He fell
into a protracted illness and became dropsical.
And he died after a year, confessing these things.

18. I went with Theodore and other brothers

to the monastery of those called Tabennesiots, where Theodore had seen the apparition. As we were with him in the garden of the monastery, which lay along the river, about thirty villagers came to him and fell down before him. He refused such a thing and raised them up. As all were weeping, one of them besought him saying, 'Yesterday evening I gave my daughter who is fifteen years old in marriage to a man. And today when she was compelled to take food, she was overtaken with cramps and is lying speechless. It is clear to all who see that a poison has been put into either her food or her drink. The doctors who can be found here have given her up. Therefore, we beg you, deign to come to my house and pray for her. For we know that if you invoke Christ, he will grant you [the life of] my daughter.' When he did not want to go to [the man's] house, they wept and entreated him; and he said, 'You said that I should go to your house, to pray for your daughter; but God embraces and fills all things; he is not limited by place. Let us therefore invoke him here and he will give life to your daughter over there.' While all the others heard the word as a pledge of the child's life, Theodore turned to prayer with all the monks who were with him. He bent his knees three times and invoked God intensely. When he paused, he said, 'God has granted life to your daughter. Go with confidence.'

Amid the sound of a crowd of men and women weeping near the monastery—for she was expected to expire—the child's father came from the opposite bank, carrying a silver cup filled with water. In tears, he brought it to Theodore

Theodore heals
a sick girl

Cf. Ws 1:7.

and said, 'I am a man of little faith. I beg you at
least to invoke the name of God upon this water
for her, for I believe that God will listen to you
and will make of this water a medicine of salvation for my daughter.' Theodore took the cup,

Mt 14:19.
looked up to heaven and prayed with tears, and
made the sign of the cross of Christ over the
water.

The child's father took the water and went to
his house with the crowd. After three or four
hours he returned with a few of his friends and re-

Ac 2:11.
latives, relating *the marvels of God* which He had
done with him. He said, 'My brothers were able
by force to open the corners of my daughter's
mouth and pour in a small portion of the water.
Immediately there was an abundant excretion
below, and the girl was saved.'

A certain Silvanos, an Alexandrian living in
the Bendelian quarter who was an Arian and a
stone dealer, was with the child's father. Witness-

Ac 2:11.
ing *the marvels of God,* he glorified God.

19. After that, Theodore took about a hun-

**Silvanos is
punished by
God for his lack
of confidence in
Theodore's
holiness**

dred and twenty monks and led them to an island
in the river to collect the material the Egyptians
call rushes, which goes into the preparation of the
mats. Among them was a Theban called Silvanos,
who was the leader of twenty-two linen-weaver
monks. From this number was his second, called
Macarios, the elder brother of holy Theodore—of
the same mother but not the same father.[1]

On the ninth day, one of the monks came and
announced that some of the monks who had gone
with Theodore had brought Silvanos in a boat,
about to expire. They were in the moorings of the
river, which are a mile from Phbow—for we were

in that monastery. We went to meet him, and we found them on the road, carrying Silvanos on a bed, unconscious, neither hearing nor speaking; it was the third day since he had lost consciousness. And as he continued for three more days taking neither food nor drink, Theodore the Alexandrian, Pecoš, Psahref, Pšentaesi, Elourion, and Isidore, men well-pleasing to God,[2] *raised their hands to heaven*, and with many tears made supplication to God to have mercy on Silvanos. While they were still praying, I heard Silvanos say, '*Blessed are you O God*, who has chastised me and had mercy on me.' Then I said in a loud voice, 'Blessed be God', and they completed the prayer.

2 M 15:21.

Tb 8:5.

Theodore gave him food, having me as his attendant. And before dawn, Silvanos called all those in the monastery to assemble near him. He sat on the bed while I stood beside him. With Elourion proclaiming in a loud voice to the crowd what he was saying, he said, 'Listen to how this happened to me. On the fourth day of the week on the island, Theodore was standing, teaching the brothers who had formed a circle around him. He stopped speaking and moving from the place where he had been standing he showed to [our] eyes two small vipers, saying, "Let someone kill them. They came about my feet as I was speaking; and in order that none of the brothers might be troubled, I made as it were a vault with my feet and hid them."[3] After they were killed, he said that an angel had appeared to him and said, "Some of the monks who are with you are negligent about their own salvation". And [he said], "He told me the names of some. And about one of them he said also that the sentence had been pronounced by God, ordering that he be expelled from the monastery; and this man is dwelling in Phbow."[4]

'When I heard these things, I scorned Theodore in my heart, saying, "Is he not the brother of my Macarios? Did not Macarios' mother bear him also? Where does the vainglory of this one come from? Macarios is very humble." Then someone with a human aspect came to me in shining clothes and with an exceedingly fearsome face, and said, "Do you not fear God either, thinking such things about his servant?" Confounded and full of shame, I felt as if he had given me a slap in the face. After that I no longer knew where I lay or how I came here, until God healed me.' Hearing this we all glorified God.

20. A few days later, Theodore arrived at the monastery and ordered the brothers to assemble. He talked to them and told them to wait for his coming. Then he went with two of those who were with him to the house in which the monks used to eat. A certain young monk came out of the house; he grabbed hold of him and dragged him to a certain vaulted house. He compelled him to say what he had been doing, showing that it was he who had been indicated by the angel and who had been ordered expelled from the monastery. As he did not want to speak, Theodore began to tell him his first action and asked him if any of the monks knew about it. Falling at Theodore's feet, he begged him to keep silent about his other actions and [only] to expel him from the monastery. When Theodore indicated him to the assembled throng of the brothers, he

Cf. Lk 23:40.

Theodore corrects some brothers' secret sins which were revealed to him

confessed that God had truly revealed what concerned him to his servant and that he had justly
been ordered expelled from the monastery.

Theodore ordered him cast out and spoke at
length to the brothers. At night, he went privately to each one of the other brothers who had been
accused by the angel. He related to each one the
sins he had committed after holy baptism and
amazed each one, persuading them by further
speech to appease God by repentance. As for
them, realizing how much God had spared them,
they were eager to reveal themselves to all. But
Theodore prevented them, saying that most of
the brothers were unable to bear such tidings. He
added that besides the harm done to those who
were still *infants in Christ,*[1] there might also be a
snare for some of those who confessed in the reproach they would receive from one of those who
were not yet firmly established. But each one of
them revealed himself privately to the holy men
who were with Pecoš and Pšentaesi, entreating
them to pray for them to God.

21. These things happened during the Forty
Days. Then, in the days of the Passover, on the
third day of the week,[1] late in the evening, when
all the monks from the eleven monasteries under
Theodore were assembled in Phbow[2] — it is in fact
a custom with them to assemble there in order to
celebrate the feast of the holy Passover together[3] — many were asking Theodore to interpret the sayings of Holy Scripture that they had
not understood. He made clear to each one what
he was seeking, according to the question he had
put, and said, 'It is good to say a pretty thing before you! An unclean spirit came and laughed at

1 Co 3:1.

Theodore warns
the brothers
against fasting
beyond their
strength

one of us saying, "Last night, as the monks were staying away from the meal according to custom,[4] this one was among those who stayed away. But when I visited him during the night, I found him hungry and very negligent" — for it is the custom of the demons to sit by and attack the passions of men. "I suggested thoughts to him and kindled his hunger; then I persuaded him to steal some loaves of bread and to eat them secretly. And now the thief is sitting in the monks' midst, having become a transgressor of his own resolution, that is to make the prolonged fast with them." '[5]

And Theodore said to the monks, 'Let no one constrain himself to fast beyond his strength, because your bodies have become weak from the excessive *ascesis*. Let those then who are exceedingly weak eat every evening except Friday.'[6] That man rose up in the midst of the crowd of monks — we were indeed more than two thousand together — and fell at Theodore's feet, accusing

1 K 19:13.

himself. Theodore *covered his face with his goat skin* and did not let him be manifested to the

2 Co 11:29.

crowd, saying, *Who is weak, and I am not weak?*[7]

Theodore knows from a distance the frivolous conduct of some of the brothers

22. Likewise the blessed Theodore once went with forty brothers into mountainous and uninhabited places to get wood for work, and sent as many others for the same purpose under the direction of the holy Isidore, a man full of all meekness and of sagacity according to Christ. The distance between them was a day's journey long. Now, on the first day when Theodore's company had begun cutting the wood, when they had stopped working and gathered together at evening for the customary prayers, he urged

them saying, 'As you know, there was an urgent
need to complete the work for which we have
come here. But during the twelfth prayer,[1] as we
knelt on the ground, the Holy Spirit revealed to
me that in the other mountain four of the brothers who have brought themselves up well from
childhood have fallen — they will return to their
former state however, once they have been admonished by my lowliness. It is necessary therefore to disregard this work so that both we and
those in the other mountain be found in Phbow
on Saturday.' He called two of the brothers and,
enjoining them not to mention these things to
anyone, he sent them to the other mountain to
tell those who were there with Isidore to be in
Phbow on Saturday. So he came to the monastery
on Saturday after sunset, bringing all those who
were with him. The others were already there.
Finding all assembled, he came to the church. At
the time he usually gave an instruction to the
monks, he stood in their midst and, while Theodore the Alexandrian interpreted, said:

23. 'You know, brothers, that the life of monks
and of ever-virgins surpasses the way of life of
men and is angelic.[1] Those who lead this way of
life have died to the common way of life of men
and live *for him who died and was raised for
them.** Refusing *to live for themselves,*† they *crucify* themselves *with Christ.*‡ Each of us, choosing
this life, came here renouncing the poverty of his
parents; he ought therefore to live according to
Christ, having as model and pattern those of us
who preceded him. To those of us who desire to
attain to his kingdom, God has given, as roads
leading to it, not only the holy Scriptures, but

Theodore rebukes the brothers

*2 Co 5:15.
†*Ibid.*
‡Ga 2:20.

also the life of these servants of his and their grounding in the faith of Christ.

Ga 5:7.

'Some of us, however, who were running this course well have slipped, but have not fallen. Four of the brothers whom we sent to the mountain, finding themselves alone, began to tell jokes to one another, to make sport, and to laugh aloud, so that *the Holy Spirit whom they grieved*[2]

Cf. Eph 4:30.

revealed to me their names and their offences, that they might be ashamed and correct themselves with tears and groanings. Brothers, what have you done with the word of Jeremiah saying to God, *Lord Almighty, I did not sit in their assembly when they played, but I had respect for your hand;*

Jr 15:16-17.

I sat alone, for I was filled with bitterness?[3] How did you not remember Job saying, *If I have been walking with jesters* let such and such sad thing

Jb 31:5.

come upon me? Or how have you forgotten Paul's words which you continually recite? Do you not know that God examines the little defeats of his saints as if they were great, for their salvation? Have you not heard Solomon's saying, *Like the crackling of thorns under the cauldron, so is the*

Qo 7:6.
laughter of fools? and again, *Of laughter I said,*
Qo 2:2.
It is a madness; and again, *Better anger than*
Qo 7:3.
laughter. Therefore, come to your senses and hear the Apostle saying, *Let your laughter be turned in-*
Jm 4:9.
to mourning[4] *and your joy into sadness,* that you may not experience that somber sentence of the Saviour, *Woe unto you who laugh now, for you*
Lk 6:25.
shall weep and mourn.[5] Rather take up with zeal the voluntary mourning and voluntary weeping which last a short time, that you may not experience the involuntary ones which are eternal. Let each one of you say to God, *I am ready for*
Ps 38(37):17.
stripes.'

He was still speaking when the four, as by a single decision — although they were separated from each other — declared that they were those who were accused, wailing and weeping with a loud voice, looking to the east and casting themselves down before God. And they entreated the crowd of the brothers to pray for them. All prayed with copious weeping, and the *synaxis* was concluded as usual. But those men, taking what the blessed Theodore had said as provisions for their whole life, improved so much that everyone in the monastery took each of them as a model and a pattern for salvation. Such in fact was their life even before this slight offence.

24. There was a certain monk called Mousaios. He was a Theban, and under the aforementioned Silvanos. He was sent with Silvanos and the other brothers under him to an island in the river to collect and pickle the so-called charlock for the brothers' food. On their fifth day there, he was called for alone by Theodore, but did not want to obey, saying, 'I will come with all my brothers after we have finished the task assigned to us'. He was led to the monastery even against his will, and he found Theodore weeping bitterly in [his] cell. Pšentaesi and Isidore stood by him. Theodore looked at him for a long time and said, 'Why was I informed of the death, not of your body — which would have been better — but of your soul? Did I not visit you night and day in your cell, saying, "*Your soul is meditating evil things?* You have thoughts that are more grievous than any sin. Such thoughts have been the ruin of many." And when you said that those foul ideas were the suggestions of demons, I said, "The demons have not yet been permitted to at-

Theodore expels Mousaios, who was indulging in worldly thoughts

Cf. Jb 27:4.

tack you; but by becoming so full of weeds, you prepare broad pasture for demons, drawing them upon yourself by evil counsels." Did I not tell you, "In you is fulfilled the word of the Proverbs which says, *Like a farm is a man who has no sense; like a vineyard a man lacking in mind. If you leave it, it gets all dry and full of weeds; it becomes abandoned and its fences of stones are broken down"?*[1]

Pr 24:30-31.

And then he said, 'Where have your evil ways led you?' And when he said that he had had no new thought, except those Theodore knew, Theodore said to him, 'When you were sitting behind the hut, what did you think and what did you set in your heart?' He said that they were suggestions of the demons; and Theodore replied, 'Till this hour no demon was ever permitted to attack you; now, because you have set such evil things in your heart, it is useless for you to dwell here. It has therefore been ordered that you be expelled from the monastery.' He delivered him to four young monks, and ordered them to lead him to his own home. When he was by the monastery gate, he was seized with a demon and he set off like a roaring bull to his own village, loosed by the four monks.

25. Near Ptolemais in the Thebaid, Theodore

Theodore knows of Carour's death from a distance

had built a monastery and caused it to be inhabited by monks.[1] Among them was one called Carour—which means 'short' in Theban. Theodore rebuked him very often for being slothful about nightly prayers. There was a great distance from there to the monastery called Phbow, where Theodore was sitting with all the brothers after sunset. But suddenly he became filled with joy and

said, 'I announce to you the good news of the   Cf. Lk 1:72.
mercy that God has worked for Carour in Ptolemais. Just now He has taken his soul from his
body into heaven with much glory, because he
kept with exactitude to the doctrines of the
Church and, with his other virtues has preserved
his body completely chaste. His other defects,
[God] has wiped out with the various diseases He
brought upon him.' Eight days later, two brothers from there came and amazed us all by informing us of the day and hour in which Carour had
died.

26. Once, when Theodore had all the brothers
[near him], he said to Psahref,[1] who was the first   Theodore detects
of all in Phbow, 'Send to the cell of Patchelphios,   and corrects
and make him come with the young man found   Patchelphios'
with him in the cell. Send also for his elder son.'[2]   heresy
When they came, Theodore said to Patchelphios,
'Say what you were teaching this young man during the night'. And he said, 'What I was teaching
him? Fear of God.' Theodore said, 'God himself
denounced you through an angel; tell the truth, if
your teaching is Light.' But he refused, and Theodore said to everyone, 'He was teaching him that
there is no resurrection of the flesh, calling the nature of the flesh evil'. Then he said to Patchelphios, 'Say if this is so or not'. Patchelphios' son
cried out, 'Me too he tried to persuade to think this
yesterday evening'. Then someone who was called
Or and was eunuch from his mother's womb, said
to Theodore with great boldness, 'Make the young
man who has been deceived remember!' Theodore
said, 'The soul of this young man as well as of Patchelphios' son has become like steel and has received nothing of his teaching'.

To the young man he said, 'God has accepted your resolution'. And to the superior[3] of the house in which the young man dwelt he recommended that he not rebuke him at all for having left the house secretly by night and without his permission. Then he spoke at great length from the holy Scriptures to Patchelphios about the resurrection of our mortal flesh from the dead, and he insisted that *this mortal* flesh of ours *must* rise up in glory from the dead, *immortal and incorruptible.* Patchelphios, weeping in front of the crowd of brothers—for what Theodore had said was enough to lead him to faith—threw himself down, consenting to the doctrines of the Church and asking everyone to pray for him, so that God might also wipe out this sin of his. The brothers prayed with joy and Patchelphios confessed to God in a loud voice and with many tears.

27. Once we went by boat with Theodore to an island to gather fire wood. As we, the Greek [brothers], were still in the boat, Theodore disembarked from another boat with many monks—for he had arrived before us—and began to make a tent. But a big boy called Patrick, who came from Myra in Lycia and was in our boat, cried out, calling for help. And we saw a great black asp clinging with its fangs to the heel of his right foot. A young Theban, a monk, who was with us on the boat, took the beast by the tail and snatched it away from Patrick's foot with difficulty; he killed it, beating it against the wall of the boat, and threw it dead into the river.

Patrick was weeping and all of us were expecting him suddenly to fall down dead; but Theodore came up, made the sign of the Cross of

Margin notes:

1 Co 15:52-54.

Theodore heals the monk Patrick who had been stung by an asp

Christ upon the mark of the beast's fangs, and said to Patrick, [still] weeping, 'Do not be afraid. Christ has healed you'.

Cf. Ac 9:34.

The next day some of the monks said, 'We did not believe Theodore and we were expecting Patrick to die during the night. Seeing him in good health, we bless Christ, and we marvel at Theodore for being so well-pleasing to Him.' The one who killed the beast also remained unharmed.

28. Many other monks coming from Phbow by boat reached the island, and we were three hundred in number. About the eighth hour of the 26th of the month of Athyr*, Theodore called all of us and gathered us near himself, and he told Theodore the Alexandrian to interpret what he was going to say to all: 'God revealed to me long ago what I have to say, but told me to keep silence for a while. Now, as I was standing, I have just been ordered to say it to you, and it is this: In almost every place where the name of Christ is being preached, many of those who have sinned after holy baptism have kept the apostolic faith in which we also stand and have wept for their sins. The Lord, accepting the genuineness of their repentance, has wiped out their sins. Therefore all those among you who up to this day have wept truly over the sins committed after your baptism, shall know that you have received forgiveness. Let each of you, therefore, *confess to the Lord his mercies* and say, *You have changed my grief into joy; you have stripped off my sackcloth and girded me with gladness.*'[1]

Theodore has a revelation concerning the forgiveness of sins.
*22 Nov. 354.

Ps 107(106):8.

Ps 30(29):11.

29. He continued to exhort the brothers with many more words. And as it was about to be the tenth hour, Theodore called four of the brothers

A letter from
Antony confirms
his revelation
by name and we all heard him telling them, 'Our
brothers who are coming from Alexandria with
Theophilos and Copres are getting near this
place. Now, that they might not pass us by una-
wares, go to the promontory of the island and signal to those who are in the boat that comes
around the bend of the river, so that they may
moor at the island. Theophilos, who is steering,
knows the safe moorings, and he will pull in
there.'

The brothers went, and after waiting a little,
they saw the boat coming around the bend. They
recognized Theophilos steering and they were astonished. They made signs to them and made it
clear that Theodore was on the island, and they
came back announcing that the boat had come.
All were astonished and followed Theodore who
went to the moorings and who received on land
the monks coming down from the boat, *greeting*
them with a holy kiss.

Rm 16:16.

After the greeting, as we were all in a circle
around him, he said to them, 'Come with joy, for
you have seen our father Antony'. They said, 'He
sent you a letter through us'. And they gave him
the letter. He read it and grew filled with joy.
Then he gave the writings to Elourion, ordering
him to read them to the brothers, while Theodore
the Alexandrian again interpreted, for it was
written in the Egyptian language.[1] It said:

'Antony to his beloved son Theodore, greetings
in the Lord. I knew that *the Lord God will not do*
anything without revealing his instruction to his
Am 3:7.   *servants the prophets,* And I thought that I need
not declare to you what God has revealed to me a

long time ago. But when I had seen your brothers who were with Theophilos and Copres, He enjoined me to write to you and to declare to you that in almost all parts of the world, many of those who worship Christ in truth but have sinned after their baptism have wept and mourned, and God, accepting their weeping and their mourning, has wiped out the sins of all those who have walked in this way until the day this letter shall be given you. Read it to your brothers, therefore, that they may rejoice in hearing it. Greet the brothers. The brothers [here] greet you. I pray that you may be healthy in the Lord.'

All of us who were present, hearing this, threw ourselves on our faces before God, and wept so much that, when the priest who was present had brought the prayer to an end, Theodore said, 'Believe me when I say that all the heavenly rational creation rejoiced also in this weeping of yours. God has indeed received our prayer and has wiped out the sins of some of us monks who are presently so bitterly weeping here. It is with foreknowledge of them that he has spoken as I have said and our father Antony has written.' We were all filled with great joy, and Theodore said to me, 'Ammon, the things that we have said here secretly, and the other things that you have seen and heard from us, you will tell them in public and in the streets'.

Cf. Ac 22:15.

30. During my third year in the monastery, a friend of my father saw me at the gate of the monastery with Besarion, the servant of God, who was then the monastery's porter.[1] He entreated me, saying that my mother had been

Ammon goes to visit his family and stays in Mount Nitria

mourning since the day I left my family and that
my father, having gone to all the monasteries in
Egypt and Augustamnica and not found me, was
lamenting me as dead. When I heard this, I
asked the man of God Theodore to send two
monks with me, so that I might see my mother
and comfort her, and then return with them. But
he said to me, 'Your mother has become a Christian. As for you, you shall dwell in those parts
from now on. Therefore, I advise you to dwell in
Mount Nitria, for especially in that place are holy
men, well-pleasing to God.' He meant Theodore,
the companion of the holy Amoun, who was still
alive, Elourion and Ammonios who both died not
long after, the holy Pambo and the servant of
God Pior,[2] who had both received from the Lord
gifts of healing, and the holy men who were with
them, whose names I have passed over in silence,
not to lengthen my writing. As he sent me on my
way, I kissed him with many tears, and asked him
to pray for me so that I might go and see my parents. After seeing them I dwelt in Mount Nitria.

1 Co 12:9.

August 355.
**The Arian
persecution**
8 Feb. 356.

31. Six months later, in the days of Constantius, the blessed pope Athanasius was driven out
by the Arians.[1] The holy monks who were then in
Egypt and Alexandria as well as the ever-virgins
and the zealous lay folk suffered many evils and
were destroyed by molestation. The bishops of
Egypt were exiled by Sebastian, the Egyptian
Duke who was the successor of Syrianos, who had
slain with arrows many ever-virgins in the church
of holy Theodore the Bishop, and by Artemios,
the successor of Sebastian. Many were flogged to
death, and the holy bishops from the West were
exiled. Absolutely indescribable evils were perpe-

June 356.

8 Feb. 356.

A.D. 360.

trated by the Arians, whose leader was the cruel George.[2] Then I used to tell those who were with Pior and Pambo and the other priests dwelling in Mount Nitria what the man of God Theodore had said about this persecution, that it would be hard and that it would eventually end.

A.D. 357-358.

32. As the evils of the Arians were increasing, four monks came to Mount Nitria, sent by Theodore with a letter to the monks dwelling on the Mount. Following Theodore's instructions, they looked for me and, when they found me, they gave me the letter. It was Saturday evening. The next day, Sunday, I read it first to the priests privately, then on their authority to the whole throng of monks. It said:

Theodore's comforting letter to the monks in Mount Nitria

'Theodore to the beloved brothers in Mount Nitria: priests, deacons and monks, greetings in the Lord. I want you to know that *the pride of* the Arians *has gone up* to God and that *God has visited his people and seeing the afflictions* that they endure has had mercy on them. He has promised to have mercy on his Church and to deliver it from these afflictions. The time has come therefore when the Church will be delivered from these persecutions. Indeed God said of the Arians, *I will punish Babylon, and will take from her mouth what she has swallowed.* And of the Church, *Who is there among you that saw this house in its former glory?*[1] *For the last glory of this house is going to surpass the first.* Therefore, brothers, *since we have these promises,*[2] comfort those who are suffering from [the Arians] in those parts, that no one's faith may be turned aside, for *the sins of the* Arians *have not yet ended.* The

Cf. Ps 74(73):23.
Ex 4:31; Lk 7:16.

Jr 51:44.

Hag 2:3.9.
2 Co 7:1.

Gn 15:16.

brothers who are with me greet you. May the
Lord keep you in good health, beloved brothers.'

When I read this, all the brothers praised God.
A man called Hagios, one of the priests, said to
me smiling, 'And we too say to you, *Now we no*
longer believe because of what you said'. By command of Heraclides the priest, I gave this letter to
Isaac, also called Chrysogonos, who was then a
monk in Mount Nitria, but was later appointed
deacon of the Church of Hermopolis Parva by the
most holy bishop Theodore, to send it to the most
holy bishop Dracontios who was in exile.[3] And I
think that our God-fearing brother and fellow-
minister Dioscoros,[4] the successor of the holy Isidore, will be able to find it if he looks for it.

33. In the ninth month of the sixth year after
pope Athanasius was driven out, Julian, an idola-
ter, became Emperor and exiled him to the Thebaid. After making many threats against the
Christians, he came to a quick end in Persia and
was not able to fulfil any of his threats against the
Christians. And so all of us who had heard Theodore glorified God, seeing after so many years the
fulfilment of what he had said. And we expected
without any doubt that the madness of the Arians
against us would also be abolished. Now, after so
many years, we see this.

34. I dared to write these things in obedience
to the order of Your Holiness. Of what I saw near
Theodore, I left out many things which many
would not be able to hear, because I feared that
my letter might come into the hands of people
who are little and still *infants in Christ.*[1] But
when the blessed pope Athanasius arrived, in the

Jn 4:42.

**Death of Julian
the Apostate**
3 Nov. 361.

A.D. 363.

**Athanasius gives
a testimony
about Theodore
and Pammon**

1 Co 3:1.

presence of my lowliness and of other clerics of
the Church of Alexandria in the Great Church,
he said something about Theodore to Ammonios
of blessed memory, who had become bishop of
Elaearchia, and to Hermon, the bishop of Bubas-
tis, which it is necessary to call to the mind of
Your Piety—[although] I think that Your Holiness was also there and heard it. [So], I shall write
what he said.

As the bishops I have mentioned were marvelling at blessed Antony, the pope Athanasius (who
had often conversed with him) said to them: 'I
have seen in these times also great men of God:
Theodore, the holy man of the Tabennesiot
monks, and, in the region of Antinoopolis, a father of monks called Apa Pammon. They have
recently died. For when I was driven out by Julian
and was expecting to be killed by him — for of this
true friends had informed me — the two men
came to me at Antinoopolis on the same day. As I
planned to hide with Theodore, I embarked on
his boat which was covered on all sides. Apa
Pammon also sent us on our way. The wind was
not favorable, and in anguish of heart I was praying. Then the monks of Theodore's company disembarked to tow the boat. While Apa Pammon
was comforting me in my anguish, I said, "Believe me when I say, My heart is not so confident
in time of peace as in the times of persecution. Indeed I believe that, *suffering for Christ*[2] and   Ph 1:29.
strengthened by his mercy, I will find his mercy
even more if I am killed." I was still saying this
when Theodore looked at Apa Pammon and
smiled. And as Apa Pammon nearly laughed, I
said to them, "Why did you laugh when I said

this? Do you judge me a coward?" Theodore said
to Apa Pammon, "Tell him why we smiled." Apa
Pammon said, "You ought to say it." And so Theodore said, "In this very hour Julian has been

A.D. 363.

killed in Persia. God has indeed foretold of him,
He who is haughty and contemptuous shall achieve

Ha 2:5.

nothing at all. A Christian emperor will rise up

Jovian, 363–4

who will be famous but short-lived. Therefore
you need not trouble yourself to go to the
Thebaid but go secretly to the court. You will
come across him on the road, and he will indeed
receive you, and you will return to the Church.
And so, this [emperor] will quickly be taken by
God to Himself." And so it happened. Therefore
I believe that mostly among monks there are many
hidden people well-pleasing to God. These also
were indeed unknown, just as also the blessed
Amoun and the holy Theodore, who dwelt in
Mount Nitria, and the servant of God, the ex-
cellent old man Pambo.'

Ammon gives a
testimony about
Theodore before
Athanasius

35. The bishop Ammonios marvelled at the
blessed Pior and Elourion and Ammonios and
Isidore, the priest of the anchorites, and the holy
Macarios, all of whom Your Holiness has seen in
Mount Nitria. He also questioned me about the
holy anchorites of Scethis, Paisios as well as Paul
and Pšoi his brothers, and Isaiah, Pisyrous, Issac,
and Paul. And he asked me if I had also seen
Theodore the Theban. When I said that I had
lived three years with Theodore, he ordered me
to tell [him] anything I had seen with him. When
I had told him some of the things I have written
above—for to His Holiness I kept my words con-
cise—the pope marvelled and said, 'Having

known the man personally, I believe these things
to be exact'.

36. Now that I have also written to Your Holi-   Conclusion
ness the things I have heard from the blessed
pope Athanasius, I add an entreaty, that you
would deign to pray for me always, asking unceasingly that the mercies of God may be upon
me. Salute the brothers who are with you. Those
who are with me address Your Holiness. May the
all-holy God of all things preserve you many years
for the churches in good health for his glory and
praying for me, My Lord, most holy brother.

LETTER OF THEOPHILOS TO AMMON

37. Theophilos, to my lord, beloved brother,
and fellow-minister, Ammon, greetings in the   Theophilos'
Lord. Knowing the good zeal of your piety, we   response to
welcome you for your memory of the saints. You   Ammon
have gladdened us by sending in writing the
things that we had often heard in discourse. Then
let it be that we may all have our portion and
communion with the blessed Theodore. By not
neglecting our request but granting us this, too,
you have profited us, beloved and most longed-
for. Salute the brothers who are with you; the
brothers who are with us address you in the Lord.
May you have good health in the Lord, beloved
and most longed-for brother.

Notes to the Letter of Bishop Ammon
(Am. Letter)

Am. Letter   1   ¹ἡγιασμένον: This is the only instance in our Greek texts of this
qualificative being applied to a man. But see G¹ 96, where it is
found in a quotation of 2 Tm 2:21.
  ²The addressee of this letter is very probably Theophilos, the patriarch of Alexandria (385–412), although Lefort, VC, p. LII,
thinks it might be another Theophilos.

Am. Letter   2   ¹This text is quoted also in G¹ 9.

Am. Letter   3   ¹In Hors. Test. 52 we find the same quotation of Lm 3:27–28,30,
(without v. 29, as here). There is also a quotation of Lm 3:27 in
Pach. Letter 3: 13.
  ²In Hors. Test. 20, this text is quoted in an exhortation to chasti-
ty, which seems to be the meaning here as well.
  ³This text is quoted also in SBo 105; Pach. Letter 5:11 and Hors.
Test. 11.
  ⁴The first part of 2 Co 7:1 is quoted below, ¶ 32. This text is quoted also in Theod. Instr. 3:5. There is an allusion to it in G¹ 49.

Am. Letter   4   ¹On the vocation of Theodore the Alexandrian, see SBo 89 (= G¹
94).
  ²This text is used again below, ¶ 23, and it is quoted also in S¹ 3.
  ³Theodore, who had been Pachomius' interpreter, continued to
fulfill that role under Horsiesios: see SBo 91 (end).

Am. Letter   5   ¹The same text is quoted again below, ¶ 34, in a similar context.
  ²The same text is quoted again below, ¶ 10.

Am. Letter   6   ¹The same expression is used in Pach. Instr. 1:39.
  ²Lit. 'The voice of the feet of the rain.'

Am. Letter   7   ¹See SBo 91; G¹ 95.

Am. Letter   9   ¹This is the only instance where ἡγησάμενος is used for
ἡγούμενος
  ²In Scripture this expression is applied to Enoch.
  ³In G¹ 123 this expression is applied to the other Theodore, the
Alexandrian.
  ⁴This text is quoted about Athanasius below, ¶ 12.
  ⁵On the vocation of Theodore, see SBo 29–32; G¹ 33–35. About
the problems concerning Theodore's age, see SBo 31, note 3. The
age thirteen given by Ammon is probably exact.

Am. Letter 10   ¹Here (Halkin, p. 101,32) and in three other places (Halkin, pp.
104, 12; 104,15 and 111,9), Ammon calls the church of the monastery ἐκκλησία, term that is never used with that meaning in G¹ or
Paral. We find the same use of ἐκκλησία only in Draguet Fragment
1: 4. There is another instance in SBo 184; see *ibidem*, note 2.

Am. Letter 12 ¹τὸν μονήρη βίον: this expression, which is not common in pachomian literature, is found once more in G¹ 150, in Athanasius' letter to Horsiesios (Halkin, p. 95,16).
²Alexander was patriarch of Alexandria from 312 to 328. This confirms the dating of Pachomius' conversion in 313. What is said here confirms also the mention by SBo 10 of Pachomius spending three years in Seneset before joining Palamon.
³This is probably the same vision that is narrated in SBo 103 (= G¹ 102). There is something similar in Paral. 17-18.
⁴This text was quoted above, ¶ 9.

Am. Letter 13 ¹Athanasius was appointed bishop in 328. In the same year Theodore came to Tabennesi. Since Pachomius began to receive novices in 324, Elourion was among the ancients if he was already in the community at that time. Surprisingly enough, he is never mentioned in the Coptic sources.

Am. Letter 14 ¹The mention of the diocese of Nitentori shows that the monastery in question was Tabennesi. It has not been named yet in the Letter. It was the only pachomian monastery existing when Theodore joined Pachomius.
²The meaning seems to be that he alternated the times of prayer and of sleep, spending the same amount of time at each.
³There is a reminiscence of the same text in SBo 184.
⁴Mt 25:20 is quoted in Hors. Instr. 4: 2.
⁵See v.g. SBo 34.

Am. Letter 16 ¹It was for his gift of clairvoyance that Pachomius was called to explain himself at the Synod of Latopolis.
²Cf. G¹ 48.
³This text is quoted in a similar context in G¹ 48.
⁴There is another allusion to Gehasi's leprosy in Draguet Fragm. 2: 2. The theme is classical; see H.L. 17 (Macarios of Egypt).

Am. Letter 19 ¹This is the only time this Macarios is mentioned. He is probably distinct from the Macarios who was leader of Phnoum shortly after Pachomius' death. See SBo 137.
²Apart from Isidore, who was not mentioned before, all these are ancient pachomian monks.
³D.J. Chitty has shown that a similar story read in the *De oratione* of Evagrius (formerly attributed to Saint Nilus) is based on the text of Ammon. See SBo 98, note 6 and Chitty, 'Pachomian Sources Reconsidered', pp. 39-41.
⁴We close the quotation after διάγει (Halkin 108,35) instead of closing it after ὀνόματα (Halkin, 108,33).

Am. Letter 20 ¹The same expression is used again below, ¶ 34.

Am. Letter 21 ¹Wednesday of Holy Week.
²G¹ 134 states that Theodore added three monasteries to the nine established by Pachomius: two in the region of Hermopolis, and one near Hermonthis. Since Ammon speaks of eleven monasteries, we may suppose that one of Theodore's foundations was made at a later date.

³The pachomian monks assembled twice a year at Phbow, for the Passover and at the end of the year. About these two meetings, see SBo 71, notes 2 and 3; SBo 144, note 3.
⁴Cf. Jer. Pref. 5.
⁵About the fast during the six days of the Passover, according to early christian customs, see *La liturgie*, pp. 254-255.
⁶Theodore gives the same advice he had received from Pachomius in the past; see SBo 35.
⁷This text is quoted also in Hors. Test. 13.

Am. Letter 22   ¹The Rules of Pachomius speak of an Office of Six Prayers, but not of Twelve Prayers. When Ammon wrote this, he had been gone from the pachomian monastery a long time and he had spent many years in Nitria, where the practice of the twelve prayers was common. This can easily explain his mistake. On the history of the tradition of the twelve prayers (or twelve psalms), see *La liturgie*, pp. 324-339.

Am. Letter 23   ¹Although there is a text in SBo 107 where Pachomius distinguishes the purity of marriage from the angelic purity chosen by the monks, the theme of the 'angelic life' is not prominent in pachomian literature. Neither is the theme of the superiority of monastic life over the life-style of other people that we find here from Ammon's pen.
²Eph 4:30 is often quoted. See SBo 101; Pach. Instr. 1: 45; Hors. Test. 19 and 53.
³This text is quoted also in Hors. Test. 42.
⁴Pachomius quotes this text in Pach. Letter 3: 6. Note that this quotation from James is introduced here by the words: 'hear the Apostle saying', which is unusual. The title 'the Apostle' ordinarily means Paul.
⁵This malediction is quoted in Hors. Test. 41.

Am. Letter 24   ¹There is a clear allusion to this text in G¹ 49.

Am. Letter 25   ¹There is no mention of a monastery near Ptolemais in the Life. Is this a fourth foundation made by Theodore? Ptolemais is only a few miles from Šmin-Panopolis, where Pachomius had already founded three monasteries.

Am. Letter 26   ¹Psahref appears also as the superior of Phbow in SBo 185 (= G¹ 138), at the time of Artemios' perquisition.
²τὸν υἱὸν αὐτοῦ τοῦ πρεσβύτερου (correcting Halkin's misprint: πεσβύτερου) could also mean 'his son the priest'.
³προεστῶτι; apart from here, προεστώς is never used in our texts. We find it in G², though.

Am. Letter 28   ¹This text is quoted also in Theod. Instr. 3: 28 and in Hors. Test. 42.

Am. Letter 29   ¹In Bohairic, the Coptic dialect of the Delta, the 'Egyptian' epistragy proper, clearly distinguished from the Thebaid; see SBo 185, note 2.

Am. Letter 30 [1]This may be the same Besarion who is mentioned in a fragment about Horsiesios from a *Synaxarium* of the eleventh or twelfth century, published by Lefort under the *siglum* S[15] (VS, p. 351-360; VC pp. 400-405).
[2]Theodore, Amoun's companion, is mentioned in SBo 2 (= G[1] 2). Pambo, who lived with Amoun, and Pior, who lived with Antony, were among the first to settle in Mount Nitria.

Am. Letter 31 [1]Constantius, son of Constantine, reigned over the Eastern Empire from 337 to this death in 361. After his brother Constans' death in 350 he reigned also over the Western Empire.
[2]George occupied the throne in Alexandria from February 357 to October 358. He returned shortly before Constantius' death in 361, but was imprisoned by Julian the same year.

Am. Letter 32 [1]Although Horsiesios quoted Hag 2: 4-9, in Hors. Letter 1: 5, he omits this part of v. 9; but he quotes it in Hors. Letter 3: 2.
[2]This text is quoted above, ¶ 3.
[3]See H.L., 10 and 46.
[4]A monk of Mount Nitria, Dioscoros was one of the Four Tall Brothers who were involved in the Origenist dispute with Theophilos. He was made bishop of Hermopolis in 394 and attended the Council of Constantinople the same year. He was later deposed by Theophilos in his battles against Origenism. He died in Constantinople in the early fifth century.

Am. Letter 34 [1]This text was quoted above, ¶ 20.
[2]Ph 1:29 is quoted also in Theod. Instr. 3: 5 and Hors. Test. 5.

∂raguet fragment 1
(∂raguet 1)

I N THAT MONASTERY, the following thing happened: Two of the brothers who fulfilled the weekly service quarrelled. One of them, boiling over with anger, struck the other. The latter could not stand it and in his turn gave him a blow.[1]

Quarrel between two brothers

2. What had happened between them was reported to the blessed archimandrite Pachomius.[1] Calling them before the whole community,[2] he questioned them and they confessed their faults. The one who had rashly given the blow, he expelled from the monastery. As for the other, he excommunicated him for a week,[3] saying, 'Why did you not master yourself when you received a blow, but instead answered in the same way to the one who had done you evil?'

Severe judgement from Pachomius

3. There was an old man called Gnositheos who, as is the meaning of his name, had knowledge of God. He was in his eightieth year of age. When the first one was being expelled from the monastery, he exclaimed from the midst of the brothers, 'I am a sinner, brothers, and I leave with him; *if anyone is without sin,* let him stay here.'[1] Unanimously the whole community of the brothers followed the old man, saying, 'We are also sinners; we are going with you'.

Intervention of an old monk

Cf. Jn 8:7.

111

Pachomius
repents

4. When he saw that they were all leaving, the blessed Pachomius ran in front of them, threw himself on his face at the door, covering his head with dust, and asked everyone for forgiveness. They entreated him to rise and they went to the church.[1] There they prayed, and entreating their abba, they forgave also the brothers who were at fault.

He meditates
in the church

5. Entering into himself, the blessed Pachomius made this reflection, 'If the murderers, the sorcerers, the adulterers, and others, having committed all kinds of evil, flee to the monastery to be saved through penance, who am I to expel a brother from the monastery? All the more so since our Saviour Christ says in the Gospels, *Whatever you bind on earth shall be bound in the heavens, and whatever you loose on earth shall be*

Mt 18:18.

loosed in the heavens. And when the blessed Peter asked the Saviour, *If my brother sinned against me, how many times shall I forgive him; as often*

Mt 18:21.

as seven times?[1] the one who *has the power to for-*

Mt 9:6.

give sins told him, *Peter, I do not tell you seven*

Mt 18:22.

times, but seventy times seven. [2] And the teaching given to the Apostles by the Lord in the Prayer and recited during the Eucharist,[3] is *Forgive us our debts, as we forgive those who are in debt to*

Mt 6:12.

us.[4] And again, *Pardon and you will be par-*

Lk 6:37.

doned.'[5]

He draws con-
clusions from
the incident

6. Remembering those precepts, he condemned himself and judged himself unworthy of the mysteries of Christ and decided not to approach them for three weeks and not to taste anything at all. And he established for his monastery[1] this rule, that whatever the sin a brother has committed, he must not be expelled from the

monastery, but [must be] corrected according to
his sin, even by corporal punishment if he deserves it. This way he would not be abandoned in-
to the hands of the devil and [the father] would   Cf. 1 Co 5:5.
not be reproached for the loss of a soul.[2]

Notes to Draguet Fragment I

Draguet I, 1   [1]This story has many similarities with the apophthegm 21 of
            Macarios the Egyptian: PG 65:269d (English translation by Benedicta
            Ward, *The Sayings of the Desert Fathers*, p. 111). According to A. de
            Vogüé, 'L'anecdote pachômien du "Vaticanus graecus" 2091', this
            apophthegm is one of the sources of our fragment.

Draguet I, 2   [1]The title 'archimandrite' is not found in any early pachomian docu-
            ment either in Greek or in Coptic, except in late title-heads of a few
            Coptic documents. The title is given to Pachomius in H.L. and in the
            two late liturgical hymns in Bohairic published by Lefort in an *appen-
            dix* to the Bohairic Life (see VB, pp. 218,24 and 221,21). D.J. Chitty
            believed that the term comes from Syriac, where the monastic enclosure
            was frequently called μάνδρα, a 'fold'; see *The Desert a City*, p. 41,
            note 68.
              [2]Lit. 'the brotherhood' (ἐπὶ πάσης τῆς ἀδελφότητος). The ex-
            pression is rare in pachomian literature; we find it only once in G[1],
            where it occurs in Antony's letter (Halkin, p. 96,14), and once in
            Theophilos' letter, at the end of Am. Letter (Halkin, p. 121,15), and
            once also in Paral. 7 (Halkin, p. 130,24).
              [3]I.e. he separated him from the Eucharist.

Draguet I, 3   [1]This is very similar to the apophthegm 7 of Bessarion: PG 65:141b
            (English translation, *The Sayings*, p. 35). According to de Vogüé,
            'L'anecdote pachômien du "Vaticanus graecus" 2091', this
            apophthegm is another source of our fragment.

Draguet I, 4   [1]Ἐκκλησία is not a term commonly used for the monastery oratory in
            the pachomian texts. See Am. Letter 10 note 1.

Draguet I, 5   [1]There is a clear reference to Mt 18:21 in Hors. Test. 54.
              [2]Pachomius uses this text in exhorting a monk to forgive his brother;
            see Pach. Instr. 1:59.
              [3]Lit. 'in the mysteries'.
              [4]This sentence from the Lord's Prayer is quoted twice by Horsiesios;
            see Hors. Test. 9 and 54.
              [5]This exhortation of the Lord to pardon is quoted by Pachomius in a
            long series of biblical texts about pardon; see Pach. Letter 7:3; it is also
            quoted in Pach. Instr. 1:38.

Draguet I, 6   [1]The expression: 'his' monastery would seem to indicate that this incident happened at an early time when there was yet only one pachomian monastery (*sic* R. Draguet, 'Un morceau grec inédit. . .', p.
274). But the pachomian authenticity of our text is doubtful.

   [2]Hors. Test. 3 exhorts the brothers to walk in the footsteps of the
fathers in order to avoid this fate (1 Co 5:5). Pachomius' attitude
toward sinners will evolve; the *Life* shows that he did not hesitate to
expel bad elements, although he was full of understanding and patience. See references given by R. Draguet, 'Un morceau grec
inédit. . ., pp. 275-276.

Draguet fragment II

(Draguet II)

ABBA ZANOS said: There are many monks who have left behind father and mother, brothers and sisters, family and relatives, servants and maids, friends and acquaintances, means and possessions, for the salvation of their souls, whose first commitment and entry into the monastery were praiseworthy and agreeable, but who finished blameworthy and reprehensible. So they glorified God and profited men by their beginning, but God was saddened, men scandalized, and the demons made joyful by their end.

Many monks who start well finish badly

2. This happened to them because they did not give themselves to a pure obedience and an unsolicitous detachment. Therefore they were neither authentically committed to Christ nor worthily disengaged from the devil.[1] Materially and in the eyes of men they had renounced the world, but spiritually they shared in Gehazi's leprosy*[2] and in that of Ananias and Sapphira.†

Because they were not totally committed to Christ

*2 K 5:27.
†Ac 5:1-11.

They were wounded not by leprosy but by shameful and unclean thoughts, and they were snatched away not by bodily death but by falling into their passions as into a tomb. For an unclean soul is the tomb of the spirit, while an earthly body is the tomb of the soul, and very rightly so. Indeed, whoever loves gold hates Christ,[3] and whenever the beginning is disreputable, the whole is rejected. In fact the idea of a

115

wicked deed will not come easily to the one who is
not readily disposed to it.

3. I do not say these things lightly but instructed by my own sufferings and trials. For I know
what the devil has done in me. He shot thoughts
into my spirit and blinded my heart, and did not
cease to assail, upset, and counsel me until he
could fetch me out of the monastery of the Tabennesiots. He dragged me by his shrewd halter,
tripped me up by worldly desires, and kicked me
with temptations until he hurled me into covetous-
ness and then sunk me into the pit of fornication.

4. I come from the city of Memphis. Leaving
behind father and mother, brothers and sisters, I
became a monk. After three years I began to be
assailed by the thought of going to my parents
and relatives according to the flesh, with the idea
of saving them, making them monks, and trans-
forming my father's house into a monastery.[1] I
had already begun to accomplish the services as
burdens and to make excuses saying, 'There is no
salvation in this place'.

5. I could not find a clever pretext. But then it
happened that Abba Theodore was sent to Memphis on some errand. With a wicked mind and
evil desires, I drew up a letter that I gave to one of
the brothers, persuading him to say, 'Your father
is sick and he sends this letter asking you to come
with all haste to tonsure him'.

6. When the brother arrived, I took the letter
and went to show it [to Abba Theodore], entreating [him] to let me go for a few days. But Theodore said to me, 'My child, sit down with the patience of God and be quiet; it is not opportune for
you to go to your father'. Since I was seeking a

**Abba Zanos
himself has been
the victim of
the devil**

**He was tempted
to go back to
his family**

**He tried an
artifice**

**He finally left
the monastery**

pretext, I felt grated by these words, I said things I should not have said and I left.

I found one of the brothers who was light-headed like me and shared my foul thoughts and he was easily baited into such schemes. Being of one mind, we left the monastery and, finding a boat, we sailed the whole day. That brother left me, however, and returned to the monastery.

7. Since I did not find anyone to make the journey with me, I walked absolutely alone. And all of a sudden, looking behind me I saw a nun.[1] She was a very good-looking and beautiful woman, and she said to me, 'Hello, Abba!' And I said to her, 'Peace to you, Amma. Where are you going?' She answered, 'I am a virgin from the monastery of the Tabennesiots,[2] and I am going to my family according to the flesh'. And with those words the thought of fornication began to beset and disturb me. I was no longer able to stay the burning. I locked her in my embrace and, so it seemed, I tossed her down and stripped her naked; whereupon she gave me a slap, and I saw the whole place looking like fire. Then I arose, having ejaculated, but she had disappeared. And forthwith I heard in the air laughter and clapping, as if from a numerous crowd. A fever and a shivering immediately seized me and I stayed lying there from the third to the ninth hour.

8. Then a caravan of wheat-sellers came that way. They picked me up and carried me off to Oxyrynchos, where I remained, suffering very much. My eyes were turned backward and the fever, the shivering, and the headache were unyielding and unceasing, so much so that the physician in charge of the hospital said to the administrator of the hospital, 'There is no cure for him'.

He was tempted and struck by the devil under the appearance of a woman

He was carried off to the hospital at Oxyrynchos

He was cured by
bishop Sarapion
who sent him
back to his
monastery

9. I spent eleven months in that kind of
weakness. Then by the Providence of the man-
loving God, Bishop Sarapion came to Oxyrynchos on some business.¹ The administrator of the
hospital brought him to me. Seeing me in such a
state of suffering he said, 'Where are you from,
brother, and what happened to you?' Three
brothers sat me upright, one sitting behind me,
the second holding my hands, and the other wip-
ing away the fluid flowing from my ears and my
nostrils. Then I said to him, 'Master, have mercy
on me. I was from the monastery of Abba Pacho-
mius² and the demons led me astray in this manner.' He called the bishop of the place and some
clerics. He performed an expiation rite, anointed me with holy oil, and said, 'Behold, through
the prayer of the holy Fathers, the Lord heals
you; return to the monastery where you have renounced [the world]. For the tree bears fruit
where it has been planted. Do not become an
empty cloud or like *chaff in the desert*, for both
are *driven about by the wind.**³ Become rather *a
fruitful olive tree bearing fruit in the house of the
Lord*,† that is, in the monastery. See to it, my son,
that you do not allow impure thoughts to linger
in the earth of your heart, lest you harvest the
sheaves in hundredfold aches and torments. Be a
swift runner returning gracefully to where you
came out disgracefully, lest some further trial
overtake you, and there be no longer any cure
from it for you.'

*Jude 12;
Jr 13:14;
Cf. 2 P 2:17.
†Ps 52(51):8;
Cf. Ho 14:7.

Another
unpleasant
meeting with
the devil on
returning to
his monastery

10. I spent seven days seeking in vain for a fellow traveller. On the eighth day, when I was
asleep, I saw the demon in the habit of that nun,
and he said to me, 'You have become my consort!

Even though that gluttonous old Sarapion has
separated you from me, accept a hernia as a sou-
venir of our intimacy every day of your life.' And
he gave me a kick under the navel. From that
hour on until now I have been suffering very
much, but also giving thanks to God who through
this fleeting pain freed me from such an unclean,
wicked and cruel demon.

Notes to Draguet Fragment II

Draguet II, 2 ¹The opposition of the terms is very clear in Greek: 'they were neither
authentically committed (συνετάξαντο) to Christ, nor worthily disengaged (ἀπετάξαντο) from the devil.'
²The theme of Gehazi's leprosy is classical. See Am. Letter 16, note 4.
³The author plays on words: 'Whoever indeed loves gold (χρυσὸν)
hates Christ (χριστόν)'.

Draguet II, 4 ¹The temptation for a monk to leave the desert in order to bring his
family to monastic life was not unusual; see v.g. H.L., c. 35. 8-9 (John
of Lycopolis).

Draguet II, 7 ¹Lit. a 'canonical woman' (γυναῖκα κανονικὴν). There is a similar
'affair' in H.L., c. 23.
²Pachomius founded two monasteries of virgins: the first in Tabennesi, where his sister Maria lived; and the other in Tsime. Theodore
founded yet another at Bechne, near Phbow. See SBo 27(= G¹ 32) and
G¹ 134.

Draguet II, 9 ¹This Sarapion could very well be the bishop of Nitentori (diocese of
Tabennesi), mentioned in the Life of Pachomius.
²Above, ¶ 3, he said that he was from 'the monastery of the Tabennesiots'. If we take into account the role played by Theodore in the
story, the monastery in question must have been either Phbow or
Tabennesi.
³This quotation is a combination of Jr 13:24 and Jude 12. Jr 13:24 is
quoted also in Pach. Letter 3: 13.

fROM the history of the monks in egypt

(hma)

Ed. Festugière, pp. 39-40

WE SAW ALSO another man in the Thebaid called Ammon,[1] father of three thousand monks who are called Tabennesiots and have a great way of life.[2] They wore goat skins and ate with face covered and head bowed down, lest any should see his neighbor,[3] and they practised such a silence as to seem to be in the desert.[4] Each one accomplished his own practices in secret; it was only for the sake of appearances that they sat at table and seemed to eat, trying to escape each other's notice. Some of them, indeed, would once or twice bring their hands to their mouths, after taking a bit of bread or olives or of the things set before them; and when once they had tasted each type of food they would be satisfied with this nourishment.

The way of life of the Tabennesiots

2. Others quietly chewed their bread, paying no attention to the others,[1] and so showed their endurance. Still others would taste the cooked dishes[2] only three times and abstain from the rest. I marvelled at all this as was proper and I did not let go of the profit to be gained from this account.

Their discretion at table

Notes to the History of the Monks in Egypt

HMA 3:1 ¹We do not know anything else about this Ammon who lived at the time the HMA was written (394) or certainly shortly before. About the several monks called Ammon (Amoun, Ammoun, Ammonos, Ammonios, etc.); see C. Butler, *The Lausiac History of Palladius*, II, *Texts and Studies* VI, 2 (Cambridge, 1904) p. 190, n. 16. We do not know which of the pachomian monasteries the author of HMA visited. 'Tabennesiots' is a generic name for pachomian monks.

²The figure three thousand is certainly an exaggeration. According to Palladius, who himself tends to exaggerate, the Great Monastery of Phbow counted thirteen hundred monks (according to c. 32: 8) or fourteen hundred (according to c. 18: 13), which could correspond to the figures given by Jerome (Jer. Pref. 2). The other monasteries counted between two and three hundred monks, according to Palladius (c. 32: 9). The figure of three hundred would therefore be more plausible here than that of three thousand.

³Of course they did not wear only the goatskin; about the various items of clothing see Jer. Pref. 4 and Pr. 81. Pr. 90 states that the monks do not go to eat without their goatskin. The guarding of the eyes and the covering of the head during meals are prescribed by Pr. 29 and 30.

⁴Cf. Pr. 31 and 33.

HMA 3:2 ¹ἀπροσποιήτως τε τῶν ἄλλων εχοντες: about the meaning of this difficult expression, see A.-J. Festugière, *Enquête sur les moines d'Egypte* (*Historia Monachorum in Aegypto*), p. 35, n. 12.

²τῶν ζωμῶν: Although ζωμός generally means sauce, or broth, it seems in this context to correspond to the *pulmentum* (cooked dish) of Jerome's *Pachomiana latina* rather than to the broth (Jerome's *liquamen* = γάρος) that only the sick could eat. See Pr. 44–46. About the γάρος (and γαρέλαιον), see G¹ 64, note 1.

The full text of the *Historia monachorum in Ægypto* is translated as *The Lives of the Desert Fathers* (Cistercian Studies Series, Nbr. 34).

from the lausiac history of palladius
(h.l.)

Ed. Butler,
p. 26, 17-19

Excerpt from Chapter Seven:
   About the monks of Nitria.

Arsisios of
Nitria

T HAT MAN SAID that he also knew Pachomius of Tabennesi, a prophet and archimandrite of three thousand men, of whom I will speak later.[1]

Excerpts from Chapter Eighteen:
   About Macarios of Alexandria.

Excerpt A:

Ed. Butler,
p. 48, 1-6

1b. His *ascesis* was this:[1] anything he ever heard, this by every means he put into practice.[2] He heard from some that the Tabennesiots eat their food uncooked throughout Lent,[3] so he decided that for seven years he would eat no food that had passed through fire. He ate nothing except for raw vegetables, if they could be found, and soaked pulse.

Macarios
imitates the
ascesis of the
Tabennesiots

Excerpt B:

12. He heard that the Tabennesiots had a great way of life. He then changed his clothes, putting on the secular habit of a laborer and went up to the Thebaid — a fifteen-day journey

Ed. Butler,
p. 52, 1-53,13
Marcarios comes
to Tabennesi

through the desert. Coming to the monastery[1] of the Tabennesiots he asked for their archimandrite,[2] named Pachomius, a most worthy man who had the gift of prophecy but from whom was hidden what concerned Macarios. Meeting him, Macarios said, 'I beg you, receive me into your monastery that I may become a monk.'

13. Pachomius said to him, 'Now you are an old man and cannot practise *ascesis!*[1] The brothers are ascetics, and you cannot bear their toils. You will be scandalized and you will leave, speaking ill of them.' He did not receive him either the first or the second day, and up to seven days. But when he remained firm, [and] kept fasting, he said again to him, 'Receive me, Abba, and if I do not fast and work like them, order me to be cast out'. He persuaded the brothers to receive him. The number of that one house is of fourteen hundred men to this day.[2]

14. Shortly after he entered it was Lent, and he saw each one practising a different *ascesis*: one eating at evening, another every other day, another every five days; another again remained standing all night and sitting during the day. So he soaked a great quantity of palm leaves and stood in a corner; till the Forty Days were fulfilled and the Passover came, he did not touch bread or water, neither did he bend his knee or lie down. He took nothing except a few cabbage leaves, and this on Sunday, that he might give the appearance of eating.

15. Whenever he went out for his own needs, he came back quickly and stood there. He spoke to no one, did not open his mouth, but stood in silence. Except for the prayer in his heart and the palm leaves in his hands, he did nothing.

He is received
as a monk

Macarios' *ascesis*
during Lent

Pachomius'
monks are upset

When all the ascetics saw this, they quarrelled with the superior saying, 'Where did you get this fleshless man for our condemnation? Either cast him out or know that we are all withdrawing from you.' Hearing about his way of life, Pachomius prayed God to reveal to him who he was.

16. It was revealed to him. He took Macarios by the hand and led him to the oratory, where the altar was. He said to him, 'Come, good old man; you are Macarios, and you hid yourself from me. For many years I have longed to see you. I am grateful to you for having buffeted my children, that they might not be haughty about their own ascetic practices. Return then to your own place, for you have sufficiently edified us. And pray for us.' Then he withdrew as requested.

Macarios' iden-
tity is revealed
to Pachomius

Chapter Thirty-two:
　　About Pachomius and the Tabennesiots.

Ed. Butler,
p. 87, 18-96,5

1. Tabennesi is a place so called in the Thebaid, where lived a certain Pachomius, one of those men who so walk in righteousness as to be deemed worthy also of prophecies and angelic visions. He became a great lover of men and of his brothers.

Pachomius' call
and the Rule of
the Angel

Thus, as he was sitting in his cave,[1] an angel appeared to him and told him, 'As concerns yourself, you have reached perfection; there is no need for you to continue sitting in your cave. Come, go forth and assemble all the young monks and dwell with them;[2] and legislate for them according to the rule I give you.' And he gave him a bronze tablet on which this was written:[3]

2. You shall permit each one to eat and to drink according to his strength, and you shall assign work also according to the strength of the eaters,[1] and not prevent them from fasting or eating.[2] But entrust the hard work to those who are stronger and eat, and the lighter work to those who are weaker and more ascetic. Make separate cells in the court and let them stay three in each cell.[3] But let the meals of all be sought at one house.

3. Let them sleep not lying down, but let them make reclining chairs of masonry and sleep sitting on these chairs after covering them with their blankets.[1] At night let them wear linen tunics and be belted. Let each of them have a tanned goatskin without which they may not eat.[2] When they go to Communion on Saturday and Sunday, let them loosen their belts, lay aside their goat skins and go in with the hood only.[3] He prescribed[4] for them hoods without nap, as for children, and he ordered a sign in the form of a cross to be put on them in purple.[5]

4. He ordered that there should be twenty-four classes and to each class[1] he assigned a Greek character, beginning with alpha, beta, gamma, delta, and so on. So when he asked questions and busied himself with so great a crowd, the senior would ask the second, 'How is the Alpha class?' or 'How is the Zeta?' Or again, 'Give greetings to the Rho,' following a particular meaning of the characters. 'To the simpler and purer you shall assign the Iota, but to the more difficult and devious the Xi.'

5. And so he adjusted the character to each class according to their dispositions, tempera-

ments, and lives; but only those who were spiritual knew the meanings.[1]

It was written on the tablet: A stranger from another monastery having another rule shall not eat or drink with them, nor enter into the monastery unless he finds himself on a journey. Anyone who has come to stay with them, they do not receive into the innermost parts for a period of three years,[2] but he performs the more laborious works, and then enters after three years.

6. While eating they shall cover their heads with their hoods, so that a brother may not see his brother chewing. Nor shall one talk while eating or cast his eyes anywhere besides his own plate or table.[1]

Meals and the twelve prayers

He laid down that in the course of the day they should make twelve prayers, and at the lamp-lighting time twelve, and in the nightly vigils twelve, and at the ninth hour three. When the multitude goes to eat, he laid down that a psalm should be sung before each prayer.[2]

7. As Pachomius objected to the angel that the prayers were too few, the angel said to him, 'I arranged these so that even the little ones might achieve the fulfillment of the rule without grief. As for the perfect, they have no need of legislation, for they have dedicated all their life to the contemplation of God by themselves in their cells. I have laid down rules for all those whose mind has not attained knowledge, so that at least fulfilling like servants the duties of monastic life, they may be established in confidence.

The prayer of the perfect monks

8. The monasteries abiding by this rule are many and count seven thousand men. The first and great monastery is the one where Pachomius

The Great Monastery

himself lived.[1] It gave birth to all the other monasteries, and it has thirteen hundred men,[2] among
whom was the good Aphthonios who became my
true friend and is now the second in the monastery. They send him to Alexandria to sell the produce of their work and to purchase the necessities,
since he is not one to be made to stumble.[3]

The other
monasteries

9. There are other monasteries of more than
two hundred and three hundred men. When I
went to Panopolis I found one of them having
three hundred men. In this monastery I saw fifteen tailors, seven smiths, four carpenters, twelve
camel drivers and fifteen fullers. They work at
every craft, providing for the women's monasteries and for prisons from their surplus.

10. They even raise swine.[1] When I criticized
this practice, they told me, 'It is a custom we have
received in the tradition, to raise them with the
winnowings and the vegetable left-overs and all
that is left over and thrown out, that it not be
wasted. The swine are to be killed and the meat
sold, but their feet must be given to the sick and
the old, because the country is small and heavily
populated.' For the Blemmyes people live near
them.

11. Those who do the service for the day rise
early and busy themselves, some about the kitch-
en, some about the tables. They work at them until [meal] time, setting and putting on each table
loaves, compounded charlock, olives, cheese
made of cow's milk, the animals' feet, and small
vegetables. Then some come to eat at the sixth
hour, others at the seventh, others at the eighth,
others at the ninth, others at the eleventh, others
at late evening, and others every other day, so
that each letter knows its own proper hour.[1]

The raising of swine (marginal)

Hours of meals (marginal)

12. It was also the same with regard to their work. One works the land as a farmer, another the garden, another works at the forge, another at the bakery, another in the carpenter's shop, another in the fuller's, another weaving the big baskets, another in the tannery, another in the shoe-shop, another at calligraphy, another weaving the soft baskets. And they learn all the Scriptures by heart.

Various crafts

Chapter Thirty-three: The Women's Monastery.

Ed. Butler, p. 96, 6-97,20

1. They also have a monastery of about four hundred women, with the same constitution and the same way of life, except for the goat skin. The women are across the river and the men opposite them. When a virgin dies, the other virgins prepare her body for the burial; they carry it and place it on the bank of the river. The brothers cross over on a ferry, with palm leaves and olive branches and carry the body across with psalmody. Then they bury it in their own tombs.[1]

Burial of a virgin

2. No one goes over to the women's monastery. A tailor from the world crossed over through ignorance, looking for work. A young [sister] who had come out—for the place is deserted—met him involuntarily and gave him this answer, 'We have our own tailors'.

Story of a sister who was falsely accused

3. Another [sister] saw them talking. Some time later, on the occasion of a quarrel, she accused falsely that [sister] before the community, by a diabolical insinuation [and moved by] great wickedness and boiling temper. A few others joined her in this nasty act. The other was so

She committed suicide

grieved at undergoing such an accusation, of a thing that had not even come to her mind, that not being able to bear it, she threw herself secretly into the river and died.

4. Then the slanderer realized that she had slandered out of wickedness and committed that crime. She also could stand it no longer; she went and hanged herself.

When the priest came, the other sisters told him what had happened. Then he ordered that the Eucharist should not be offered for either of them. Those who had not effected a reconciliation between the two, he excommunicated and deprived them from the Eucharist for a period of seven years for their complicity with the slanderer and for having believed what was said.

Chapter Thirty-four:
     The Nun Who Feigned Madness.

1. There was another virgin in the same monastery who feigned madness and demon-possession. The others had so much contempt for her that they never ate with her, which was her own choice. Strolling about the kitchen she did all kinds of services. She was, as the saying goes, the sponge of the monastery, and she fulfilled the word of the Scripture, *If any one among us thinks of himself as wise in this world, let him become a fool that he may be wise.*[1] She used to serve with a rag around her head, while all the others have their hair closely cropped and have hoods.

2. Not a single one of the four hundred ever saw her eating during all the years of her life. She

never sat at table or received a piece of bread, but was satisfied with the crumbs she wiped off the tables with a sponge and what she got scouring the pots. She never abused any one, she never murmured or spoke either little or much, although she was boxed, abused, cursed, and loathed.

Her ascesis and humility

3. Now an angel appeared to the holy Piteroum, a most proven anchorite dwelling at Porphyrites, and said to him, 'Why do you think highly of yourself for being pious and for dwelling in a place such as this? Do you want to see a woman more pious than yourself? Go to the women's monastery at Tabennesi and there you will find one with a diadem around her head. She is better than you are.

An angel revealed her holiness to Abba Piteroum

4. 'While being cuffed around by such a crowd, she has never taken her heart away from God. As for you, while dwelling here you wander about the cities in your mind.'

Piteroum came to the sisters' monastery

So, he who had never gone away went to that monastery and asked the teachers to let him enter the women's monastery.[1] They dared to let him enter since he was a man of great reputation and of great age.

5. He went in and asked to see all of them. But that one did not show up. Finally he said to them, 'Bring them all to me; there is one missing'. They told him, 'We have one in the kitchen, who is "shaky"'—for this is what they call the afflicted ones. He said to them, 'Bring that one also to me; let me see her'. They went to call her but she did not obey, perhaps because she sensed the matter or it had even been revealed to her. They seized her forcibly and told her, 'The holy Piteroum wants to see you'—for he was renowned.

He asked to see all the sisters

He revealed the
virtue of the one
who feigned
madness

6. When she came, he saw the rag around her forehead and fell down at her feet saying, 'Bless me!' She likewise fell down at his feet saying, 'You bless me, lord!' They were all amazed and they told him, 'Abba, take no insult, she is "shaky"'. Piteroum said to all of them, 'You are ones who are "shaky"; for she is my Amma and yours' — for this is what they call the spiritual women — 'and I pray to be found worthy of her on the day of judgement.'

The sisters
confessed the
wicked things
they used to do
to her. Then she
went away

7. When they heard this, they fell down at her feet. They all confessed various things: one how she had poured the leavings of the plate over her; another how she had beaten her with her fists; another how she had blistered her nose. In a word, they all confessed various outrages.

After praying for them, he departed. A few days later, the [virgin] left the monastery, being unable to bear the praise and the reverence of the sisters, and burdened by their apologies. Where she went, where she took refuge, and how she died, nobody knows.

Notes to the Lausiac History

H.L.   7:6 [1] This Arsisios of Nitria, whom Palladius calls 'Arsisios the Great' (H.L. 7: 3) was a contemporary of Antony and Pachomius. He survived both of them.

H.L. 18:1b [1] This Macarios of Alexandria is, as D.J. Chitty put it, 'a survival from the first adventurous generation, whose experience was to set more sober lines for their successors.' A convert at the age of forty in c. 333 and ordained priest some time after 340, he is the first known priest of Kellia, in Nitria. If he outstripped all others by his *ascesis*, stability in one place was not his main characteristic; apart from an occasional visit to Pachomius, he maintained four cells in four different places. He died in 393 at the age of one hundred.

See D.J. Chitty, *The Desert a City*, pp. 32-33. There is also a Coptic Life of this Macarios in *ADMG* - 25, pp. 235ff.

²We find the same attitude in young Antony who, after visiting various pious men endeavoured to realize in himself the virtues of all; see *Vit. Ant.*, c. 4.

³This detail is not confirmed either by the Rules or by the Life of Pachomius.

H.L.18:12 ¹ἀσκητήριον; this is not a pachomian term. It is used only once in G¹ (¶ 19; Halkin, p. 12, 11) where it is the name given the small dwelling where Pachomius lived with his brother John. It corresponds to *manšopi* in the parallel text of SBo 21. *Manšopi* means 'dwelling' in general, but is also often used for 'cell' in Pachomian texts. Note also that G³ has replaced the ἀσκητήριον of G¹ 19 by μοναστήριον.

².This term of 'archimandrite' is not pachomian either; see Draguet I, 2, note 1.

H.L. 18:13 ¹Actually Macarios was one year younger than Pachomius.

²In c. 32, 8, Palladius will give the figure of thirteen hundred monks for the Great Monastery (Phbow). These figures are not inconsistent with the indications given by Jerome (Jer. Pref. 2, note 1), but they must be accepted with some reservation.

H.L. 32:1 ¹σπηλαίῳ; this is yet another non-pachomian term. In G¹ it is used only once (Halkin p. 2, 4) in a quotation of Heb 11:38. Pachomius never lived in a cave; nevertheless, in S¹ 8, after his wrangle with John, he descended into an underground place in order to pray. According to SBo 12, when Pachomius was still living with Palamon, he used to leave his cell during the night and go to the tombs in the desert and pray. It seems that it was there he saw a second time the vision he had had in Tabennesi four years earlier. These tombs were in fact caves that are still visible on the side of the mountain. For a description of Palamon's desert and of these tombs, see L.-T. Lefort, 'Les premiers monastères pachômiens', pp.393-397.

²In fact, Pachomius' very first disciples were not people who were already monks, but poor peasants of the surrounding villages who came to live near him because he was good to them; see S¹ 10.

³Sozomen claimed that the tablet was still preserved in his time (H.E., III, 14, 9).

H.L. 32:2 ¹The meaning is probably 'according to the strength they acquire through eating'.

²Cf. Jer. Pref. 5.

³The 'court' is not a pachomian term. Moreover, pachomian monks did not live three in a cell. Except for one obscure text of Hors. Reg. 17, that seems to imply that two brothers shared the same cell, all our sources indicate that each monk had his own private cell.

H.L. 32:3 ¹About these reclining seats, see Pr. 87, with note 2.

²The expression μηλωτὴν αἰγείαν εἰργασμένην is strange. First, because μηλωτὴ αἰγεία is a pleonasm; μηλωτή by itself means a goat skin. Second, because the participle εἰργασμένην (from ἐργάζομαι) does not mean anything specific. (See R. Draguet, 'Le chapitre de HL', pp. 100-102.)

About the clothing of the pachomian monks, see Jer. Pref. 4 and Pr. 81.

[3] This means that, when going to Communion, the brothers wore neither their goat skin (or *melote*) or their linen mantle (that could be attached to the hood), but only their tunic (or *lebiton*).

[4] ἐτύπωσεν corresponds to the Coptic word tôs, commonly used with this meaning in pachomian texts.

[5] The clause 'as for children' refers to the wearing of the hoods, not to their make; cf. Cassian I, 3 where the constant wearing of the hood (*cucullus*) is explained as an imitation of the children's innocence and simplicity. The Rule (Pr. 99) prescribes that the hoods be marked with the sign of the community and the sign of the house, but there is no question of 'the sign of the cross'. Even the Hors. Reg. having a long section on the sign of the cross (¶¶ 7-10) do not mention it on the monks' clothes. In fact, even in the text of H.L. the words 'in the form of the cross' (τύπον σταυροῦ) are not original; they are absent from the excellent *codex* O; see R. Draguet, 'Le chapitre de HL', pp. 110-111.

H.L. 32:4 [1] These classes correspond probably to the tribes of which Jerome speaks in his Preface to the Rule (¶ 2, note 9). They are occasionally mentioned in the Life; see SBo 26, note 5.

H.L. 32:5 [1] There is here an indirect witnessing to the existence of a mysterious language used by Pachomius, especially in some of his letters; see H. Quecke, *Die Briefe Pachoms*, p. 28. See also our introduction to Pachomius' letters in Volume III.

[2] About the reception of guests, see ¶ 51-52; cf. SBo 40 (= G¹ 40). On the reception and formation of postulants, see Pr. 49. According to this Pr. 49, the new comer shall stay *a few* days at the gatehouse; Theod. Instr. 3: 16 speaks of *a month*, but there is nowhere required the period of three years mentioned here by Palladius

H.L. 32:6 [1] Cf. Pr. 29-30.

[2] This has undergone many transformations through the transmission of the text. See our *excursus* on the tradition of the twelve psalms, in *La liturgie...*, pp. 324-339.

H.L. 32:8 [1] This must be Phbow. Nevertheless Phbow (often called the Great Monastery) was first only in importance; Tabennesi was anterior in time.

2 In H.L., c. 18, 13, above, the figure was fourteen hundred. Some manuscripts have harmonized the figures.

[3] Pachomius seems to have had problems at times in finding a brother suitable for such a delicate job; see Paral. 21-23.

H.L. 32:10 [1] There is no trace of this either in the Rules or in the Life.

H.L. 32:11 [1] Although the indications of the Life and of the Rules are not absolutely clear and perhaps not entirely consistent, it seems that there were two meals served every day in the pachomian communities, one at noon and one in the evening, after a *synaxis* that may have been held at the ninth hour. Everybody had to go to the noon meal; but after the *synaxis*, in the evening, each one could go either to the refectory or to his cell; see Jer. Pref. 5; Pr. 103; etc. The great diversity described here by Palladius, however, has nothing in common with pachomian customs.

H.L. 33:1 ¹Pachomius founded two monasteries of women: one in the village of Tabennesi, near the brothers' monastery, and one at Tsmine. Theodore founded one at Bechne, a mile from Phbow. Is Palladius speaking of one of these? The monasteries of Tabennesi and Bechne were certainly not across the river from the brothers' monastery. Was Tsmine in that position? The expression of G¹ 134, εἰς Τομηνὲ, (on the use of εἰς for ἐν in G¹, see Festugière, *La première Vie grecque*, p. 136) can hardly be understood of a monastery on the other side of the river in front of Tsmine. D.J. Chitty supposed that Palladius was referring to that monastery, since he mentioned in c. 32:9, that he visited one of the monasteries of the monks near Panopolis. It is not impossible; but the argument is weak. (See Chitty, *The Desert a City*, p. 24 and note 71). About the burial of a sister, see a more detailed description (without the ferry!) in SBo 27 (= G¹ 32).

H.L. 34:1 ¹This text is quoted also in SBo 95; note here the change of the second person plural ('If any one among *you*...') into the first person plural ('...among *us*...').

H.L. 34:4 ¹These 'teachers' correspond to the 'elders appointed to the virgins' ministry' of Pr. 143.

apophthegmata
about pachomius and theodore
(apoph.)

ONE DAY, the body of a dead man was carried on the road. Our great father Pachomius came across it and saw two angels behind the bed,[1] following the dead man. Reflecting about them, he prayed God to reveal to him what had happened. Then the two angels came to him, and he said to them, 'Why is it that you who are angels follow the dead man?' The angels told him, 'One of us is the [angel] of Wednesday and the other of Friday. Because this soul did not miss fasting on Wednesday and Friday until the time of its death, we have followed its body, since it has kept the fast until death. For this cause therefore we have also glorified it, because it has contended in the Lord.'[2]

The angels of Wednesday and Friday

II

PG 65:304;
G³ 160

Abba Macarios went once to Abba Pachomius of the Tabennesiots. Pachomius asked him, 'When brothers do not live with discipline, is it good to correct them?' Abba Macarios said to him, 'Correct and judge justly those under you; but outside, judge no man. For it is written, *Is it not of those who are inside that you are the judges? But of those who are outside, God is the judge.*'[3]

About the correction of brothers

1 Co 5:12-13

137

PG 65:189;
G³ 195

III

The work of
the soul

A brother questioned him saying, 'What is the
work of the soul, which we now consider to be
secondary, and what is that which is secondary
and which we now consider to be the work?' The
old man said, 'Everything that is done as a commandment of God is the work of the soul; but to
work and to hoard [goods] for a personal motive,
this is what we must consider as secondary.' Then
the brother said, 'Explain this matter to me.' So
the old man said, 'Suppose you hear that I am
sick and you ought to visit me, and you say to
yourself, "Should I leave my work and go now? I
would rather finish [my work] first and then go."
Then another pretext comes along and you will
perhaps never go. Or again another brother says
to you, "Lend me a hand, brother"; and you say,
"Should I leave my work and go to work with
him?" Now, if you do not go, you neglect the
commandment of God which is the work of the
soul, and you do what is secondary, that is, the
work of your hands.'⁴

Notes to the Apophthegmata

Apoph. 1   ¹κράββατος: bed or couch on which the body lay.
²This apophthegm is recorded by Bousset (*Apophthegmata. Studien
zur Geschichte des ältesten Mönchtums* [Tübingen, 1923] p. 168) in the
first Armenian recension (Arm. XVIII, 53). J.-Cl. Guy has mentioned it
among the nominative apophthegmata of the systematic collection
(*Recherches sur la tradition grecque des Apophthegmata Patrum, Subsidia hagiographica* 36 [Brussels, 1962] pp. 174-175 and 242); and D.J.
Chitty found it also in the collection contained in the Bodleian Ms.
Cromwell 18 (see 'Pachomian Sources Reconsidered', p. 55).
³This is Macarios the Alexandrian; about him, see H.L., C. 18: lb, note 1.
⁴In G³ this teaching is attributed to Theodore, Pachomius disciple. It is
found also in the Latin and Greek collections of *Apophtegmata* (PL
73:1039-1040; PG 65:189). In the Greek collection of *Apophthegmata*, it
is attributed to Theodore of Pherme.

pachomian rules

the Rules of
saint pachomius

Jerome's preface
(Jer. Pref.)

1. However sharp and polished a sword may
be, it becomes sullied with rust and loses the bril-
liance of its former beauty if it is kept a long time
in the sheath. Therefore, as I had been sorrow-
ing over the death of the holy and venerable
Paula[1]—in this not acting contrary to the precept of the Apostle, but sighing over the refresh-
ment lost by many through her death—I received the books sent to me by the man of God,
the priest Silvanus, who had himself received
them from Alexandria that he should bid me to
translate them. He said that in the communities
of the Thebaid and in the monastery of Metanoia (the name of which by a happy conversion
has been changed from Canopos into Penitence)
lived many Latins, who did not know the Egyptian and Greek languages in which the precepts
of Pachomius, Theodore, and Horsiesios were
written.[2] These were the first in the Thebaid and
Egypt to lay the foundations of cenobitic life[3] according to the precept of God and of the angel
who was sent by God for this very purpose.[4]

Because I had remained mute for a long time
and suffered my grief in silence,[5] and [because]
the priest Leontius and the other brothers who
had been sent to me with him kept pressing me, I
summoned a scribe and I dictated those writings

Text: Boon
pp. 3ff.

1 Th 4:13.

141

in our language, as I had found them translated
from Egyptian into Greek. I did this to obey the
command—not to call it the request—of such
great men, and to break my long silence under fair
auspices, as they say. Returning to my former
studies I [thought I] would [in so doing] bring re-
pose[6] to the soul of that holy woman who had always burnt with love for the monasteries and had
meditated[7] here on earth on what she was going to
see in heaven. Also, the venerable virgin of Christ,
her daughter Eustochium,[8] would have something
to give the sisters as a rule of conduct and our
brothers would be able to follow the example of
the Egyptian, that is the Tabennesian monks.

2. They have in each monastery fathers and
stewards, weekly servers, ministers, and a master
of each house. A house has, more or less, forty
brothers who obey the master and, according to
the number of brothers, there are thirty or forty
houses in one monastery, and three or four houses
are federated into a tribe.[9] They either go to work
together or they succeed each other in the weekly
service according to their rank.

3. The first to enter the monastery sits first,
walks first, says the psalm first, stretches his hand
out first at table, and communicates first in
church. Among them, account is taken not of
age, but of [the time of] profession.

4. They have nothing in their cells except a
mat and what is listed here below; two *lebitonaria*
(which is a kind of Egyptian garment without
sleeves), and a third one, already worn, for sleeping and working, a linen mantle, two hoods, a
goat skin which they call *melote*, a linen belt, and
finally shoes and staff to go on journeys.[10]

5. The sick are sustained with wonderful care and a great abundance of food.[11] The healthy practise a greater abstinence. They all fast twice a week, Wednesday and Friday, except during the Passover and the Fifty Days [of Eastertide]. On other days those who want to do so eat after noon and the table is set again at dinner time on account of those who are tired,[12] the old, and the boys, and on account of the very severe heat. There are some who eat a little the second time, others who are satisfied with one meal, either at noon or in the evening; and some taste a little bread and then go out. All eat together. Anyone who does not want to go to table receives in his cell only bread with water and salt, either daily or every other day, as he wishes.[13]

6. Brothers of the same craft are gathered into one house under one master. For example, those who weave linen are together, and those who weave mats are considered one family. Likewise tailors, carriage makers, fullers and shoemakers are governed separately by their own masters, and every week they render an account of their works to the father of the monastery.

7. The superiors of all the monasteries have one head who lives at the monastery of Phbow. In the days of the Passover all assemble around him except those who are needed in their own monasteries, so that nearly fifty thousand men celebrate together the feast of the Lord's passion.[14]

8. In the month which is called Mesore, that is, August, they observe days of remission like the Jubilee.[15] Sins are forgiven everyone and those who have had any quarrel are reconciled to each other. And, as necessity requires, heads of mon-

Lv 25.

asteries, stewards, masters, and ministers are appointed.

9. The Thebans say that to Pachomius, Cornelios and Sourous (who is said to be still alive at more than 110 years of age)[16] an angel gave knowledge of a secret language, so that they might write to each other and speak through a spiritual alphabet, wrapping hidden meanings in certain signs and symbols. We have translated these letters into our language just as they are read among the Egyptians and the Greeks, following literally the text we had.[17] If we have imitated the simplicity of the Egyptian speech, we have done so out of fidelity to the text, lest rhetorical speech should alter what has been said by apostolic men filled with spiritual grace.

As for the other things that are contained in their treaties I did not want to give a foretaste, so that they may be learned from their authors, and those who find delight in the studies of the holy congregation[18] may drink from the springs rather than from the rivulets.

precepts

of our father Pachomius,
the man of God who by commandment of God
was the first founder of the cenobitic life.

(PR.)

Here begin the precepts:

W hen someone uninstructed comes to the assembly of the saints, the porter shall introduce him according to [his] rank from the door of the monastery and give him a seat in the gathering of the brothers.[1] He shall not be allowed to change his place or rank of sitting until the οἰκιακός, that is, his own housemaster, transfers him to the place he should have.[2]

2. He shall sit with all modesty and meekness, tucking under his buttocks the lower edge of the goat skin which hangs over his shoulder down his side,[1] and carefully girding up his garment — that is, the linen tunic without sleeves called *lebitonarium* — in such a way that it covers his knees.[2]

3. As soon as he hears the sound of the trumpet calling the [the brothers] to the *synaxis*[1], he shall leave his cell,[2] reciting something from the Scriptures until he reaches the door of the *synaxis*.[3]

4. And when he begins to walk into the *synaxis* room, going to his place of sitting and standing, he should not tread upon the rushes which have been dipped in water in preparation for the plaiting of ropes, lest even a small loss should come to the monastery through someone's negligence.[1]

145

5. But at night when the signal is given you shall not stand at the fire usually lighted to warm bodies and drive off the cold, nor shall you sit idle in the *synaxis*, but with a quick hand you shall prepare ropes for the warps of mats, although exception is made for the infirmity of the body to which leave must be given for rest.

6. When the one who stands first on the step, reciting by heart something from the Scripture, claps with his hand for the prayer to be concluded,[1] no one should delay in rising but all shall get up together.[2]

7. Let no one look at another twisting ropes or praying; let him rather be intent on his own work with eyes cast down.

8. These are the precepts of life handed down to us by the elders.[1] If it happens that during the psalmody or the prayer or in the midst of a reading anyone speaks or laughs, he shall unfasten his belt immediately and with neck bowed down and hands hanging down he shall stand before the altar and be rebuked by the superior of the monastery. He shall do the same also in the assembly of the brothers when they assemble to eat.[2]

9. When by day the trumpet blast has called [the brothers] to the *synaxis,* anyone who comes after the first prayer shall be punished in the manner described above and shall remain standing in the refectory.[1]

10. At night however, more is conceded to the body's weakness and anyone who comes after the third prayer shall be punished in the same manner both in the *synaxis* and at meal time.[1]

11. When the brothers are praying in the *synaxis,* let no one go out except by order of the superiors and unless he has asked and been permitted to go out for the necessities of nature.

12. No one shall divide the rushes for plaiting ropes except the person who does the weekly service. And if he is reasonably detained by some work, the directive of the superior shall be resorted to.

13. Among the weekly servers from one house some shall not be chosen to stand on the step and recite something from the Scripture in the assembly of all, but all of them, according to their order of sitting and standing, shall repeat from memory what has been assigned to them.

14. If any one of them forgets anything and hesitates in speaking, he shall undergo punishment for his negligence and forgetfulness.[1]

15. On Sunday, or at the time of the Eucharist,[1] none of the weekly servers shall be absent from his seat on the *embrimium*[2] and not responding to the psalmist. They are all [to be] from the same house that does the greater weekly service; for there is another lesser weekly service performed in the individual houses by a smaller number. If a greater number is necessary, others from the same tribe shall be called by the housemaster doing the weekly service. Without his order no one shall come from another house of the same tribe to sing psalms. Likewise, it shall not be permitted anyone at all to serve in the weekly service of a house other than his own, unless it be [a house] of the same tribe. They call a tribe a group of three or four houses—according to the population of the monastery—which

we could designate as families or peoples of a single race.[3]

16. On Sunday and in the *synaxis* in which the Eucharist is to be offered, let no one be allowed to sing psalms apart from the housemaster and the elders of the monastery, who are of some reputation.

17. If anyone is missing when one of the elders is chanting, that is, reading the psalter,[1] he shall at once undergo the order of penance and rebuke before the altar.

18. Anyone who, without an order from the superior, leaves the *synaxis* in which the Eucharist is offered shall be rebuked at once.

19. In the morning in the individual houses, after the prayers are finished,[1] they shall not return right away to their cells, but they shall discuss among themselves the instruction they heard from their housemasters. Then they shall enter their quarters.

20. An instruction shall be given three times a week by the housemasters. And during the instruction the brothers, whether sitting or standing, shall not change their place [which is] according to the order of the houses and of the individual men.[1]

21. If someone falls asleep while sitting during the instruction of the housemaster or of the superior of the monastery, he shall be forced to get up at once, and he shall stand until ordered to sit.

22. When the signal is given to assemble and hear the precepts of the superiors, no one shall remain behind. Nor shall the fire be lighted before the instruction has ended.

Anyone who neglects one of these precepts shall undergo the aforesaid punishment.

23. Without the order of the superior of the monastery, the weekly server shall not have authority to give ropes or any vessel to anyone. And without his order he shall not be able to give the signal for [the brothers] to gather whether for the midday *synaxis* or for the evening *synaxis* of the Six Prayers.[1]

24. After the morning prayer, the weekly server on whom this work is enjoined shall ask the superior of the monastery about the various things he believes necessary and about when they ought to go out to work in the fields. And according to his directives, he shall go around the individual houses to find out what each one has need of.

25. If they seek a book to read, let them have it; and at the end of the week they shall put it back in its place for those who succeed them in the service.

26. When they are working at mats, the ministers shall ask each of the housemasters in the evening how many rushes are required per house. And so he shall dip the rushes and distribute them in the morning to each in order. If in the morning he notices that still more rushes are needed, he shall dip them and bring them around to each house, until the signal is given for the meal.

27. The housemaster who is completing the weekly service and the one taking up the service for the coming week and the superior of the monastery shall have the responsibility of observing what work has been omitted or neglected. They

shall have the mats that are usually spread out on the floor in the *synaxis* shaken out. And they shall also count the ropes twisted per week, noting the sum on tablets and keeping the record until the time of the annual gathering, when an account shall be given and sins forgiven everyone.[1]

28. When the *synaxis* is dismissed, each one shall recite something from the Scripture while going either to his cell or to the refectory. And no one shall have his head covered during recitation.

29. And when they come to eat, they shall sit in order in [their] appointed places, and cover their heads.[1]

30. When you are ordered by the superior to pass from one table to another, you shall do it at once, without contradicting him at all. Nor shall you dare to stretch out your hand at the table before your housemaster. And you shall not look around at others eating.

31. Each master shall teach, in his own house, how they must eat with manners and meekness. If anyone speaks or laughs[1] while eating, he shall do penance and be rebuked there at once; and he shall stand until another of the brothers who are eating gets up.[2]

32. If someone comes late to eat,[1] without [being detained by] an order of the superior, he shall likewise do penance, or return to his house without eating.

33. If anything is needed at table no one shall dare to speak, but he shall make a sign to the ministers by a sound.[1]

34. When you come out of the meal you shall not speak while going back to your own place.[1]

35. The ministers[1] shall eat nothing but what has been prepared for the brothers in common, nor shall they dare to prepare special foods for themselves.

36. The one who strikes the signal to assemble the brothers for meals shall recite while striking.

37. The one who dispenses sweets to the brothers at the refectory door as they go out shall recite something from the Scriptures while doing so.[1]

38. The one who receives the things that are handed out shall receive it not in his hood but in his goat skin; and he shall not taste what he has received until he reaches his house. The one who portions out [the sweets] to the others shall receive his portion from the housemaster. In the same way, the other ministers shall receive theirs from another, claiming nothing for themselves at their own discretion. What they receive shall be enough for three days. And if anyone has anything left over, he shall bring it back to the housemaster who shall put it back in the storeroom to be mixed with the rest and given out to all the brothers.

39. No one shall give more to one than another has received.

40. If some sickness is alleged, the housemaster[1] shall proceed to the ministers of the sick and receive from them whatever is necessary.

41. If one of the ministers is sick himself, he shall not have permission to enter the kitchen or storeroom to get something for himself; but the other ministers shall give him whatever they consider he needs. Nor shall he be permitted to cook for himself what he desires; but the housemasters shall get from the other ministers what they consider he needs.

42. Let no one who is not sick enter the infirmary. The one who falls sick shall be led by the master to the refectory for the sick. And if he needs a mantle or a tunic or anything else by way of covering or food, let the master himself get these from the ministers and give them to the sick brother.

43. Nor may a sick brother enter the cell of those who are eating and eat what he wants, unless he is led there to eat by the minister in charge of this matter. Nor shall he be permitted to take to his cell any of the things he has received in the infirmary, not even a fruit.

44. Those who cook the meals shall themselves serve them in turn.

45. Let no one touch wine or broth outside the infirmary.[1]

46. If someone is sent on a journey and falls sick on the road or in the boat, and has the need or the desire to eat some fish broth or some other things that are used at meals in the monastery, he shall not eat with the other brothers but by himself. And the ministers shall give to him abundantly so that a sick brother may not be saddened in any way.

47. No one may dare visit a sick brother without the superior's leave. And except by order of the housemaster not even a relative or a blood brother shall be authorized to serve him.

48. If someone omits or neglects any of these [precepts], he shall be corrected with the customary rebuke.

49. When someone comes to the door of the monastery, wishing to renounce the world and be added to the number of the brothers, he shall not

be free to enter.[1] First, the father of the monastery shall be informed [of his coming]. He shall remain outside at the door a few days and be taught the Lord's prayer and as many psalms as he can learn.[2] Carefully shall he make himself known: has he done something wrong and, troubled by fear, suddenly run away? Or is he under someone's authority? Can he renounce his parents and spurn his own possessions? If they see that he is ready for everything, then he shall be taught the rest of the monastic discipline: what he must do and whom he must serve,[3] whether in the *synaxis* of all the brothers or in the house to which he is assigned, as well as in the refectory. Perfectly instructed in every good work, let him be joined to the brothers. Then they shall strip him of his secular clothes and garb him in the monastic habit. He shall be handed over to the porter so that at the time of prayer he may bring him before all the brothers; and he shall sit where he is told.[4] The clothes he brought with him shall be given to those in charge of this matter and brought to the storeroom; they will be in the keeping of the superior of the monastery.[5]

50. No one living in the monastery may receive anyone to eat; he shall send him to the guesthouse door to be received by those in charge of this matter.

51. When people come to the door of the monastery, they shall be received with greater honor if they are clerics or monks. Their feet shall be washed, according to the Gospel precept, and they shall be brought to the guesthouse and offered everything suitable to monks. If they

Jn 13:14–15.

wish to join the assembly of the brothers at the
time of prayer and *synaxis*, and they are of the
same faith,[1] the porter or the guestmaster shall
inform the father of the monastery and they shall
be brought in to pray.[2]

1 P 3:7.

52. If seculars, or infirm people or *weaker
vessels* — that is, women — come to the door, they
shall be received in different places according to
their calling and their sex.[1] Above all, women
shall be cared for with greater honor and dili-
gence. They shall be given a place separate from
all areas frequented by men, so there may be no
occasion for slander. If they come in the evening,
it would be wicked to drive them away; but, as we
have said, they shall be lodged in a separate and
enclosed place with every discipline and caution,
so that the flock of the brothers may freely tend to
its duty and no occasion for detraction be given to
anybody.

53. If someone presents himself at the door of
the monastery and says he would like to see his
brother or his relative, the porter shall inform the
father of the monastery, who will call the housemaster and ask him whether the man is in his
house. Then, with the housemaster's permission,
he shall be given a trustworthy companion and so
shall be sent to see his brother or relative. If it
happens that the latter brought him some of the
foods which are allowed to be eaten in the monastery, he may not receive them himself, but he
shall call the porter who shall receive the gifts. If
they are of a kind to be eaten with bread, the one
to whom they were brought shall receive none of
them, but they shall all be taken to the infirmary.
But if they are sweets or fruits, the porter shall

give him some of these to eat as he is able, and he shall carry the rest to the infirmary. The porter may not eat any of the things brought; but he shall give the donor either some charlock — which is a cheap kind of herb — or some bread or some small vegetables. As for the aforesaid foods brought by parents or relatives, which need to be eaten with bread, the one to whom they have been brought shall be taken by the housemaster to the infirmary, where he will eat from them once only. The rest shall stay in the hands of the minister of the sick who himself may not eat any of these things.[1]

54. If it is reported that one of the relatives or family of those living in the monastery is sick, the porter shall first inform the father of the monastery, who will summon the housemaster and question him. They shall choose a man of proven faith and discipline and send him with the brother to visit the sick person. And he shall receive as much provision for the journey as the housemaster decides. If it is necessary for him to remain and eat outside, he shall by no means do this in the house of his parents or relatives. He shall stay instead in a church or in a monastery of the same faith. If his parents and relatives have prepared foods and served them, they shall not accept or eat anything at all except what they customarily eat in the monastery. They shall not taste broth or drink wine or take any of the other things which they do not customarily eat.[1] If they receive anything from the parents, they shall eat just as much as it is necessary for the journey. They shall give the rest that remains to their housemaster who will take it to the infirmary.

55. When someone's close relative dies, he shall not be allowed to attend the funeral unless the father of the monastery orders it.

56. No one should be sent out alone on any errand without a companion.

57. And if, on their return to the monastery they see at the door someone looking for one of his relatives living there, they shall not dare go tell him or call him. And they may not, in any circumstance, talk in the monastery about what they have done or heard outside.

58. When the signal is given to go to work, the housemaster shall lead them, and no one shall remain in the monastery except by order of the father. And those who go out shall not ask where they are going.

59. And when all the houses are gathered, the housemaster of the first house shall go before them all, and they shall proceed according to the order of the houses and of individuals. They shall not speak to each other, but each one shall recite something from the Scriptures.[1] If perhaps someone comes along and wants to speak to one of them, the porter of the monastery whose task it is shall come and answer him; and they shall use him as intermediary. If the porter is not at hand, the housemaster or another appointed to this task shall answer those who might come along.

60. At work, they shall talk of no worldly matter, but either recite holy things[1] or else keep silent.

61. No one shall take his linen mantle with him when going to work, except with the superior's permission. And in the monastery no one shall

walk around wearing that same mantle after the
synaxis.[1]

62. At work no one shall sit without the superior's order.[1]

63. If the leaders of the brothers find it necessary to send someone on a journey, they may
not do so without the master's order. And if the
leader himself must go off somewhere, he shall
delegate his office to the next in rank.[1]

64. If the brothers who are sent out on business
or are staying far away eat outside the monastery,
the weekly server who accompanies them shall
give them food but without making cooked dishes, and he shall himself distribute water as is done
in the monastery. No one may get up to draw or
drink water.

65. When they return to the monastery, no one
shall remain out of his rank.[1] When they come to
their houses they shall hand over the tools they
used for work and their shoes to the second — the
one after the housemaster. He shall take them at
evening into a special cell and secure them there.

66. At the end of the weekly service, all the
tools shall be brought to one house, so that those
who come next in the service may know what to
distribute to each house.

67. No one apart from the boatmen and the
bakers shall wash his tunic or any other monastic
clothes except on Sunday.

68. They shall not go to do laundry unless one
signal has sounded for all. They shall follow their
housemaster and do the washing in silence and
with discipline.

69. No one shall do the laundry with his clothes
drawn up higher than is established.[1] When the

washing is done, all shall return together. If someone stays behind or is not present at the time they go to do the laundry, he shall inform his master, who shall send him with someone else. And when he has washed his clothes he shall return to his house.

70. In the evening, they shall take up the dry tunics and give them to the second — the one who is after the housemaster — and he will put them in the cell. But if they are not dry, they shall be spread out in the sun the next day until they are dry. But they shall not be left in the heat of the sun after the third hour. And when they are brought in they shall be lightly softened. The brothers shall not keep them with themselves but shall hand them over to be stored in the cell until Saturday.[1]

71. No one shall take vegetables from the garden unless he is given them by the gardener.

72. No one on his own authority shall take palm leaves for basket-plaiting, except the one in charge of the palms.

73. For the sake of discipline, no one should dare eat still unripe grapes or ears of corn. And no one shall eat at all anything from field or orchard on his own, before it has been served to all the brothers together.[1]

74. The cook shall not take any of the food before the brothers eat.

75. The one in charge of the palm trees shall not eat any of their fruits before the brothers have first had some.

76. Those who are ordered to harvest the fruits of the palm trees shall receive a few from the master of the harvesters to eat on the spot. And when

they have returned to the monastery, they shall receive their portion with the other brothers.

77. If they find fallen fruits under the trees, they shall not dare to eat them, but they shall put them together at the foot of the trees as they pass by.[1] Also the one who distributes [the fruits] to the other harvesters may not taste them, but shall bring them to the steward who shall give him his portion after he has given some of them to the other brothers.

78. Let no one put away in his cell anything to eat, except what he has received from the steward.

79. As regards the small loaves given to the housemasters to be distributed to those who dedicate themselves to greater abstinence and do not want to eat in common with the others, they must see to it that they give them to no one as a favor, not even to someone going away. Nor shall they be put in common, but they shall be distributed in good order to them in their cells when they want to eat. And with these loaves they shall eat nothing else except only salt.

80. No one may cook foods outside the monastery and the kitchen. When they go out, that is, to work in the fields, they shall receive vegetables seasoned with salt and vinegar and prepared for long storage in summertime.

81. In his house and cell, no one shall have anything except what is prescribed for all together by the law of the monastery: no woolen tunic, no mantle, no soft sheepskin with unshorn wool, not even a few coins, no pillow for his head or various other conveniences. They shall have only what is distributed by the father of the mon-

astery through the housemasters. This is their
equipment: two linen tunics plus the one already
worn, a long scarf for the neck and shoulders, a
goat skin hanging from the shoulder, shoes, two
hoods, a belt and a staff. If you find anything
more than this, you shall take it away without
contradiction.[1]

82. No one shall have in his own possession little tweezers for removing thorns he may have
stepped on. Only the housemaster and the second
shall have them, and they shall hang in the alcove
in which books are placed.

83. If anyone is transferred from one house to
another, he may take nothing with him but what
we have mentioned above.

84. No one may go out into the fields, walk
around in the monastery or go outside the monastery wall, without requesting and receiving the
housemaster's permission.[1]

85. Let care be taken that no one reports words
from house to house, from monastery to monastery, from monastery to field or from field to
monastery.[1]

86. Anyone who has been journeying by land
or water, or working outside, shall not speak in
the monastery about what he has seen happen
there.

87. For sleeping, either in the cell or on the
roof — on which they rest at night during times of
great heat[1] — or in the fields, one must always use
the reclining seat alloted to him.[2]

Text: csco 159,
p.80 ff.

88. No one shall speak to another[1] in the place
where he sleeps.[2]

No one, after he has been in bed and slept, shall
get up in the morning[3] to eat or drink during a

time of fast. And no one shall spread anything on his reclining seat except a mat.

89. No one shall enter the cell of his neighbor without first knocking.

90. Nor should one go in to eat at noon before the signal is given. Nor shall they walk around in the village[1] before the signal is given.

91. No one shall walk in the community without his goat skin[1] and his hood, either to the *synaxis* or to the refectory.

92. No one shall go to oil his hands in the evening unless a brother is sent with him; no one shall oil his whole body unless he is sick, or bathe or wash it immodestly contrary to the manner established for them.[1]

93. No one shall oil or bathe a sick man[1] unless ordered.

94. No one may speak to his neighbors in the dark.

95. Nor shall you sit[1] two together on a mat or a carpet.

No one may clasp the hand or anything else of his companion; but whether you are sitting or standing or walking, you shall leave a forearm's space between you and him.[2]

96. No one shall draw a thorn out of a man's foot, except the housemaster or the second or another so ordered.

97. No one shall shave his head without his housemaster['s permission]; nor shall a man shave another without being ordered; nor shall a man shave another when both are seated.[1]

98. No one shall change anything in his wardrobe without his housemaster['s permission]. Nor shall they take anything in trade without his ap-

proval. And no one shall add anything to his wardrobe contrary to what has been established for them.[1]

99. All the goat skins shall be belted up;[1] and all the hoods shall bear the sign of the community and the sign of their house.

100. No one shall leave his book unfastened when he goes to the *synaxis* or to the refectory.

101. Every day at evening, the second shall bring[1] the books from the alcove and shut them in their case.

102. Either in the village[1] or in the fields, no one shall go to the *synaxis* or to the refectory with shoes on his feet or clad in his mantle.

103. No one shall leave his mantle[1] in the sun until the signal is given at noon for the meal.

The one who neglects all these things shall be rebuked.

104. No one shall take a shoe or any other object to oil it but only the housemasters.[1]

105. When a brother has been injured and is not bedridden but is up and around, if he needs a garment or a bit of oil, his housemaster shall go to the stewards' place to get them for him until he is well again; then he shall return them to their place.

106. No one shall receive anything from another without his housemaster['s permission].

107. No one shall sleep in a locked cell; nor shall anyone get a locked room except by order.[1]

108. No one, not even the farmers, shall enter the stables without being sent, except the herdsmen.[1]

109. Two men shall not sit together on a barebacked donkey or on a wagon shaft.[1]

110. When you arrive at the monastery mounted on a donkey, you shall dismount and walk ahead of it, except in case of necessity.[1]

111. No one may go to the shops except those in charge, who go for the needs of their work; nor may they go before the signal is given for eating, except for work needs. In that case the superior of the monastery shall be informed first and he shall send the weekly server.[1]

112. No one shall go to the breadboards place;[1] and no one shall enter a house[2] unless he is sent.

113. No one shall take anything on trust from another man, not even from his own brother.[1]

114. No one shall eat anything in his cell.[1]

115. When any man in charge goes away, the housemaster of his tribe[1] shall take care of his house in everything in which the second may need him. He shall give the fast days' instructions, one in his own house, the other in the house of his fellow [master].[2]

116. About the bakery:
No one shall speak when the kneading is done in the evening, nor shall those who work at the baking or at the boards in the morning. They shall recite together[1] until they have finished. If they need anything, they shall not speak, but shall signify it by a knock.[2]

117. No one shall go to the baking without being ordered. No one shall loiter in the oven-house when the bakers are baking, except only those appointed.[1]

118. About the boats:
No boatman shall put out a craft, not even a skiff, from port without [the permission of] the superior of the monastery. Aboard a boat no one shall go

to the hold to sleep. Nor may they take a secular aboard to sleep.

119. Nor [shall they take aboard] any *weaker vessel* without the permission of the superior of the monastery.

1 P 3:7.

120. No one shall light a fire in his house before the brothers have been so commanded.[1]

121. The one who arrives late for one of the Six Prayers at evening, or does not recite, or laughs or talks, shall do penance in his house during the Six Prayers.[1]

122. Sitting in their houses, they shall not speak ... [1]but they shall reflect on the words spoken by the housemaster.[2]

123. Reflecting on the instruction, they shall not plait or draw water until the housemaster says so.

124. No one shall take soaked rushes without [the permission of] the weekly server of the house.

125. Whoever breaks a clay vessel or who dips a batch of rushes three times shall be rebuked during his Six Prayers.[1]

126. After the Six Prayers, when all separate for sleep, no one may leave his cell except in a case of necessity.[1]

127. When a brother dies among the brothers, they shall all together accompany him to the mountain. No one shall remain behind unordered, nor shall anyone sing psalms without being ordered.

128. Proceeding to the mountain, they shall not sing psalms two by two. No one shall take his mantle with him while going to the mountain. They shall not neglect to respond, but shall maintain unison.

129. The infirmarian shall remain behind in case a brother should fall sick. This is the way [of doing things] wherever someone may be sent.

130. No one may walk ahead[1] of his housemaster and his leader.[2]

Text: Boon, p. 48ff

131. No one may stay out of his rank. If anyone loses anything he shall be publicly rebuked before the altar. And if what he has lost is from his own clothing, he shall not receive it for three weeks; in the fourth week, once he has done penance, he shall be given what he has lost.

132. Whoever finds a thing shall hang it up for three days in front of the *synaxis* of the brothers, so that the one who recognizes it may take it.

133. For all reproofs and teachings whose measure is determined in writing, the housemasters shall suffice. But if there is any novel fault, it shall be referred to the superior of the monastery.

134. No one shall make abode in a house without his permission; and any new matter shall be decided by him.

135. Every rebuke shall be made this way: those who are rebuked shall remove their belt and shall stand in the major *synaxis* and in the refectory.

136. Anyone who has left the *Koinonia*[1] of the brothers and afterwards does penance and comes back shall not return to his rank without the superior's order.

137. In the same way, if a housemaster or a steward sleeps outside one night without the brothers, and afterwards does penance and comes to the assembly of the brothers, he shall not be permitted to enter his house or take his rank without the superior's order.

138. Everything that is taught them in the assembly of the brothers they must absolutely talk over among themselves, especially on the days of fast, when they receive instruction from their masters.[1]

139. Whoever enters the monastery uninstructed shall be taught first what he must observe; and when, so taught, he has consented to it all, they shall give him twenty psalms or two of the Apostle's epistles, or some other part of the Scripture.[1]

And if he is illiterate, he shall go at the first, third, and sixth hours to someone who can teach and has been appointed for him. He shall stand before him and learn very studiously with all gratitude. Then the fundamentals of a syllable,[2] the verbs, and nouns shall be written for him, and even if he does not want to, he shall be compelled to read.

140. There shall be no one whatever in the monastery who does not learn to read and does not memorize something of the Scriptures. [One should learn by heart] at least the New Testament and the Psalter.

141. No one shall find pretexts for himself for not going to the *synaxis*, the psalmody, and the prayer.

142. One shall not neglect the times of prayer and psalmody, whether he is on a boat, in the monastery, in the fields, or on a journey, or fulfilling any service whatever.

143. Let us speak also about the monastery of virgins: No one shall go to visit them unless he has there a mother, sister, or daughter, some relatives or cousins, or the mother of his own children.

And if it is necessary to see them for any evident reason, and if some paternal inheritance is due them from the time before their renunciation of the world and their entry into the monastery, or if there is some obvious reason, they shall be accompanied by a man of proven age and life; they shall see them and return together. No one shall go to visit them except those we have just mentioned.

When they want to see them, they shall first inform the father of the monastery, and he shall inform the elders appointed to the virgins' ministry. These shall meet [the virgins] and with them see those whom they need with all discipline and fear of God. When they see the virgins, they shall not speak to them about worldly matters.[1]

144. Whoever transgresses any of these commands shall, for his negligence and his contempt, do penance publicly without any delay[1] so that he may be able to possess the kingdom of heaven.

precepts and institutes

of our father Pachomius,
the man of God who by commandment of God
was the first founder of the Koinonia of holy Life.[1]

(Inst.)

about the rule of the assembly,[2] and how to assemble the brothers for the instruction which is useful to their souls, according to what is pleasing to God and in conformity to the advices and rules of the saints.[3]

Text: CSCO 159, p. 80, 23-32.

God has given us [that rule] in the light of the Scriptures for the liberation of ignorant souls, that they might glorify God *in the light of the living,* and that they might know how *they ought to behave in God's house,* without lapse or scandal, not inebriated by what is pleasing to God[4] but standing in the norm of truth, according to the traditions of the *apostles and prophets,* in the manner they teach us how to celebrate in God.[5]

Ps 56(55):13.

1 Tm 3:15.

Eph 2:20.

[This is] how [the brothers] shall assemble daily in the house[6] for prayer and fasting, in the light of the Scriptures. Those who minister well are those who follow the norm of the Scriptures.

Text: CSCO 159, pp. 33ff.

This is the ministry that the minister[7] must carry out.

1. He shall gather the brothers at the time of prayer according to the norm fixed for them.[1]

They shall carry out their ministry according to their canon, set down for them.[2]

They shall give no one grounds to complain against them, but [will follow] their rules.

They shall not let anyone come and go against the norm of the Precepts.[3]

2. To those who ask for a book, they shall bring it.[1]

3. If someone comes from outside in the evening and fails to receive his work for the next day, they shall give it to him in the morning.[1]

4. Or if someone has finished the work he was doing, [the minister] shall inform the steward [and he shall do] what he is told or what he is sent to do.

5. The minister shall not let anything be found spoiled in any of the shops where they work at each craft; neither shall he let any of the things outside the houses be spoiled. For all the things that will be found spoiled in the shops[1] he shall be punished by the steward according to their rule. He shall himself punish the one who is found to have spoiled the thing, according to the sentence of the steward, without whose order no one shall punish a man.[2]

6. If the sun rises a third day on a garment[1] spread out, the owner shall be punished for it; he shall bow down to the ground[2] in the *synaxis* and stand in the refectory.[3]

7. For a goat skin[1] or a shoe or a belt or any other article, he will be punished according to these judgements.[2]

8. If anyone takes any object not his own it shall be put on his shoulders in the *synaxis* during one of the prayers[1] and he shall bow down to the ground; and he shall stand in the refectory.[2]

9. If they find someone contentious or arguing beyond measure,[1] he shall be punished as his deed deserves.[2]

10. If they find someone to be lying or showing hatred in his speech, or disobedient, or dissipated, or idle, or speaking in a harsh and unedifying manner, or a slanderer of brothers and of strangers; about all these, which are things contrary to the norm of Scriptures, the steward shall deliberate and pass judgement according to the nature and the degree of the fault.[1]

11. For any object lost from the house for more than three days, whether it be lost in the field or on the road, the housemaster shall be held responsible if he does not inform the steward within the three days. He shall bow down to the ground according to the established precept.

12. He shall also be held responsible for the loss of someone who has run off, if he does not notify the father of the monastery within three hours, unless he finds the man again.[1] This is the sin of the one who has lost a man through negligence. For three days he shall bow down to the ground daily, according to their rule. But if he has reported it at the time of the flight, he shall be exempt from sin.

13. When a sin is committed among the men in one of the houses, if the housemaster,[1] seeing the fault, does not notify the steward, it shall be done to him according to their canon.

14. Assembled in their house they shall do the Six Prayers in the evening, according to the rule of the assembly.[1]

15. The instruction of the Word must be given twice a week.[1]

16. No one in the house shall do anything against the directive of the housemaster.[1]

17. If the housemasters[1] judge him and find

him negligent or using a harsh language beyond measure, he shall be punished according to their canon.

He too shall do nothing without receiving the permission of the steward, in everything new outside what is established.[2]

*Cf. Pr 23:31; Si 19:2; Eph 5:18.

18. He shall not be found drunk.*[1]

He shall not sit in the lower places, by the monastery vessels.[2]

He shall not be found breaking bonds established in heaven by God to be observed on earth.

He shall not be mournful on the feast of Christ.

Cf. Rm 8:13.

He shall be master of his flesh, according to the measure of the saints.

Cf. Lk 14:8.

He shall not be found on lofty beds after the manner of the gentiles.

He shall not be of divided faith.[3]

He shall not follow the thoughts of his heart but the law of God.

Cf. Rm 13:1.

He shall not resist higher authority with swollen mind.

He shall not growl and neigh over the lowly.

*Cf. Dt 27:17; Pr 22:28; 23:10. †Cf. Pr 12:20.

He shall not be a displacer of boundaries.*

He shall not be a man crafty in his thought.†

He shall not forget the poverty of his soul.

Cf. Ga 5:19.

He shall not be overcome by the works of the flesh.

He shall not walk in negligence.

Cf. Mt 12:36.

He shall not be quick to utter idle words.[4]

He shall not pour gall in the blind man's mouth.[5]

He shall not teach his own soul wantoness.

Cf. Pr 10:23.

He shall not be overcome by the laughter of fools.

Cf. Rm 16:18.

He shall not let his heart be carried away by those who speak follies and flatteries.[6]

Cf. Ex 23:8.

He shall not let his soul be carried away by a gift.[7]

He shall not be overcome by the words of a child.

He shall not be crushed in tribulation.[8] Cf. 2 Co 4:8.

He shall fear not death but God. Cf. Mt 10:28.

He shall not deny out of fear.

He shall not forsake the light for food.

He shall not vacillate in his actions.

He shall not be fickle in his tongue, but shall be correct in righteous language, discerning and judging in truth without looking for glory but open to God and men.[9]

He shall not be blind to the knowledge of the saints.[10]

He shall not wrong his neighbor through pride.

He shall not be carried away by the desires of his eyes.

He shall not be led by the lusts of his thoughts. Cf. Si 5:2.

He shall not walk in cleverness.[11] Cf. Pr 12:5.

He shall not acquit the dishonest.[12]

He shall not praise a man in court for a bribe.*[13] *Cf. Pr 17:15; Is 5:23.

He shall not condemn a soul out of pride.† †Ibid.

He shall not be a trifler amidst children.

He shall not abandon truth, overcome by fear.[14]

He shall not eat the bread of fraudulence.

He shall not covet another's land.

He shall not oppress a soul for the spoils of others.

He shall not forget the distress of needy souls.* *Cf. Ps 9:12; 74(73):19.

He shall not swear a false oath for gain.† †Cf. Ex 20:16; Jr 5:2.

He shall not lie out of pride.

He shall not dispute for high rank.

He shall not give up[15] out of weariness.

He shall not lose his soul out of shame. Cf. Si 20:22.

He shall not set his eyes on the dainties of a table. Cf. Si 40:29.

He shall not desire beautiful clothes.[16] Text: Boon, p. 61,2–62,8.

He shall not neglect the old men, so that he may always discriminate between his thoughts.

He shall not get drunk with wine,* he shall have humility joined with truth.

When he judges, he shall follow the precept of the elders and the law of God which is preached in all the world.

If he neglects any of these, *it shall be measured out to him with the measure he has used,*[17] and he shall be paid *as his works deserve.*[18] For he has *committed adultery with the trees and the stones;* for the glitter of gold and the sheen of silver he has *set aside judgement,* and for desire of temporal gain he has enmeshed himself in the nets of the wicked.

May he receive:

the breaking of Eli* and of his branches;[19]

the curse of David called down by Doeg;†

the sign with which Cain was marked;‡

the *burial of a donkey* spoken of by Jeremiah;*

the perdition by which *the earth opened and swallowed up*† sinners;[20]

the death of the Canaanites;‡

the *shattering of the pitcher at the fountain;*[21]

the crushing of the sand on the shore hammered by salty waves;

the breaking of the splendid staff, as in Isaiah†;

that he may be *like the blind man feeling the wall* with his hand.‡

All these things shall befall him because he has not kept truth in judgement, and has acted wickedly in all that was entrusted to him.

precepts
and
judgements

of the same our father Pachomius,

(Jud.)

L*ove is the fulfilling of the law* for those who know *that the time has come for us to wake up* and that *our salvation is nearer now than it was when we came to the faith; the night is almost over, it will soon be daylight; let us give up the works of darkness*[1] which are *strifes, slanders, hatreds, and the pride of a swollen mind.*[2]

Text: Boon,
pp. 63–70.

Rm 13:10–12.
2 Co 12:20;
Ga 5:20.

1. If someone is prone to slander and to saying that which is not [true] and is caught in this sin, he shall be admonished twice. And if he is too contemptuous to listen, he shall be separated from the assembly of the brothers seven days and shall receive only bread and water until he firmly promises to convert from that vice. Then he shall be forgiven.

2. If someone is irascible and violent, and frequently gets angry without reason or for some light and unimportant reason, he shall be admonished six times. The seventh time, he shall be removed from his seating rank and placed among the last ones, and he shall be given instruction, that he may be cleansed from this agitation of mind. And when he can bring three trustworthy witnesses to promise for him that he will never

175

again do anything of the kind, he shall be given back his seating rank. Otherwise, if he remains in his vice, he shall lose his former rank and remain among the last ones.

3. If someone wants to prove something false against another so as to oppress an innocent, he shall be admonished three times. After that he shall answer for his fault, whether he is from a higher or from a lower rank.

4. If someone has the wicked habit of soliciting his brothers by words and of perverting the souls of the simple, he shall be admonished three times. If he shows contempt and remains obstinately in the hardness of his heart, he shall be isolated outside the monastery. He shall be beaten before the gates and he shall be given only bread and water to eat outside until he is cleansed from his filth.

5. If someone has the habit of murmuring and complains that he is overwhelmed by heavy work, he shall be shown five times that he is murmuring without reason and shall have the exact truth explained to him. If he is still disobedient even after that, and he is an adult, he shall be considered as one of the sick and put in the infirmary, where he shall be fed and left idle until he returns to the truth.

But if his complaint is well-founded and he is being unfairly overwhelmed by a superior, the one who has caused him offence shall be submitted to the same sentence.

6. If someone is disobedient or a wrangler or a gainsayer or a liar, and he is an adult, he shall be admonished ten times to desist from his vices. If he does not want to listen, he shall be punished

according to the laws of the monastery. But if it is by another's fault that he has fallen into these vices, and this is proved, the guilty one shall receive the punishment.

7. If someone among the brothers is caught easily laughing and playing with boys and having friendships with those of tender years, he shall be admonished three times to withdraw from their intimacy and to be mindful of honesty and of the fear of God. If he does not desist, he shall receive the very severe punishment he deserves.

8. Those who spurn the precepts of the superiors and the rules of the monastery, which have been established by God's precept, and who make light of the counsels of the elders, shall be punished according to the established order until they amend.

9. If the one who is the judge of the sins of all abandon the truth, because of the perversity of his heart or out of negligence, he shall be judged by twenty holy and God-fearing men, or ten or even only five about whom all bear witness. They shall sit and judge him, and degrade him to the lowest place until he amends.

10. If someone disturbs the minds of the brothers and is prone to talking, sowing strifes and quarrels, he shall be admonished ten times.[1] And if he does not mend his ways, he shall be corrected according to the order of the monastery until he amends.

11. If someone among the superiors and the housemasters[1] sees his brother in tribulation and does not want to find the cause of the tribulation and disregards him, the aforementioned judges shall examine the cause between the brother and

the housemaster. If they find that the housemaster, out of negligence and pride, has been op-
pressing the brother and has judged him with respect of persons and not according to truth, they
shall degrade him from his office until he amends
and is cleansed from the filth of injustice. For he
has considered the persons rather than the truth,
and has submitted to the depravity of his soul
rather than to the judgement of God.

12. If someone has promised to observe the
rules of the monastery and has begun to do so,
but abandoned them, and later on returned and
did penance, while putting forward the weakness
of his body as the reason for his incapacity to fulfil what he had promised, he shall be made to stay
with the sick and shall be fed among the idle until, having done penance, he fulfil his promise.

13. If there are boys in a house given to games
and idleness and they would not amend when rebuked, the housemaster shall admonish and rebuke them during thirty days. If he sees them
persisting in their depravity without informing
the father and they are caught in some sin, he
shall himself be punished in their stead according
to the sin that has been discovered.

14. If someone judges unjustly, he shall be
condemned by the others for his injustice.

15. If one of the brothers, or even two or three,
being scandalized by someone, leaves the house
and afterwards returns, the case between them
and the one who scandalized them shall be
judged. If the latter is found guilty, he shall be
corrected according to the rules of the
monastery.

16. If someone agrees with sinners and defends

someone else who has committed a fault, he shall
be accursed before God and men and shall be
very severely rebuked.[1] But if he has been deceived through ignorance, thinking the situation
to be other than it was in reality, he shall be forgiven. And anyone who sins through ignorance
shall be easily forgiven, while the one who sins
wilfully shall be scolded according to the measure
of his deed.

precepts and laws

*of our father Pachomius
about the Six Evening Prayers
and the synaxis of the Six Prayers
which is made in each house.*

(lec.)

The housemaster and the second must plait twenty-five fathoms of palm leaves, so that the others may work after their example. If they are absent, the one who is in charge in their place shall apply himself to accomplishing that amount of work.

Text: Boon, pp. 71-74.

2. [The brothers] shall come to the *synaxis* after they have been summoned. Nobody shall leave his cell before the signal is given.[1]

If anyone transgresses these precepts, he shall be subject to the usual reproof.

3. The brothers shall not be forced to work excessively, but a moderate labor shall incite everyone to work. Let there be peace and concord among them, and let them willingly submit to the superiors, either sitting, walking or standing, according to their rank, and competing with one another in humility.

4. When a sin is committed, the fathers of the monasteries shall have the authority to correct it and to establish what must be done.

5. The housemaster and his second shall have the authority to compel brothers to submit to penance only for individual sins either in the house *synaxis* or in the major *synaxis* of all the brothers.

6. When the housemaster is on a journey, his second shall take his place for receiving the penitence of a brother as well as for any of the other things which are necessary in the house.

7. If someone, unbeknownst to these two, goes to another house or to a brother from another house, to borrow a book to read, or any other object, and is convicted of this, he shall be rebuked according to the order of the monastery.[1]

8. The one who wants to live spotless and without contempt in the house to which he is assigned, must observe before God everything that is prescribed.

9. When the housemaster is busy, the second shall do everything that is necessary either in the monastery or in the fields.

10. To make the Six Evening Prayers after the pattern of the major *synaxis* in which all the brothers are assembled together, is a great delight. And they are made so easily that they imply no burden that would cause weariness.[1]

11. If someone has been suffering from the heat and returns from outside when the other brothers are going to celebrate the Prayers, he shall not be forced to go if he cannot.

12. When the housemaster teaches the brothers about the holy way of life, no one shall be absent without very serious necessity.

13. The elders who are sent outside with the brothers shall have the same jurisdiction as the housemasters for all the time they are there, and everything should be subject to their decision. They shall give the instructions to the brothers on the appointed days. And if some quarrel arises among the brothers, it will be the responsibility of

the elders to hear and judge the case and scold the culprit, so that at their command the brothers may immediately make peace wholeheartedly.

14. If one of the brothers has a grievance against his housemaster, or the housemaster himself has some complaint against one brother, brothers of proven life and faith must hear the case and bear judgement, but only if the father of the monastery is absent or has gone somewhere. First they shall wait for him, but if they see that he is prolonging his absence, they shall hear the case between the housemaster and the brother lest a greater grievance arise from the delay in judgement. Let the housemaster and the subject, as well as those who hear the case, do everything according to the fear of God and not give any occasion of discord.

15. About clothing:
If someone has more than what is prescribed, he shall bring them to the storeroom keeper without being warned by the superior, and he may not enter or ask for them. They shall be at the disposal of the housemaster and the second.[1]

Notes to the Rules of Saint Pachomius

Jer. Pref.   [1]Paula, born in 347, died on 26 January 404. Jerome's translation of the *Pachomiana* was therefore undertaken toward the end of 404. About Paula see G. del Ton, *S. Paola Romana* (Milan, 1950).

[2]Around the year 390 Theophilos, bishop of Alexandria (385-412) and the uncle of Cyril, destroyed the sanctuary of Sarapis at Canopos, about twenty miles northeast of Alexandria, and built in its place a monastery to which he invited pachomian monks. The name of the place was then replaced by the Greek name *Metanoia*, which means Penitence or Repentance. See P. Ladeuze, *Etude sur le cénobitisme pakhômien*, p. 202 and H. Bacht, *Das Vermächtnis*, pp. 9-10.

[3]The technical name for the assembly of all the pachomian communities in the Coptic documents is the Greek name *Koinonia* to which corresponds τὸ κοινόβιον in the Greek documents; see G[1] 54, note 5.

[4]Jerome cannot depend on the *Lausiac History*, which was written much later (419 420). He may have known the text of the Rule of the Angel that Palladius incorporated into his Lausiac History or — more probably — he depends here on a tradition corresponding to the anecdotes we read in the Life of Pachomius. See S[1] 6; SBo 22; G[1] 23; cf. also SBo 17; G[1] 12.

[5]Lit. 'devoured my grief' (*dolorem meum ... deuoraram*).

[6]'... *et sanctae feminae refrigerans animam.*' The substantive *refrigerium* is found also in Hors. Test. 14 (quotation of Ac 3:20) and 30. On this concept, see A. Parrot, *Le refrigerium dans l'au-delà*, (Paris, 1947); and J. Quasten, 'Vetus superstitio et nova religio. The Problem of Refrigerium in the Ancient Church of North Africa', in *The Harvard Theological Review* 33 (1940) 253.

[7]'... and had meditated' or '... and had prepared'; the latin word *meditari* can mean both.

[8]About the role played by Eustochium in Jerome's life, see J. Steinmann, *Hieronymus—Ausleger der Bibel* (Cologne, 1961) p. 367.

[9]The existence of 'tribes' is mentioned only once in the Life (SBo 26 — G[1] 28) and twice in the Rule (Pr. 15 and 115). See SBo 26, note 5.

[10]We find the same list of monastic garments in Pr. 81 with only a few minor divergences in the vocabulary. The linen mantle (*amictus lineus*) of Jer. Pref. 4 corresponds to the scarf (*sabbanus longior*) of Pr. 81; and the linen belt (*balteus lineus*) of Jer. Pref. 4 corresponds to the *zona* of Pr. 81. For a detailed study of the clothes of the pachomian monks, see R. Draguet, 'Le chapitre de HL', (1944) pp. 95-111; see also SBo 19 note 1 and SBo 120, note 1. In the expression *'duo lebitonaria ... et uno iam adtrito'* it is difficult not to understand the words '*et uno iam adtrito*' of a third tunic; but R. Draguet, p. 95 understands that the pachomian monks had only two tunics, a good one and a worn one. The same latin expression recurs in Pr. 81 and the Greek *Excerpta* mention only two *lebitonaria* at that place. As for the *cucullus*, it was really a hood covering the head and the neck and had little in common with modern cowls.

[11]On the care for the sick brothers, see Pr. 40-47, 92, 105 and 129; Pach. Letter 5: 2 and Hors. Reg. 24. See also B. Steidle, '"Ich war krank, und ihr habt mich besucht" (Mt 25, 26)', in EuA 40 (1964) 443-468; 41 (1965), 36-46, 99-113, 189-206.

[12]'*propter laborantes*' could also be translated: 'on account of those who work'.

[13]Although the indications of the Life and of the Rules are not absolutely clear and perhaps not entirely consistent, it seems that there were two meals served every day in the pachomian communities, one at noon and one in the evening, after a *synaxis* that may have been held at the ninth hour. Everybody had to go to the noon meal; but after the *synaxis*, in the evening, each one could go either to the refectory or to his cell; cf. Pr. 103.

[14]This figure is certainly an exaggeration. Earlier in his Prologue, Jerome said that each monastery was composed of thirty or forty houses of forty monks. Fifty thousand monks would therefore make more than thirty monasteries! Although three foundations were added by Theodore (see G[1] 134) and a few may have been founded later on by Horsiesios, who died after 387, the number of monasteries in the *Koinonia* cannot have reached the figure thirty by the year 404.

¹⁵The Egyptian month of *Mesore* corresponds to the period from July 27 to August 24 of our calendar. About the two annual meetings of all the brothers of the *Koinonia*, see SBo 71, notes 2 and 3.

¹⁶Sourous (*Syrus* in Jerome's Latin) was one of the first three disciples, along with Pšentaesi and Pšoi (see SBo 23). He became the leader of the monastery of Phnoum (see SBo 58), and died of the plague in 346, shortly before Pachomius (see SBo 119; G¹ 114). Jerome is therefore mistaken in stating that he was still alive and 110 years old in 404. Jerome is confusing him with another Sourous, perhaps 'Sourous the Younger' who replaced Theodore as father of the monastery of Tabennesi (see SBo 78).

¹⁷Lit.: 'putting the same elements as we found them.' (*eadem ut reperimus elementa ponentes*).

¹⁸*Congregatio* is probably a translation for *koinonia*.

Pr. 1   ¹The newcomers were entrusted to the porter who took care of their instruction until they were ready to be introduced in the community; see Pr. 49.

²The rank (*ordo*) in the community was important, and respect for it is often stressed; see Pr. 13, 20, 63, 65, 131, 136, 137. See also F. van Beneden, 'Ordo. Über dem Ursprung einer kirchlicher Terminologie', in *Vigiliae Christianae* 22 (1969) 161-179.

Pr. 2   ¹This was one of the several uses of the goat skin, probably to prevent the tunic from getting dirty or worn out.

²This recommendation is better understood if we remember that the pachomian monks, as other Egyptian monks, had only their *lebiton* to cover their body and did not use any underwear. See Cassian, Inst. I, 10.

Pr. 3   ¹This mention of the trumpet (*uocem tubae*) is probably a paraphrase by Jerome. In fact, the signal was given by knocking a hammer or something like it on a piece of wood.

²The Greek *Excerpta* (recension A) have: 'he shall leave his *house*.'

³We translate by *synaxis* both the word *collecta* at the beginning of this precept and the word *conventiculum* at the end. The Greek *Excerpta* have συναξίς in both cases; and we know that Jerome often translated the same word in two or three different ways.

Pr. 4   ¹There was a very close unity between prayer and work in pachomian monasteries; the monks constantly prayed during their work and they did weaving and plaiting during the *synaxis*.

Pr. 6   ¹'*ut oratio finiatur*' corresponds to the Greek εἰς τὸ προσεύχεσθαι, which shows clearly the meaning.

²Cf. Cassian, Inst. II, 2.

Pr. 8   ¹We incline to think that this sentence should be considered as the conclusion of the first group of seven precepts rather than the beginning of a new series.

²Cf. Cassian, Inst. II, 10.

Pr. 9   ¹Cf. Cassian, Inst. III, 7.

Pr. 10 ¹At this point, the Greek *Excerpta* (recension A) have a precept that was omitted by Jerome: 'If anyone is found praying before the doors of the *synaxis* without being ordered [to do so], he shall be rebuked in the same manner'.

Pr. 14 ¹'for his negligence and forgetfulness'; the Greek *Excerpta* have: 'for neglecting the texts [to be] learned by heart' (ὡς ἀμελήσας τῶν ἀπο στήθους).

Pr. 15 ¹According to the practice of the Church of Egypt at that time, the Eucharist was celebrated on Saturday evenings and Sunday mornings. See SBo 25, note 4.
²*Embrimium* corresponds to the Coptic word m̄rôm, meaning *mat, cushion.*
³This last sentence has all the appearances of an explanation added by Jerome.

Pr. 17 ¹'*psallente . . . id est legente psalterium*': the clause 'that is, reading the psalter', absent from the Greek text, is probably an addition of Jerome. It is not always clear in our pachomian documents whether ψάλλειν – *psallere* means 'chanting' or 'singing' in general or more precisely 'singing psalms'.

Pr. 19 ¹It is not perfectly clear whether the expression *'finitis orationibus'* refers to prayers made in the individual houses or to prayers made in the large *synaxis* of all the brothers, after which they returned to their individual houses. Cf. Pr. 122

Pr. 20 ¹According to all the other indications of the Rules and of the Life, three instructions (κατήχησες) were given each week by the father of the monastery (one on Saturday and two on Sunday), and two by the housemasters (on Wednesday and Friday); see SBo 26 (G¹ 28); G¹ 77, 110, 131, 145; Pr. 115, 138; Inst. 15; Leg. 12. The three instructions mentioned in the present ¶ are certainly the instructions given by the father of the monastery, since the brothers must listen to them standing or sitting 'according to the order of the houses'. The mention 'by the housemasters', at the beginning of the ¶, is absent from the Greek text and must be considered as an unhappy addition by Jerome. See below, Pr. 115, note 2.

Pr. 23 ¹The Greek *Excerpta* have simply Μηδεὶς χωρὶς τῆς κεφαλῆς καλεσῇ τοὺς ἀδελφοὺς εἰς τὴν σύναξιν. Therefore the words 'whether for the midday *synaxis* or for the evening *synaxis* of the Six Prayers' are probably a gloss of Jerome. There was a *synaxis* of all the brothers of the monastery in the morning and a celebration called the 'Six Prayers' in the individual houses in the evening. Whether there was another assembly of all the brothers of the monastery in the evening, possibly after the ninth hour, is doubtful. If there was one it was perhaps the celebration that Jerome calls *collecta meridiana*. See A. Veilleux, *La liturgie*, pp. 292-315.

Pr. 27 ¹There were two annual meetings of all the brothers of all the monasteries, one for the Passover and the other one in the month of *Mesore*, at the end of the year in the Coptic calendar. The Life mentions only the administrative character of the second meeting, but it seems that at least at a second stage of the evolution it was also the occasion for a mutual forgiving of offences. See SBo 71, notes 2 and 3.

Pr. 29   [1]Cf. Cassian, Inst. IV, 17.

Pr. 31   [1]The Greek *Excerpta* add: 'out of impulsiveness' (προπετείᾳ φερόμενος).
[2]The exact nature of this penance is not clear.

Pr. 32   [1]'... late to eat'; the Greek *Excerpta* say: '... late at the prayer before eating'.

Pr. 33   [1]The Greek *Excerpta* have only: 'he shall make a sound'.

Pr. 34   [1]'*donec ad locum tuum peruenias*' could mean either 'until you have returned to your place [in the refectory, to continue your meal]' or 'until you have returned to your house [or cell]'. The Greek *Excerpta* understood: 'until you have reached your house'.

Pr. 35   [1]*Ministri*; the Greek *Excerpta* have: 'none of the superiors'.

Pr. 37   [1]The *tragemata* (κορσενήλια) were a kind of sweet food distributed to the brothers after the meals. About the etymology of the word, see L.-T. Lefort, 'Un mot nouveau', in *Muséon* 26 (1923) 27–31; see also A.-J. Festugière, *La première Vie grecque*, p. 56, note 1. Cf. Hors. Reg. 42

Pr. 40   [1]The Greek *Excerpta* have: ὁ ἀββάς.

Pr. 45   [1]This broth (*liquamen*) is called γάρος in the Greek *Excerpta*. It corresponds to the Coptic *čir* that W.E. Crum (*Coptic Dictionary*, pp. 780B–781A) translates by *brine, small salted fish* or *pickle*. Cf. γαρέλαιον in G[1] 64, note 1 (= SBo 61: *karella*).

Pr. 49   [1]'wishing to renounce the world': renunciation (ἀπόταξις) is one of the most fundamental aspects of monastic life. To become a monk is 'to renounce the world' or simply 'to renounce'. See G[1] 24 (Halkin, p. 15, 3): τῷ κόσμῳ ἀποτάξωνται; G[1] 39 (Halkin, p. 24, 9-10):   τῶν μοναχῶν ἀποτασσόμενος; Am. Letter 23 (Halkin, p. 111, 17-18): τῇ πενίᾳ τῶν γονέων ἀποταξάμενος; Theod. Inst. 3, 20: 'having renounced all they had for this vocation'. In the Coptic documents, the monk is often called an *apotaktikos*; see SBo 185 (VB p. 166, 10-11).
[2]'as many psalms as he can learn' may be a gloss of Jerome. The Greek *Excerpta* have simply 'psalms'.
[3]'what he must do and where he must serve' is not in the Greek *Excerpta*.
[4]Cf. Pr. 1
[5]The Greek *Excerpta* read 'they will be given into the authority of the *Koinonia*, at the discretion (γνώμην) of the father of the monastery'.

Pr. 51   [1]This was written at the time of Arianism. See the story of the search made by the duke Artemios (SBo 185; G[1] 138). 'If ... they are of the same faith ...' is not mentioned in the Greek *Excerpta*, probably because it was no longer relevant at that time.
[2]See SBo 40; G[1] 40.

Pr. 52   [1]Boon reads: '*iuxta ordinem praepositi et sexus sui*', with the Mss MCX; we prefer to read '*iuxta ordinem* propositi *et sexus sui*' with the Mss EBW. Cf. SBo 37, note 3: 'according to their habit (*schêma*)'.

Pr. 53   [1]Cf. Theod. Instr. 3, 17.

Pr. 54   [1]Cf. Pr. 45.

Pr. 59   [1]The Greek *Excerpta* have only: 'they shall recite'. Cf. Cassian, Inst. II, 15.

Pr. 60   [1]Here again the Greek *Excerpta* have only 'recite'; Jerome is prone to add specifications!

Pr. 61   [1]The mantle, mentioned in connection with the sick brothers in Pr. 42 (also in Pr. 105 in Jerome's translation), was used during the night and at the morning *synaxis* to protect against the cold. Pr. 102, which seems to be in contradiction with Pr. 61, speaks probably of the evening *synaxis* during which the mantle could not be used. See R. Draguet, 'Le Chapitre de HL', pp. 104-105.

Pr. 62   [1]The Greek *Excerpta* have: '. . . no one shall sit *to work* . . .'

Pr. 63   [1]'*Ductores fratrum in itinere si necessarium habuerint aliquem mittere* . . .'; this precept concerns probably the fathers of the monasteries; but the expression '*ductores fratrum*' is unusual. The modifications introduced in the text by the manuscripts of the *recensio brevis* show that their scribes encountered some difficulties also.

Pr. 65   [1]'no one shall remain out of his rank'. The text of the Greek *Excerpta* is better: 'no one shall remain behind without being ordered'.

Pr. 69   [1]See above, Pr. 2, note 2.

Pr. 70   [1]Cf. Leg. 15 and Hors. Test. 26.

Pr. 73   [1]Cf. Cassian, Inst. IV, 18.

Pr. 77   [1]The Greek *Excerpta* add: 'and the one who is appointed shall collect them'.

Pr. 81   [1]Cf. another description of the clothes of the pachomian monks above, Jer. Pref. 4, note 1.

Pr. 84   [1]According to the Greek *Excerpta*, one must request permission from the father of the monastery.

Pr. 85   [1]The Greek *Excerpta* read: 'from monastery to monastery or from field to field'.

Pr. 87   [1]The clause 'on which . . . great heat' is absent from the Greek *Excerpta*.
    [2]The pachomian monks slept not on a bed but on a type of reclining seat which is mentioned not only in Pr. 87-88, but also in the *Life*; see G[1] 14, 79, and probably also 144 (see *ibidem*, note 1); cf. also Paral. 30; HL c. 32, 3 and Cassian, Conf. I, 23, 4. There are other examples of the same custom in the monastic literature; see R. Draguet, 'Le chapitre de HL', pp. 87-90.

Pr. 88   ¹The Coptic fragment begins here. We will translate from the Coptic text, giving the more significant Latin variants in the notes.
²'in the place where he sleeps'; the Coptic text is confirmed by the Greek *Excerpta*; Jerome has: 'after he has gone to sleep'.
³Jerome has 'during the night', which probably makes the text clearer.

Pr. 90   ¹'Nor shall they walk around in the village (*hm̄ptime*)' is different from the expression of Pr. 91: 'No one shall walk in the community (hn̄tsoouhs̄)'. Although Jerome translates '*in monasterio*' in both cases, there is no reason to believe that the Coptic word *time* (the village) was another name for the pachomian monastery. The meaning here is purely and simply *village*. We know that Tabennesi and Phbow were founded in deserted villages and that the brothers built a monastery for Pachomius' sister in the village of Tabennesi at some distance from the monks' monastery.

Pr. 91   ¹The meaning of *rahtou* (here and in Pr. 99) is not clear. W.E. Crum (*A Coptic Dictionary*, p. 312b) translates vaguely: 'a monkish garment'. We follow Jerome who understood it as another name for the goat skin (*pellis-pellicula*).

Pr. 92   ¹'. . . wash it immodestly contrary . . . for them'; Jerome writes: '. . . wash it naked, unless his illness is evident'.

Pr. 93   ¹'a sick man'; Jerome: 'another'.

Pr. 95   ¹'sit'; Jerome: 'sleep'.
²Cf. Cassian, Inst. II, 15; A forearm's space: lit. a *cubit*.

Pr. 97   ¹Jerome: 'No one shall shave his head without the superior's permission'. The Recension A of the Greek *Excerpta* corresponds to Jerome's text, while Recension B corresponds to the Coptic text.

Pr. 98   ¹Cf. Hors. Test. 26.

Pr. 99   ¹Jerome adds: 'and they shall hang from the shoulders'.

Pr. 101   ¹'shall bring'; Jerome has: 'shall number'.

Pr. 102   ¹in the village'; Jerome has: 'in the monastery'; cf. above, Pr. 90, note 1.

Pr. 103   ¹'Mantle': this is the usual meaning of *pres̆*. Jerome has a more general term: *vestimentum*.

Pr. 104   ¹'but only the housemasters'; we follow the Coptic text published by Lefort in *Oeuvres de s. Pachôme*, (*CSCO* 159: p. 32, 1-2): *eimêti en̄rm̄nêï m̄mate*. In anterior publications Lefort had given a slightly different text: '. . . but only those in charge': *eimêti en̄rm̄nran m̄mate* (*Muséon* 1927, p. 38,A,24-25; also in Boon, *Pachomiana latina*, p. 157). We have not been able to check with the manuscript itself. Jerome has: 'except the one delegated for the service and the housemaster'.

Pr. 107   ¹'without an order'; Jerome has: 'unless the father of the monastery has permitted it for reason of age or illness'. The Greek *Excerpta*, like Jerome, have also: 'without the permission of the father'.

Pr. 108 ¹Jerome: 'No one, unless he is sent, shall go to the farm, except the herdsmen, the ox-drivers and the farmers.'

Pr. 109 ¹'Wagon shaft' is an hypothetic translation, the Coptic word *mrêh* being a *hapax*. The Greek *Excerpta* did not translate it.

Pr. 110 ¹'except in the case of necessity'; Jerome: 'except in the case of illness'.

Pr. 111 ¹Jerome adds: 'to carry what is necessary'.

Pr. 112 ¹These 'bread-boards' were boards on which the loaves were placed before or after the baking. Cf. Pr. 116 and Hors. Reg. 40.
²'a house'; Jerome: 'another cell'.

Pr. 113 ¹Cf. above, Pr. 98; also Leg. 7 and Hors. Test. 26.

Pr. 114 ¹Jerome adds: 'without the master's permission; not even the poorest fruit or anything of the kind.'

Pr. 115 ¹The meaning is obviously '*another* housemaster of his tribe'. So Jerome understood: 'another housemaster of the same nation and tribe'. About the tribes, see above, Jer. Pref. 2, note 1 and also SBo 26, note 5.
²At a very early stage the word κατήχησις, was reserved in christian terminology for the person who was being prepared for baptism. But the word κατήχησις, absent from the New Testament, kept its broad meaning of instruction or teaching for a very long time. This broad meaning was maintained particularly in writings that reflected the popular mentality, traditions, and language. See A. Turck, 'Catéchein et Catéchésis chez les premiers Pères' in *Revue des sciences philosophiques et théologiques* 47 (1963) 361-372. And before the word κατήχησις, attracted by κατηχούμενος had been reserved for the baptismal *catechesis*, it had acquired, especially in the Church of Alexandria and in Egypt, another more or less technical meaning, as the name of a religious instruction inspired by the Scripture that was given in the church to the community of the faithful on certain days of the week. See *Apost. Trad.*, c. 35, ed. Botte, pp. 82-83; *Apost. Const.*, ed. Funk, T.I, p. 538. In Alexandria that practice was quite old; Jerome tells us that around the year 200 Clement (who was a layman) was 'κατηχήσεων *magister*'. The historian Socrates informs us that during his time there were *synaxes* held on the fast-days, Wednesday and Friday, during which the Holy Books were read and commented by the '*didascaloi*' (*Hist. Eccl.*, V,22; PG 67:636). He adds that custom went back to the time of Origen, who had preached in the church especially on those days. (See Origen, *In Exod.*, hom. VII,5, ed. A Baehrens [*Die griechischen christlichen Schriftsteller der ersten drei Jahrhunderte*, Origen VI], 1920, p. 211.) It is probably that usage that was spread from Alexandria to the whole of Egypt and that we find in the pachomian monasteries. About the number of instructions, see above, Pr. 20, note 1.

Pr. 116 ¹'They shall recite together'; Jerome has: 'They shall also keep silence and only sing something from the psalms or from [other parts of] the Scriptures'. In pachomian literature, the Greek word μελετᾶν used in Coptic (= Latin *meditari*, to meditate) expresses the action of reciting something—usually a text from the Scripture—either in a low voice or within one's heart. The words 'meditation' and 'to meditate' having a very different connotation in our modern languages, we use 'to recite — reciting — recitation' to translate the words of the family μελετᾶν-*meditari.* See also G¹ 58, note 1.

²Jerome has 'give a sign to those who can bring what they need.'

Pr. 117   ¹We find a long series of precepts concerning the work at the bakery, in Hors. Reg. 39-54.

Pr. 120   ¹'... before commanded'; Jerome has: '... unless it is lighted for all together'.

Pr. 121   ¹'shall do penance in his house during the Six Prayers' is the most normal translation of the Coptic *efnametanoei h̄m̄pefeï h̄m̄psoou n̄sop.* It was also L.-T. Lefort's early translation: *'aget paenitentiam in domo sua per sex orationes'* (in A. Boon, *Pachomiana latina,* p. 165) or *'aget paenitentiam in domo sua in sex orationibus'* (in *Muséon* 1927, p. 53). We see no good reason to translate as he did in *Oeuvres de s. Pachôme...* (*CSCO* 160, p. 33): *'fera six fois la métanie en sa maison'.* In our pachomian documents we find *nsoou n̄sop* or *nsoou n̄sop n̄s̆lêl* used indifferently as synonyms. *Sop* is a common Coptic word with the ordinary meaning of 'occasion', 'time', 'turn'. (See W.E. Crum, *A Coptic Dictionary,* p. 349b). *Soou n̄sop* literally means 'six times' and the article *n* placed before *soou* shows that it is a technical expression: 'the six times'. The addition of *n̄s̆lêl* makes the expression a bit more difficult, since *nsoou n̄sop n̄s̆lêl* is as unusual in Coptic as its literal translation is in English ('the six times of prayer'). Crum (*A Coptic Dictionary* p. 351a) gives a second, conjectural, *sop* with the meaning of 'measure' as in 'one hundred measures of bricks'. Our *sop* could be related to this one and could mean 'section', 'piece', 'part'. In that case *sop* would correspond to the Greek μέρος used in Coptic rubrics for a section to be read at the Office. And we know from the Regulations of Horsiesios that the pachomian monks used to learn by heart sections of the Scripture which they called *meros.* The 'Six Prayers' or, more literally, the 'Six Sections (of Prayers)' is probably the name of an Office during which a reader or each one of the readers recited six sections of the Scripture by heart (see Pr. 125). For a longer study of the Office of the Six Prayers, see A. Veilleux, *La liturgie,* pp. 306-313. See also G¹ 58, note 1.

Pr. 122   ¹One word of the Coptic manuscript is illegible. Jerome's text is 'they shall not engage in worldly talks'.

²Jerome: 'but if the housemaster has taught something from the Scripture, they shall reflect on it among themselves, relating what they have heard or what they can remember.' Cf. Pr. 19.

Pr. 125   ¹'during his Six Prayers'; this expression seems to indicate that more than one person used to recite a series of six prayers or six sections of the Scripture. See above, Pr. 121, n. 1. Jerome does not have the personal pronoun: he writes: 'during *the* Six Prayers'.

Pr. 126   ¹This precept is found only in the Latin version. It may have been omitted in the Coptic manuscript by *homoeoteleuton.*

Pr. 130   ¹Here the Coptic fragment of the Precepts ends.

²'ahead of his housemaster and his leader (*ante praepositum et ducem*).'

The Latin word *ducem* is certainly a translation of the Greek ἡγούμενον, which is confirmed by the Greek *Excerpta* (recension B): ἔμπροσθεν τοῦ ἡγουμένου. It is the only time this name is given to the superior in the Precepts. It is found once also in Hors. Test. 7 (Boon, p. 112,12). (It should be added to the list established by A. de Vogüé in '*Le nom du supérieur*', p. 18.)

Pr. 136 [1]The *communio* of the Latin translation corresponds certainly to a *Koinonia* in the Coptic original and the Greek translation used by Jerome.

Pr. 138 [1]Cf. above, Pr. 19 and 122.

Pr. 139 [1]Cf. above, Pr. 49.
[2]*Elementa syllabae* probably means the characters of the alphabet.

Pr. 143 [1]Cf. SBo 27; G[1] 32.

Pr. 144 [1]'without any delay'; the Greek *Excerpta* read: 'without any contradiction' (ἀντιλογία).

Inst. Proemium   [1]We have the Coptic text of the *Praecepta et Instituta*, but this title is found only in the Latin translation.
[2]Although they are not consistent, the Coptic texts normally distinguish the 'assembly' (*sôouh*) from the *synaxis* or place of the assembly. Jerome translates both by *collecta*.
[3]'of the saints'; Jerome writes: 'of the elders (*praecepta maiorum*)'.
[4]Jerome has: 'not inebriated with any passion'.
[5]In the Coptic text, the whole paragraph, from the beginning to this point, constitutes only one sentence composed of a whole series of paratactic propositions.
[6]Jerome writes: 'in the house of God'.
[7]Jerome writes: 'the Church ministers', which is obviously a gloss.

Inst. 1 [1]Cf. Pr. 23.
[2]The Coptic text passes from the singular (He shall . . .) to the plural (They shall . . .).
[3]Cf. Pr. 84. This ¶ clearly refers the 'minister' to other sets of rules or legislative documents, and quite definitely to the *Praecepta* (n̄kôt). The substantive *kôt*, from the verb *kôt*, meaning 'to build', is the exact equivalent of the Greek οἰκοδομή, which is the name given to the *Praecepta* in the Greek *Excerpta*. There their title is Αὕτη ἡ ἀρχὴ τῶν οἰκοδομῶν (Recension B). Many of the following ¶¶ here correspond to ¶¶ of the *Praecepta*.

Inst. 2 [1]Cf. Pr. 25.

Inst. 3 [1]A few words of the Coptic manuscript are missing. We translate from Jerome's text, although it is a bit more elaborated.

Inst. 5 [1]Jerome adds: 'and the damage is due to negligence'.
[2]Cf. Pr. 133.

Inst. 6 [1]The Coptic text has *štên*, a garment in general; in his translation Lefort mistakenly read *prês̆*, mantle or blanket (see: *Oeuvres de s. Pachôme, CSCO* 160, p. 35,8, with note 24).

[2] Lit.: 'make his *metanoia*'.

[3] See Pr. 70 and 103.

Inst. 7   [1] The Coptic word *s̆aar* means a 'skin', but it has become a technical term to designate the goat skin, one of the monastic garments.

[2] 'according to the judgements' refers probably to the *Praecepta ac Judicia*, on which some of the following ¶¶ seem to depend. The Coptic word used for 'judgements' (*hap*) corresponds to the Latin *judicia*.

Inst. 8   [1] Lit.: 'during one section of prayer (*n̄ousop n̄s̆hil̄l*)'. See also Pr. 121, note 1.

[2] We modify Lefort's punctuation; cf. Inst. 6.

Inst. 9   [1] Jerome adds: 'or contradicting the order of the superior'.

[2] Cf. Jud. 2.

Inst. 10   [1] Cf. Jud. 1 and 3. 'the steward shall deliberate and pass judgement'; Jerome's text is different: '. . . the father of the monastery shall be informed and he shall punish'. The last part of this ¶ ('according . . . fault') is translated from Jerome's text, as the Coptic manuscript is mutilated.

Inst. 12   [1] The first sentence is translated from Jerome's Latin, as the Coptic text is mutilated. But the expression *pater manasterii* must correspond to the Coptic *oikonomos* as in Inst. 11.

Inst. 13   [1] The Coptic expression *pethm̄pêi* has to be considered as a synonym of *prôme hm̄pêi*, 'the man of the house', i.e. the housemaster. Jerome correctly translated it by *praepositus* here and in Inst. 16. We do not see any reason for Lefort to translate it here by '*celui qui est à la maison*', and by '*celui qui est préposé à la maison*' in Inst. 16. Cf. Hors. Test. 16.

Inst. 14   [1] Jerome paraphrases: 'They shall carry out six prayers and psalms according to the order of the major assembly which is celebrated by all the brothers in common.'

Inst. 15   [1] This confirms that the *Praecepta et Instituta* were directed to the housemaster who gave the instruction twice a week, while the father of the monastery did it three times a week. See above, Pr. 20, note 1. At the end of this ¶ Jerome adds: 'by the housemaster'.

Inst. 16   [1] On the meaning of *pethm̄pêi* see above, Inst. 13, note 1. Note the difference between 'no one in the house' (*n̄nelaau n̄rôme hm̄pêi*) and 'the housemaster' (*pethm̄pêi*), which confirms that the latter is a technical term.

Inst. 17   [1] We consider *nethm̄pêi* as the plural of *pethm̄pêi* (see Inst. 13, note 1 and Inst. 16, note 1) although we would normally expect *nethm̄nêi*, and therefore we translate by 'the [other] housemasters' and not by 'those who are in the house'. Jerome had some problems and here again he paraphrased: '*Si omnes fratres qui in una domo sunt. . .*'. According to this ¶, therefore, the housemaster is judged by the other housemasters of the same monastery and not by the members of his house.

[2] Cf. Pr. 133.

Inst. 18   ¹This scriptural quotation occurs again in this same ¶ 18 and also in Pach. Letter 3:4 and 7 and in Pach. Instr. 1:45. The rest of the Coptic manuscript is very mutilated, and we have constantly used Jerome's translation to fill the gaps. L.-T. Lefort has found many interesting parallels between this ¶ and a writing of the old Egyptian wisdom, the Wisdom of Amen-em-ope; see L.-T. Lefort, 'S. Pachôme et Amen-em-ope' in *Muséon* 49 (1927) 65–74.

²The meaning of this recommendation, which we translate from Latin, is obscure. There is a lacuna in the Coptic text, but the last word of the sentence can be read, 'the house', and shows that the recommendation was somewhat different in Coptic.

³This and the next three sentences are translated from the Latin version. 'of divided faith' (*duplicis fidei*) means probably a lack of sincerity or of purity of heart.

⁴Mt 12:36 is quoted about the pachomian monks in G¹ 58; there is another allusion to it in Pach. Fragm. 2: 3.

⁵Jerome's text is different: 'He shall not *put an obstacle in the blind man's way'* (Lv 19:14).

⁶Translated from the Latin version.

⁷'He shall not let'; Lefort's edition in *Oeuvres de s. Pachôme, CSCO* 159; p. 35, 30 has *emefapata*, but his anterior editions in *Muséon* 1927, p. 46 and in A. Boon, *Pachomania latina*, p. 161 have *emeuapata.*

⁸Theodore uses this text from 2 Co 4:8 twice: in Theod. Instr. 3:19 and 39.

⁹The words 'looking for glory' are translated from the Latin, the Coptic text being lacunose. At the end of the sentence Jerome adds: 'and alien to fraud'.

¹⁰Jerome's text is different: 'He shall not ignore the way of life of the saints nor be blind to their knowledge.'

¹¹Jerome: 'He shall never forsake truth.'

¹²Jerome: 'He shall hate injustice.'

¹³Pr. 17:15 is quoted also in Hors. Test. 43. Jerome has: 'He shall not be respecter of persons for the sake of bribes.'

¹⁴The Coptic text is lacunose. This and the next three lines are translated from the Latin version.

¹⁵Jerome: 'He shall not desert justice.'

¹⁶The Coptic fragment ends here.

¹⁷We find the same quotation in S² 7 and Hors. Test. 7 and 16.

¹⁸This theme of the reward according to each one's works with reference to Mt 26:27 and Rm 2:6 is frequent. See SBo 27 (= G¹ 32); Pach. Letter 5: 12; Pach. Fragm. 2: 3; Hors. Test. 27 and 33.

¹⁹I.e. his sons.

²⁰The same text is quoted in Pach. Letter 5: 7 and there is an allusion to it in Paral. 3.

²¹The same text appears in Hors. Test. 52 as a part of a longer quotation.

Jud. Proemium   ¹Rm 13:10 is quoted also in SBo 29 (= G¹ 34) and Hors. Test. 55; Rm 13:11 in Hors. Test. 6, 38 and 41; Rm 13:12 in Hors. Letter 4: 3.

²We have the same quotation in S² 14.

Jud. 10 [1]In Hors. Test. 24 (Boon, *Pachomiana latina,* p. 126,1-2) we find the same expression about the housemaster.

Jud. 11 [1]*'de maioribus et praepositis'*: we give to *'praepositi'* the meaning it usually has in Jerome's translation. But *'maiores'* could also mean 'elders', and *'praepositi'* superiors in general.

Jud. 16 [1]Cf. Hors. Test. 24 (beginning).

Leg. 2 [1]Cf. Pr. 3.

Leg. 7 [1]Cf. Pr. 98 and 113; Hors. Test. 26.

Leg. 10 [1]Cf. Inst. 14.

Leg. 15 [1]Cf. Pr. 70 and Hors. Test. 26.

the Regulations of horsiesios

(hors. Reg.)

1. ...but again, *Their eyes shall fall at their feet, and their tongues shall dry up in their mouths.*[1]

2. Therefore, brothers, let us know with assurance that these are not mere words or formulas,* but that these things will come to pass. Let us fear mightily lest we be in any way a scandal in the place *where two or three are assembled in the name* of Jesus; for he is with them and *in their midst,*[1] as he has said. We have already heard in the Gospel the great punishments of the Lord; for example the ones [inflicted] upon him who was invited to the wedding hall. Although he too entered and seated himself with the others, when it was noticed that he did not have a wedding garment the king did not hesitate to have him *bound hand and foot and thrown into the outer darkness, where there will be weeping and grinding of teeth.*[2] Let us then be attentive to the pitiful grinding of teeth to discover its nature, especially because they are lasting and the pain of darkness is forever.

3. Let us also consider attentively the five foolish virgins. They too carried their lamps with them and came along with the wise ones, awaiting the bridegroom until the middle of the night. However, the door was closed on them and they heard the lord say to them, *I do not know you;*

Text: CSCO 159, pp. 82-99.

Zc 14:12.

The fear of God
*Cf. Ps 19(18):3.

Mt 18:20.

Mt 22:1-13.

Mt 22:13.

Example of the five foolish virgins
Mt 25:1-13

Mt 25:12.

Lk 13:25.

where are you from? O what a deep sigh, what an endless sorrow! For after remaining with their fellow virgins until the middle of the night, their sisters were admitted into the wedding hall, while they were refused admittance.[1]

The fear of God

4. Let us have in us the fear of the words of God; let us awaken from the slumber of perdition and of eternal death. Let us not be found in the desires of the flesh and the pleasures of this age. May the father of Jesus not cut us off from the vine;*[1] may we not be wise in our own eyes†; let us not transgress one of his least commandments; let us not be called 'little ones'.[2] Let us all remain in the true vineyard, so as not to be cast away as a branch, and to wither away and be cast in the fire to burn; for if a branch is cast away from the vine, where will it go? Indeed, is the vine lord of this age alone, or is it lord as well of the endless ages? Jesus is the Lord. . . .

*Jn 15:6.
†Cf. Rm 11:25.

Mt 5:19.

Cf. Jn 15:6.

12 lines are missing

Let us recall Christ's judgement

Rm 14:10;
2 Co 5:10.

5. . . . will all arrive; *for all must stand before the tribunal of Christ, and each one will receive what comes from his body to the extent that he has produced it, either good or bad;*[1] so that we may do God's will in all our actions, and that, avoiding the snares, the great everlasting punishments, and the terrible torments, we may rather inherit *what no eye has seen, no ear heard, nor the heart of man conceived, what God has prepared for those who love him.*[2]

1 Co 2:9;
Cf. Is 64:3;
Jr 3:16.

Let us respect the canons of prayer

6. Therefore, let us guard ourselves in all things. Let us give heed with exactness to the canons of prayer, with a fear of the Lord that is worthy of him, whether at the *synaxis* or at the Six Sections, or in our houses, or anywhere, whether

in the fields or in the community.[1] Wherever we
are, even while walking along the road, we must
pray to God with our whole heart, being attentive
to prayer alone, our hands outstretched in the
form of the cross, uttering the prayer written in
the Gospel and keeping the eyes of our hearts and
bodies lifted up to the Lord, as it is written, *I lifted up my eyes to you, Lord, you who dwell in the
heaven, as the eyes of the servants fixed on their
masters' hands.*

Mt 6:9-13.

Ps 123(122):1-2.

7. At the beginning of our prayers let us sign
ourselves with the seal of baptism. Let us make
the sign of the Cross on our foreheads, as on the
day of our baptism, as it is written in Ezechiel.*
Let us not first lower our hand to our mouth or to
our beard, but let us raise it to our forehead, saying in our heart, 'We have signed ourselves with
the seal'. This is not like the seal of baptism; but
the sign of the Cross was traced on the forehead of
each of us on the day of our baptism.[1]

The sign of the Cross at the beginning of prayer
*Ez 9:4.

8. When the signal is given for prayer, let us
rise promptly;[1] and when the signal is given to
kneel, let us prostrate promptly to adore the
Lord, having signed ourselves before kneeling.
When once we are prostrate on our face, let us
weep in our heart for our sins, as it is written,
*Come, let us adore and weep before the Lord our
maker.* Let absolutely no one of us raise his head
while kneeling, for this shows a great lack of fear
and knowledge.

Kneeling down for prayer

Ps 95(94):6.

9. When we rise again, let us sign ourselves;
and after uttering the prayer of the Gospel, let us
supplicate saying, 'Lord, instill your fear into our
hearts that we may labor for eternal life and hold
you in fear'. Let each one of us say in his heart

To make the sign of the Cross again when rising

with an interior sigh, *'Purify me, O Lord, from my secret sins; keep your servant from strangers.*[1] *If these do not prevail over me, I shall be holy and free from a great sin;* and, *Create a pure heart in me, God, let a right spirit be renewed in my innermost self.*

Ps 19(18):13-14.

Ps 51(50):10.

10. When the signal is given for us to be seated, let us again sign ourselves on the forehead in the form of the cross. Then let us be seated and pay attention, heart and ears, to the holy words being recited, in accord with what we have been commanded in the holy Scriptures: *My son, fear my words, and having received them, do penance*; and again, *My son, take heed of my wisdom and incline your ear to my words.*

Again when sitting down

Pr 30:1.

Pr 5:1.

11. Let no one, in the *synaxis,* look up at anyone in the face without necessity. He who needlessly looks his neighbor in the face usually provokes laughter on the face or a smile, which brings no profit or [even] causes indignation.[1] Hence let us guard ourselves against all things that are harmful to our souls. *Let us, with our hands, raise our hearts to our Lord who is in heaven,*[2] praying with our whole heart and fulfilling the word, *Immolate before the Lord a sacrifice of benediction and offer your prayer to the Most High; call upon me on the day of your affliction and I will save you, and you will give me glory.* Let no one therefore say, 'I have not enough confidence before the Lord to cry out to him, for I am a negligent person.'

Not to look at one's neighbor during prayer

Lm 3:41.

Ps 50(49):14-15.

12. Let us consider the great mercy of God in the holy Scriptures: the son, who had squandered his fortune in debauchery and returned with all his heart to his father and humbly said to

Examples of God's mercy

him, *I no longer deserve to be called your son,*[1]   Lk 15:19.
see how God's mercy treated him! And the pub-
lican who beat his breast, not daring to raise his
eyes to heaven, and returned to his house justified
by the Lord![2] And David in what happened to   Lk 18:13-14.
him over Bathsheba[3] and Uriah, whom he had
caused to die! And the great apostle Peter, after   2 S 11-12.
he had thrice denied the Lord! Thanks to the for-   Mt 26:69-75.
giveness and mercy of the Lord, they enjoy eter-
nally the bliss of the kingdom of heaven in the
heights of God's glory. Let us also, accordingly,
trust in the abundant mercy of God, and let us cry
out to him with our whole heart at every moment.

13. When the *synaxis* is dismissed, let us recite   **To recite after**
until we reach our houses. Let no one speak to his   **the *synaxis***
neighbor as he leaves the *synaxis*. Even for mat-
ters that relate to the community, let us wait until
we reach our houses, in observance of the commandments of life.[1]

14. About the mystery of our salvation:[1] When   **The celebration**
we are summoned to it, let us prepare in great   **of the Eucharist**
fear. Let us beg the Lord with all our heart and
all our mind to make us worthy of this great gift
and to revive in us that which is pleasing to God.
Let us abandon ourselves with body, soul, and
spirit,[2] to his will, trusting in the word of the   Cf. 1 Th 5:23.
Saviour; *For, my flesh is real food, and my blood
real drink; he who eats my flesh and drinks my
blood will remain in me and I in him.* Let us re-   Jn 6:55-56.
ceive the mystery in thanksgiving, and let us re-
turn to our house with joy and gladness, without
becoming in our overall behavior a scandal to
everyone who sees us, whether a cleric or another
man, in order that they may render glory to God
as they notice all the knowledge [showing forth

in] the piety in which we are truly clothed. Let us recite also both going to and returning from the *synaxis*.

To avoid
chatting

15. Chatting, not only with strangers but with our own brothers, or shouting when speaking, we must hold as an abomination. For this is the way with the idle and with those who are heedless of their souls' fervor. On the contrary, let us take the word of God as a food of life, as it is written, *Man does not live on bread alone, but on every word that comes forth from the mouth of God does man live.*

Dt 8:3; Mt 4:4.

To learn many
sections of the
Scripture by
heart

16. Let us be wealthy in texts learned by heart. Let him who does not memorize much memorize at least ten sections along with a section of the psalter; and let him who does not recite at night recite ten psalms or five of them with a section of texts learned by heart.[1]

Nightly
recitation

17. If someone rises at night for the recitation, and the one who is in the cell with him keeps sleeping and fails to get up for the nightly recitation, the one who is awake — sleep having no hold on him because he is concerned and careful about his soul and his relationship with God — shall go outside the door of the cell and shall knock on the mat, causing the slumberer to rise and recite, so he may recite his psalms and his section of texts learned by heart before the signal is given for the *synaxis*.[1] And if he still fails to awake, he will call his name, standing outside the mat until he rises. If he is awake but refuses to rise and recite, and is not in peril because of a mortal illness, but on the contrary strong before God but lazy, let the curse that is found in the Scriptures against the slothful be his portion.

Cf. Pr 6:11;
Si 22:1-2.

18. Now, about him who is also slothful in his visible deeds. If he does not work with all his might to earn, through his own efforts, his food, clothing and all that is needful for his body, so that whether in health or stricken by illness or old age he may find someone meeting expenses for him at all times, and bread may still be found for him, and he may be placed in the porter's lodge; — if on the contrary he continues to eat from the labor of his brothers and to be clothed with what they have provided in their courage and filial generosity, even if he is a sinless child but willingly slothful, [this shall happen to him]: he shall be in the age to come like the son of a great and noble prince of the world whose father and brothers all enjoy the glory and the pleasures of wealth and of the honors that are proper to their rank — that is, of a count or a governor — whereas he lies in the abjection of beggary, with the opprobrium upon his shoulders of a beggar's clothes and shame, which penetrate and wrap him round. All are looking at his brother seated on the governor's throne, but him they see in the same place as a beggar.[1] This is how the saints and the angels will look upon the slothful in the age [to come]. Even if just and in the place of eternal happiness and in the bliss of the kingdom of heaven, he is there as a beggar.

The fate of a slothful man

19. Let us therefore guard against slothfulness in all things. And first, let us all for God's sake produce fruits from among the fruits of the Holy Spirit,*[1] and then fruits from among those that are needful to the body. Now the fruits of the Holy Spirit, which man will come to know, he will acquire through conversion and through sighs for

Let us produce the fruits of the Holy Spirit
*Cf. Ga 5:22.

the negligences he has committed, putting God's
fear within himself and believing that all the
words written in the holy Scriptures will come to
pass. He does not throw these words behind himself, in the manner of an unjust tyrant of this
world or a wicked person or a thief, who have so
cast away the fear of death as to follow the ca-
prices that will lead them to ruin, and then death
will seize them. It is impossible to escape its grip
even though its fear has been cast away, for there
is a word from the mouth of God, *On the day you*
eat of this tree you shall most surely die. So are all

Gn 2:17.

the other words which he has pronounced through
his saint; they will all come to pass, and no one will
be spared.

Hence, my beloved, let us fear God, shun the
works of malediction and clothe ourselves with

Cf. Rm 13:12.

those of benediction, that we may be found to
have confidence in the other age for ages unending. Amen.

20. Again, when we are seated at the *synaxis,*

Rules of modesty
at the *synaxis*

let us be seated with modesty. Let our garments
be gathered about us so as to cover our legs. Let
us not be overly curious during the *synaxis,* and
let us not gaze at stranger monks or at anyone
else. Let us also not trample underfoot the soaked
rushes placed before the brothers, as we come to
our seat.[1]

21. All that is useful to piety, which we have

Conclusion of
this section

not spoken here, we will teach to each other. We
will edify each other* with the doctrine of our
divine Saviour, Christ Jesus our Lord, to whom is

*Cf. Th 5:11.

glory and power unto eternity. Amen.[1]

Admonitions to the stewards.[1]

22. Let each one of us, therefore, apply himself well and carefully, in the fear of God, to the task assigned to him. The stewards will take care of every object that pertains to their ministry, so that none of these objects is damaged. They will take care lest, through forgetfulness, bread that is left soaking in water be spoiled, or lest through sloth, they make brine for two days at a time. Rather make only enough for one day, so that there will not be left more than a pickle bowl. Let them not soak so great a quantity of dates as to make date-juice in abundance, for two or three days at a time, and thus alter the taste of the dates to sourness. Let them not boil more lupines than is necessary for a week at a time; and let them take heed to wash the lupines once or twice daily, and even, if possible, to allow the water to run over them continuously, so that there will be no smell of stinking water as the brothers eat them. Again, they will take care not to let too many vegetables become spoiled, or, through negligence, damage any of the dishes, not even a small bowl. In short, we must take heed for everything in faith, for the things of the *Koinonia* are not fleshly things, like those of the world.

To prepare the brothers' food with care

Also about the stewards of the kitchen.

23. Let them take care of the porter with a cheerful countenance and poised speech; whatever they give him shall be given gladly. Whatever they cook for the brothers shall be cooked with great care in the fear of the Lord. They shall

How to cook the brothers' food

cook properly whatever they cook, whether on the open fire or on the stove. They shall be careful not to burn too much wood; only three logs at a time, according to the precept. Let them not throw too much wood on the fire: at most two handfuls. Let him who makes a fire, wherever it may be, do likewise. Likewise they shall not let the logs burn in the stove until they almost cease to blaze, but they shall add smaller pieces to the logs to avoid smoke. They shall gather together the brands in the stove so that they are not scattered, and they shall cover them with dung or anything else, so that whatever is put on the stove, wheat or lentils, may soften gradually; for an excessive flame at the outset will prevent them from softening properly. Then, when they open up the bottom of the stove, they find all the embers ready when there is need for them, and what we have to bake is properly baked. And let them stir it swiftly and carefully when the fire gets intense. Let the pots be placed side by side, so that the embers below them will be glowing.

Also about those who take care of the sick.

The food of the sick brothers

24. Let them do likewise when they bake according to the needs of the sick [brothers], whom they will care for with great compassion.

Rules concerning the cleanliness of the kitchen vessels

25. Whoever is appointed for any task of this sort, including him who distributes water and pumps for the brothers, shall wash his hands before drawing water. He will also wash the jugs properly, according to the precept, twice a week, on the two fast days; as for the basin, he will wash it once a week. He will shake the jugs and empty them each day before drawing water.

26. It behooves the stewards also not to allow, through negligence, a kettle or anything else on the fire to be damaged by leaving it there without water, or by not stirring it, including a....[1]

Care for the
vessels

*Lacuna of
6 to 10 pages*

27. ...you, pay a price for the object, as is demanded from you. I say this sincerely, so that, if you do as I say with faith and without respect of persons, God will open up to us his treasury of goods—namely, his heaven—so that the word which is written will be fulfilled for us: *The riches of the sea will turn to you, and so those of the nations and the peoples,* and, *Those who do not place their hope in men will be filled with joy.*

To pay the
price requested
for an object

Is 60:5.
Is 29:19.

28. It behooves [you] also not to sell or to buy or to do anything, large or small, without [the permission of] the superior of the community and the....[1]

Not to
sell or buy
anything with-
out permission

*7 lines are
missing*

29. Let everything, small or large, be registered at the steward's office, clearly and legibly, so that God's name may be glorified in everything we undertake. Let these be done quite properly, so that we will not be ashamed if anyone should see them. Let each one of us say, as we do anything, large or small....

About
bookkeeping

Cf. Col 3:17.

*4 lines
are missing*

... by the steward of the kitchen, the superior of the community, as well as the weekly server, him who is with the cattle and the pigs, and him who works on the farm and at whatever else, in accordance with our call.

**Let nothing
spoil**

30. Let no one let anything spoil through his negligence, knowing that it is [the fruit of] others' labor or [of] his own. Has he the right to spend it for himself or to give it away in alms for himself, for the salvation of his soul? For nothing escapes God,* not even a widow's two mites,† or a glass of fresh water.‡ One as great as Abraham has said, *From a thread to a shoe strap.*[1] As the Lord spoke to Moses from within the fire, and spelled out what he was to lay down as laws for the sons of Israel — who could discern the voice coming from within the fire — He gave them orders about everything*, including an animal that would be torn to pieces by a wild beast† or savaged by a bull.‡

*Cf. Heb 4:13.
†Lk 21:2.
‡Mt 10:42.
*Gn 14:23.

Cf. Ex 34:28,35.

*Cf. Ex 20:18–19.
†Cf. Ex 22:12,30.
‡Cf. Ex 21:35–36.

**To fulfill the
works of steward-
ship without
negligence**
*Cf. Rm 14:12;
    2 Co 5:10.

31. You have, accordingly, learned that in truth we will be questioned about every deed.* Let us not be negligent in any of them; for the works of stewardship are directives that issue from God, and we know that mercy will befall us for the care we have for the things of the brothers.

*Lacuna of
6 or 8 pages*

**Invitation
to humility.**

32. ...with a hardheartedness and brutality of this kind, 'We are able to settle a matter,' or 'He has decided because of our wisdom or courage.' Stupid as we are! If we are able, or if we have the wisdom to settle a matter outside our heart or body, let us govern our heart and body so as to present ourselves before the tribunal of God, without a stain on our body, soul, or spirit;* I refer to those whom it touches.

*Cf. 1 Th 5:23.

**Let us
accomplish our
tasks with care**
*3 lines are
missing*

33. Let us be strict with ourselves, great or small, so as to avoid, each one at his own task, any such scorn and brutality, that is, in thought...

... on the contrary, let us give glory to God who foresees all things,* and who governs them by his august angels and by men.

*Ws 6:7.

On how to act during the harvest

34. May the God of Abraham, Isaac and Jacob, and the God of Apa[1] bless us together. We wish to remind you how to act during the harvest and threshing, so that according to the law of the *Koinonia*[2] there be no negligence.

35. The superior of the community shall appoint the man who is to walk at the head of the brothers charged with doing the harvest. He will be responsible for having the brothers leave for work, and also for having them return at the proper time. Likewise, [he will be responsible for] where he wants the harvest done, or anything else concerning the work inside the community or the farming, with the agreement of the superior of the community and the housemaster of the farmers. Let no one disobey him in any task assigned to each of those who accompany him; but let us do whatever task is assigned to us cheerfully and without grumbling, that we may receive a reward before God. Let no one provoke any quarrel during work, and let no one chatter. Rather let each one do his work in the fear of God, without boasting or quarrelling, so that God's blessing may descend upon us and he may bless all the works of our hands.*

Let each do the task assigned to him

*Ps 90(89):17.

36. Let no one turn his back on his neighbor, leaving him behind him as he reaps. On the contrary, if it is possible, let us keep abreast of our brother as we reap. Let us guard our heart against boasting according to the flesh, for it is

Let us avoid boasting

God who gives strength. Let us also be careful not to despise our neighbor, so as not to be like the pharisee who despised the publican*. . .

*Lk 18:11.

2 pages are missing

Not to forget about our soul while working at perishable things

37. . . . [we] who have inherited the law of the *Koinonia* upon earth, we may inherit with them the joy of the kingdom of heaven. Hence, even if we are laboring at perishable things in order to sustain the body—which is necessary—let us be watchful not to render our soul, which is worth more than our nourishment, a stranger to eternal life under the pretext of a necessity which will disappear.[1]

To fulfill the canons of prayer

38. Let us fulfill the canons of the prayer; those of the *synaxis* and those of the Six Sections at their fixed hours in accord with the precept.

Precepts for the bakery.

39. On how to act in the kneading room.

Let all of us work together

When the time has come to make our small quantity of bread, all of us, great and little, must work at making bread in the fear of God and with great understanding, reciting the word of God with gravity, without pride, boasting, or respect of persons.[1]

Let each do quietly the work assigned to him

40. Not only anyone sitting at the 'board'[1] but also all of us who are working in the kneading room shall do in obedience whatever is assigned to each. Let each one do his work without chatting or shouting. Let absolutely no one laugh, so that there will not apply to us the reproach of the Scriptures, *They make bread for laughter.* If someone needs to ask his neighbor a question, he must do so quietly, without shouting.

Qo 10:19.

41. Let no one, great or little, eat before the

signal is given to eat. If a little one wishes to eat, he may not eat at all in the oven-room or among the brothers who are not eating; rather let him be given bread and let him go elsewhere to eat by himself. After rising from the table at the noon-day meal, we shall not eat bread again until the *synaxis* of midday is dismissed. After it is dismissed, he who is in charge of the *cace*[1] shall put enough in a basket which he shall place in a secluded place, with a bit of pure salt with which no other salt — not even the gatehouse salt — is mixed. He will place it beside the basket of *cace* so that anyone who wishes to eat may come and do so. Let him who eats not choose the *cace* at all, but let us take the [piece of *cace*] that lies at hand; we shall take it and eat it at the basket or at table when the *cace* are softened. Therefore, let the man in charge of the *cace,* in perfect charity, choose for the *cace* he will put in the basket or at table those that are good and well baked. Likewise it is only one loaf of bread that he will take for himself to eat.

Not to eat before the signal is given

42. Throughout the entire kneading, let no one, great or little, including a sick [brother], desire to bake for himself some bread different from that eaten by the brothers. Even the crusts, let no one eat them alone. The superior of the community shall reserve to himself attention in this matter; or the minister of the sick shall bring it to his notice that there should be some crusts prepared for all the sick, who will eat them in equal measure. When there are crusts, the man in charge of the *cace* will keep them and then hand them over to the infirmary. And if it is possible to bake small loaves quickly in order to give

Not to bake something special for oneself

the sick a small ration separately as well, let us
bake them well, enough to fill about five baskets.
The man in charge of the *cace* will set them apart
and hand them over to the infirmary. Let us bake
them under the directions of the superior of the
community; it is he who decides what alleviations
are to be afforded to the sick. Only, this thing
called *cole* is a daintiness. Indeed, the *cace* well
baked and white is tastier than the očcpšote; for
this latter is heavier on the heart.[1]

Those who work at the mill

43. About him who watches over the grinding
or the milling.

Let them apply themselves to the work they are
doing, in the fear of God and without any relaxation, knowing that no good deed that man does
for God shall be lost. On the contrary, our good
deeds will be a relief to us all on the day of the
great judgement.

*The kneading at evening in the kneading room,
according to the regulations regarding those who
knead in the kneading-troughs.*

The distribution of the kneading-troughs

44. At the moment of kneading, he who is in
charge of the kneading room calls out [the names
of] those whom he, with the agreement of the
head-baker, has appointed for this task. He ap-
points those who will knead and those who will
have charge of supplying water. He distributes
the kneading-troughs with fairness, without leaving aside somewhere some who are able to knead.
He shall appoint those who are to knead in the
kneading-troughs according to the order of the
houses. Let no one choose his own kneading-
trough. Let all of us in the kneading room recite,
not shouting, but softly.

45. He who is responsible for the flour measures it; let each one place his basket of flour by the kneading-trough in which he is to knead and wait for the head-baker to strike his hand on a trough or say, 'knead'. Let no one knead and let no one remove dough from the troughs unless the head-baker says to do so. We shall not knead without reciting: we may recite or pause; and if we so desire, we may recite in our heart.[1] If we need a bit of water, we shall strike the trough without saying anything, and those who have charge of supplying water will quickly bring it along. Nor will these cease to recite, and they will take care not to spill water on the feet of those who are kneading.

To start kneading when the signal is given

46. Let those who are kneading place the flour in the kneading-trough gently, so that the flour dust will not spread; and let the brim of the basket not dip into the water. They will zealously take care to arrange the flour and not leave any at the bottom of the trough. Neither will they allow the dough to stick to the sides of the trough. They must not give too much water, and the dough must not be too soft. If they raise their head above the trough and pause for a moment, let them recite standing upright, then let them go on kneading until the head-baker comes around to distribute the leaven to them.

To knead carefully

47. When they have finished the kneading, let each one wash his trough properly and empty the water out where it should be poured, so that the swineherd may take it away. After this, let them pray—and we shall give heed to pray from the start, according to the canon—and let them all return to their house still reciting, without any-

After the kneading is over

one having spoken in the kneading room, but on the contrary having observed the commandment gratefully.

On the food in the kneading room.

The same food for everyone

48. Let there be no special food for anyone working in the kneading room; let the food be the same for everyone, for those who bake and those who are appointed to any task, in accordance with what was established from the beginning by the father of the *Koinonia,* Apa, to whom God entrusted this great calling. If other fathers who have succeeded him have made canons granting special food to the bakers, they did so after Moses' manner,[1] as we have learned in the Gospel that says, *Because of your hardness of heart, Moses has allowed you to repudiate your wives, but in the beginning it was not like this.* If, for some light fatigue, a man separates himself from his brother and differs from him in his food more than do those who are to leave for the harvest or for any other task at which they will have to endure the heat, let us not allow the brothers who have been appointed for any other task in the community to eat with these,[2] since they have not set out to endure the heat and to work strenuously.

Mt 19:8.

On the contrary the unity of the *Koinonia* consists in a like measure for all, according to the saints' way of doing; thus David approached those who had not gone to war and spoke to them peacefully, giving them a share of the spoils equal to that received by those who had gone to war with him. He did not listen to those who were wicked and said, 'We will not share with them'.*

*1 S 30:21-22.

The Lord taught us likewise in the Gospel by the parable, when those who had *borne the weight of the day and the heat murmured, saying, Why have you treated us like those who have worked only an hour?* They, too, heard the reproach, *Is your eye evil because I am good?*

Mt 20:11-12.
Mt. 20:15

49. Therefore, this is what we must do with someone who is in need, little or great, being appointed for any task in our assembly, according to our calling. If anyone is overly distressed by the heat, let those in charge look into the matter; if he is really unable to eat his bread at the brothers' table, let him notify them. When he is certain before God in his heart that he is not a contemptor and that he does not wish to be different from his brothers by reason of any tradition or habit, and is not desiring enjoyment — as when we seek wine or special food — but that it is a matter of necessity and need in this case, let us say so with filial confidence, and let all that we need be brought to us, according to what is available and what God has given us at that time.* Even if all the brothers need a bit of beer or any other food that accords with the law of the *Koinonia*, the superior of the community will grant this to them generously and gladly.

But to take into account the various needs of individuals

*Cf. Ps 145(144): 15.

50. If God give those who are in front of the ovens some of the strength which he gave to the saints in the furnace,*[1] let them not seek through weakness to be different from the brothers by virtue of any tradition. However, we shall strive not to seek out what is hard to find, or what is not prepared, although within the precept; on the contrary, let us rather have the confidence to say, as did saint Paul, *I am accustomed to all this, full*

Let those who are strong bear hardships
*Cf. Dn 3.

stomach or empty stomach, to have in abundance or to be in want; I am capable of anything
Ph 4:12-13.   *in him who strengthens me, Christ Jesus.*

Let us all per-   51. And every other duty which we must perform our duties   form in conformity with the law of the holy
as one man   *Koinonia*, let us all perform with the prudence of
                       piety, as one man, as it is written; *All who believed*
Ac 4:32.   *formed but one heart and one soul;*[1] so that God
                       may bless our bread, that we may eat it with joy
                       and pleasure in the Holy Spirit, and that a bless-
                       ing may rest upon it, remain there, and not van-
                       ish rapidly; also, that the Lord may bless every
                       work we will undertake to do.

Let us do   52. All things which it behooves us to do con-
everything for   formably with our calling, let us do for the glory
the glory of God   of God, whether in matters of food or labor in the
                       fields, the *synaxis*, and conversation with seculars
                       we shall meet on the road or at the gatehouse or
                       whom we shall visit for a necessary matter
                       relating to the community. In short, let all we do
Cf. 1 Co 10:31.   or say be for the glory of God, knowing that the
                       written word is true, *The one who honors me I*
1 S 2:30.   *will honor.*[1] Indeed the words of Scripture, the
Cf. 2 Tm 3:16.   breath of God, are true and very dependable,†
†Cf. 1 Tm 1:15;   whether concerning favors or punishments.
  4:9.

To perform   53. During every occupation and in the knead-
the prayers   ing room, let us perform the prayers with zeal,
with zeal   those of the *synaxis* and those of the Six Sections
                       at their appointed hours, according to the pre-
                       cepts of the *Koinonia*,[1] with great devotion and
                       tears, praying the good God to keep for us his
                       mercy and his grace, through which he has awak-
                       ened us to renew us in his love, to give us strength
                       in our weakness, not to allow us to fall again into
                       the pit of negligence, and to place his fear, which

glows day and night, into our hearts as an ardent fire. For with such fear, not only will we shun the hell of fire and the place of *the grinding of teeth* as well as the shame which is full of dishonor in the place of glory, but we shall inherit *what eye has not seen, ear has not heard, and the mind of man has not conceived, the things which God has prepared for those who love him.* And in this age too he will give us the blessings of all the saints for everything that we shall undertake, either in the village[2] or in the field. And he will bless our bread and water, as it is written, *If you keep the commandments of the Lord your God, you will be blessed in the city and in the field*; and the rest of the blessings.

Mt 8:12.

1 Co 2:9;
Cf. Is 64:3;
Jr 3:16.

Dt 28:1-3.

54. If we clean the inside of the cup or dish, the outside will be clean, according to the word of the Lord;* and if Christ dwells in our inmost self by the faith that is in our hearts,[†] and if we produce roots and foundations in love, we shall then hear God who has appeared saying, *What you have not requested, that have I granted to you, glory and abundant riches.* And if the eyes of our hearts receive the light, and if we follow the lives of the saints, the firmness of their faith in God* and their courage in every trial, we shall then see the prosperity of Abraham, Isaac, Jacob, Job, Joseph, David, and Apa, the father of the *Koino-nia,* for he was one whom God called, blessed, loved and rendered greatly prosperous.[1]

Let us keep our inmost self pure
*Mt 23:26;
Lk 11:39.
[†]Eph 3:17.

1 K 3:13.

*Cf. Heb 13:7.

Regulations for farming.

55. Those who go out to work at the head of the brothers shall observe the time at which they must

Maintaining
observances
during farm
work

leave and the time at which they must have them return.[1] If there is any urgency in doing or finishing a task, and if we must go on working a bit at noontime or at night, let us not lose heart or grumble; however, let us by no means neglect the *synaxis*, the divine service,[2] and the refectory.

Being careful
about farming

56. The farmers will be very careful, in the fear of God, about all that concerns farming. For the extra pain each one takes beyond his neighbor will be for him as it was for him who received five talents, for him who received two, and for

*Cf. Mt 25:15.

him who received one.*[1] Hence, we must be particular about small things, so we allow nothing to be damaged through sloth.

The one in charge of irrigation.

How to irrigate
the fields

57. He shall not let the water, by day or night, cover land [already] drenched. He shall not allow much water to flow into a ditch or a lowland. He shall leave dry no portion of the field which is being irrigated, nor divide the water into two sections;[1] for this procedure of divided water will irrigate but two sections, whereas there is a possibility that three will be irrigated if you soak them one at a time, and if you do not release much water in the section. We shall take care not to uproot many reeds in the small ditches when we cultivate the field, but only those that are at the bottom of the canal; those on the edge of the canal we shall bend toward the outside and we shall put a bit of mud to stop the water; and we shall watch our step so as not to crush the stem of the reeds. When the water stops flowing, we shall be careful to place small grass [clippings] on the

portion that has been irrigated. Each day we shall inspect the main canal up to the waterwheel, for there may be a leak or some grass obstructing the water or a spot that needs a small faggot or a bit of dung, or there may be a spot that is overly soaked which requires a basket of earth, or some other useful task to be done.

The housemaster of the farmers.

58. He will inspect daily, without fail, the portion that is being irrigated. For every place that is hard to irrigate, he will appoint someone else besides the one who irrigates, (so that the water will not escape him forcibly and be wasted) until such time as the place that is hard to irrigate be soaked. For all the farm work also . . . . [1]

How to irrigate a difficult spot

2 pages are missing

59. . . . we shall also feed the calves and the small heifers in the same manner. We shall set a place apart in the stable for the donkey, so that the cattle will not injure it; let us loose it when we have finished . . . .

Care of the animals

24 lines are missing

60. . . . and not throw much of it in the alley at the cows' feet; and the green fodder, let us not throw much of it in front of them at any one time either, but only a bit at a time until . . . .

Feeding the cows

25 lines are missing

61. . . . [those] who see the cattle will congratulate the herdsman.

62. If there is any negligence in the farm work concerning any task of a man, the latter will be held responsible . . .

25 lines are missing

63. . . . God and the father of the *Koinonia*, Apa Pachomius.

64. As for us, it is with much indulgence and patience that we have laid down these things in view of right order and absence of any blame on the day when . . . .[1]

the rest is missing

Notes to the Regulations of Horsiesios

Hors. Reg. 1   [1] We do not know what this ¶ was about and how many ¶¶ there were before it.

Hors. Reg. 2   [1] Mt 18:20 is quoted also in SBo 184 and G[1] 94.
[2] Pachomius also quotes this text in an exhortation to pardon; see Pach. Instr. 1: 41.

Hors. Reg. 3   [1] Horsiesios makes reference more than once to this parable; see Hors. Letter 3: 1; Hors. Letter 4: 4 and Hors. Test. 20. There is also a reference to it in SBo 118 and another in Pach. Instr. 1: 51.

Hors. Reg. 4   [1] Horsiesios uses the image of the vine also in Hors. Instr. 3: 2 and in Hors. Test.45. See also Pachomius in Pach. Instr. 1: 37.
[2] See G[1] 126 and Hors. Letter 1: 4.

Hors. Reg. 5   [1] For other quotations of, or allusions to, the same text, see below, ¶ 31; Pach. Instr. 1: 26 and 38; Theod. Instr. 3: 10 and Hors. Test. 17.
[2] The same quotation occurs below, ¶ 53 and also in SBo 114.

Hors. Reg. 6   [1] Horsiesios is referring to some well-known canons concerning the times of prayer. Both the *synaxis (sôouh)* and the 'Six Sections' or 'Six Prayers' are technical terms. See Pr. 20, note 1.

Hors. Reg. 7   [1] About the use of the sign of the cross by the Pachomians, see H. Bacht, '*Vexillum crucis sequi*', pp. 158-162; *Idem, Das Vermächtnis*, p. 206, notes 52 and 53.

Hors. Reg. 8   [1] See Pr. 6

Hors. Reg. 9   [1] Ps 19(18):13 is quoted also by Theodore in Am. Letter 3.

Hors. Reg. 11   [1] Cf. Pr. 7.
[2] Pachomius and Horsiesios use this text often. See Pach. Instr. 1: 26; Hors. Instr. 3: 38; Hors. Test. 4.

Hors. Reg. 12   [1] We find other clear allusions to the parable of the prodigal son in S[10] 7 and Paral. 10 and 36.

²God's mercy toward the Publican is recalled also in Paral. 10 and in Theod. Instr. 3: 18.
³Bathsheba is written *Bersabee* in Coptic. The same allusion occurs in Pach. Instr. 1: 26.

Hors. Reg. 13   ¹See Pr. 28.

Hors. Reg. 14   ¹About the Eucharist see Pr. 15-18.
²1 Th 5:23 is quoted in SBo 194; see also below, ¶ 32.

Hors. Reg. 16   ¹These were the sections used in the Office of the Six Sections (or Six Prayers).

Hors. Reg. 17   ¹All the other mentions of the 'cell' in the Life and in the Rule seem to presuppose that each brother had his own private cell. See G¹ 59; SBo 64 (G¹ 69); G¹ 105; G¹ 110; SBo 202 (G¹ 144); Am. Letter 24 and 26; Paral. 1, 7, 27, 29, and 34; Jer. Pref. 4; Pr. 3, 19, 43, 78, 79, 81, 89, 107, 112, 114, 126; Leg. 2. The present text is the only one where the presence of two monks in the same cell seems to be clearly implied (it is dubious that Pr. 88 and 95 should be interpreted in this way). But this passage is so obscure that one is entitled to think that the Coptic text needs to be corrected. If the two monks are in the same cell, why should the first one need to go out and to stay at the door while he is knocking on the mat?

Hors. Reg. 18   ¹This text is obscure. The whole ¶ since the beginning is only one sentence and the manner in which the images are connected does not correspond to our Western logic. We have divided the long Coptic sentence as well as we could.

Hors. Reg. 19   ¹The expression 'the fruits of the Holy Spirit' is very often used by the Pachomians. It means not only the fruits of the Spirit listed by Paul in Ga 5:22-23, but also the virtues of the Beatitudes and all the christian virtues in general. See A. Veilleux, *La liturgie*, pp. 345-347.

Hors. Reg. 20   ¹Cf. Pr. 2 (modesty); Pr. 4 (not to trample underfoot the soaked rushes); and Pr. 7 (not to look at others).

Hors. Reg. 21   ¹This *amen* marks the end of the series of precepts concerning the *synaxis* (*sôouh*).

Hors. Reg. 22   ¹These stewards (*oikonomos*) are the housemasters entrusted with a particular weekly service in the monastery. They are often mentioned in the *Praecepta*, and the *Praecepta et Instituta* seem to be addressed to them.

Hors. Reg. 26   ¹In this lacuna was the end of the rules concerning the kitchen, and a new section began dealing with more general recommendations.

Hors. Reg. 28   ¹Cf. Paral. 21-23. In the Coptic text the superior of the community is called *rôme ntsoouhs* as in the section of the *Praecepta* extant in Coptic.

Hors. Reg. 30   ¹This expression from Gn 14:23 is used in Pach. Instr. 1: 53 and in Hors. Test. 21 to express the idea that the monk should not own anything.

Hors. Reg. 34   ¹'Apa' used without any other name means Pachomius himself.
²'The law of the *Koinonia*'; the same expression recurs again at the beginning of ¶ 51 and in Theod. Instr. 1: 4 and 5. It means the way of life of the *Koinonia* more than a set of rules.

Hors. Reg. 37   ¹This ¶ and the next one seem to refer to the time of harvest.

Hors. Reg. 39   ¹Cf. Pr. 116.

Hors. Reg. 40   ¹The 'board' on which the loaves were placed either before or after the baking. Cf. Pr. 112 and 116.

Hors. Reg. 41   ¹The *cace*—the word corresponds probably to the Greek κάκεις —must probably be assimilated to the κορσενήλιον mentioned in Pr. 37-39 (see Pr. 37, note 1) and in G¹ 111.

Hors. Reg. 42   ¹The *cole* and the *oὔcpŝote* were two types of sweet bread or cake. It is not possible to be more specific.

Hors. Reg. 45   ¹Although the reciting of Scripture was usually done in a low voice (¶ 44 recommends to do it 'not shouting, but softly'), this ¶ shows that it could also be done silently.

Hors. Reg. 48   ¹'If other fathers who have succeeded him have made canons . . .'. This seems to indicate that the author of this text is not Horsiesios but someone writing after him. Since Petronios was sick when he was appointed by Pachomius as his successor and died after a few days, only a successor of Horsiesios and Theodore could speak of 'fathers who have succeeded [Pachomius] and made canons'.
²'If . . . *a man* separates himself . . . let us not allow the brothers . . . to eat with *these* . . .' We respect the passage from singular to plural found in Coptic.

Hors. Reg. 50   ¹There are several other references to the children in the furnace. For example: Pach. Instr. 1: 15 and 25; Theod. Instr. 3: 13 and Hors. Letter 4: 4.

Hors. Reg. 51   ¹This text from Ac 4:32 is quoted also in S¹ 11; Theod. Instr. 3: 23 and Hors. Test. 50. See also SBo 194.

Hors. Reg. 52   ¹This text is quoted often; see SBo 150; G¹ 99; Pach. Instr. 1: 22.

Hors. Reg. 53   ¹Cf. above, ¶ 38. This mention of the 'precepts' (*kôt*) of the *Koinonia* may very well be a reference to the *Praecepta*.
²See another mention of the 'village' in the *Praecepta*: Pr. 90, with note 1.

Hors. Reg. 54   ¹This long series of regulations relative to the baking of bread is less surprising if we remember that the baking was done rarely—even only once a year—and represented therefore an important period of common work.

Hors. Reg. 55   [1]See above, ¶ 35.
     [2]$Pš a$: the divine service—the festival, probably the Eucharist.

Hors. Reg. 56   [1]We find several references to this parable; see: SBo 114; Paral. 41; Am. Letter 14; Pach. Instr. 1: 41; Hors. Instr. 4: 2; Hors. Test. 14 and 20.

Hors. Reg. 57   [1]The meaning of the word *pra$š$* in this context is obscure and uncertain.

Hors. Reg. 58   [1]With this lacuna a new section began, dealing with the care of the animals.

Hors. Reg. 64   [1]This is the end of our fragments. We do not know how long was the text was in its original state.

ABBREVIATIONS
of names of periodicals and series

ADMG	*Annales du Musée Guimet*, Paris.
AnBoll	*Analecta Bollandiana*, Brussels.
BKV	*Bibliothek der Kirchenväter*, Kempten.
BM	*Benediktinische Monatschrift* (later: *Erbe und Auftrag*), Beuron.
ChE	*Chronique d'Egypte*, Brussels.
CSCO	*Corpus scriptorum Christianorum orientalium*, Louvain.
DACL	*Dictionnaire d'archéologie chrétienne et de liturgie*, Paris.
EuA	*Erbe und Auftrag* (formerly *Benediktinische Monatschrift*), Beuron.
GuL	*Geist und Leben. Zeitschrift für Aszese und Mystik*, Würzburg.
HJ	*Historisches Jahrbuch*, Munich-Freiburg.
JEH	*The Journal of Ecclesiastical History*, London.
LTK	*Lexikon für Theologie und Kirche*, Freiburg.
LuM	*Liturgie und Mönchtum. Laacher Hefte*, Maria Laach.
Muséon	*Le Muséon*, Louvain.
NGG	*Nachrichten der Gesellschaft der Wissenschaften zu Göttingen*, Göttingen.
OCP	*Orientalia Christiana Periodica*, Rome.
OGL	*Ons geestelijk leven*.
Orientalia	*Orientalia. Commentarii Periodici Pontificii Instituti Biblici*, Rome.
OstKSt	*Ostkirchliche Studien*, Würzburg.
PG	*Patrologia Graeca* of Migne, Paris.

PL	*Patrologia Latina* of Migne, Paris.
PO	*Patrologia Orientalis*, Paris.
RAM	*Revue d'ascétique et de mystique*, Toulouse.
RBén	*Revue bénédictine*, Maredsous.
RHE	*Revue d'histoire ecclésiastique*, Louvain.
RHR	*Revue de l'histoire des religions*, Paris.
RHS	*Revue d'Histoire de la Spiritualité*, Toulouse.
RMab	*Revue Mabillon*, Ligugé.
SA	*Studia Anselmiana*, Rome.
Sal	*Salesianum*, (Rome) Turin.
StMon	*Studia Monastica*, Montserrat.
TGL	*Tijdschrift voor geestelijk leven*, Nijmegen.
TSK	*Theologische Studien und Kritiken*, (Hamburg) Gotha.
TU	*Texte und Untersuchungen zur Geschichte der altchristlichen Literatur.* Archiv für die griechisch-christlichen Schriftsteller der ersten drei Jahrhunderte, Leipzig-Berlin.
VS	*La Vie Spirituelle*, Paris.
ZDMG	*Zeitschrift der deutschen morgenländischen Gesellschaft*, Leipzig.
ZKT	*Zeitschrift für katholische Theologie*, (Innsbruck) Vienna.

PACHOMIAN BIBLIOGRAPHY

Amand de Mendieta, A. 'Le système cénobitique basilien comparé au système cénobitique pachômien,' *RHR* 152 (1957) 31-80.

Amélineau, E. 'Etude historique sur St. Pachôme et le cénobitisme primitif dans la Haute-Egypte,' *Bulletin de l'Institut d'Egypte*, series 2,7 (1886) 306-309.

Bacht, H. 'Pakhome—der grosse "Adler",' *GuL* 22 (1949) 367-382.

_____ . 'Ein Wort zur Ehrenrettung der ältesten Mönchsregel,' *ZKT* 72 (1950) 350-359.

_____ . 'L'importance de l'idéal monastique de s. Pacôme pour l'histoire du monachisme chrétien,' *RAM* 26 (1950) 308-326.

_____ . 'Heimweh nach der Urkirche. Zur Wesensdeutung des frühchristlichen Mönchtums.' *LuM* 7 (1950) 64-78.

_____ . 'Vom gemeinsamen Leben. Die Bedeutung des christlichen Mönchideals für die Geschichte des christlichen Mönchtums,' *LuM* 11 (1952) 91-110.

_____ . '"Meditatio" in den ältesten Mönchsquellen,' *GuL* 28 (1955) 360-373.

_____ . 'Antonius und Pachomius. Von der Anachorese zum Cönobitentum,' in B. Steidle, *Antonius Magnus Eremita, SA* 38; Rome, 1956 Pp. 66-107.

_____ . 'Studien zum "Liber Orsiesii".'*HJ* 77 (1958) 98-124

_____ . 'Mönchtum und Kirche. Eine Studie zur Spiritualität des Pachomius,' in J. Daniélou and H. Vorgrimler, *Sentire Ecclesiam, Das Bewusstsein von der Kirche als gestaltende Kraft der Frömmigkeit.*Freiburg, 1961. Pp. 113-133.

_____ . 'Pakhôme et ses disciples,' in *Théologie de la vie monastique, Théologie* 49. Paris, 1961. Pp. 39-71.

_____ . 'La loi du "retour aux sources". (De quelques aspects de l'idéal monastique pachômien),' *RMab* 51 (1961) 6-25.

_____ . 'Ein verkanntes Fragment des koptischen Pachomius-Regel,' *Muséon* 75 (1962) 5-18.

_____ . 'Pachomius der Jüngere,' in *LTK*, 7^2 (1962) Col. 1331.

_____ . 'Zur Typologie des koptischen Mönchtums. Pachomius und Evagrius.' In *Christentum am Nil (Internationale Arbeitstagung zur Ausstellung 'koptische Kunst')*. Recklinghausen, 1964. Pp. 142-157.

_____ . 'Vom Umgang mit der Bibel im ältesten Mönchtum,' *Theologie und Philosophie* 41 (1966) 557-566.

_____ . '. . . Vexillum crucis sequi (Horsiesius). Mönchtum als Kreuzesnachfolge,' *Martyria. — Leiturgia — Diakonia. Festschrift für H. Volk, Bischof von Mainz, zum 65. Geburtstag*, Mainz, 1968. Pp. 149-162.

_____ . *Das Vermächtnis des Ursprungs (Studien zum Frühen Mönchtum I)*. Würzburg, 1972.

_____ . 'Agrypnia. Die Motive des Schlafentzugs im frühen Mönchtum,' *Bibliothek — Buch — Geschichte (Kurt Köster zum 65. Geburtstag; herausgegeben von Günther Pflug, Brita Eckert und Heinz Friesenhahn)*. Frankfurt am Main, 1977. Pp. 353-369.

Batlle, C.M. 'La vida religiosa comunitària a l'Egipte del segle IV.' Un nou plantejament des de les bases. *StMon* 12 (1970) 181-194.

Biedermann, H.M. 'Die Regel des Pachomius und die evangelischen Räte,' *OstKSt* 9 (1960) 241-253.

Chitty, D.J. 'Pachomian Sources Reconsidered,' *JEH* 5 (1954) 38-77.

_____ . 'A Note on the Chronology of Pachomian Foundations,' *Studia Patristica*, Vol. II, *TU* 64. Berlin, 1957. Pp. 379-385.

_____ . 'Some Notes, mainly Lexical on the Sources for the Life of Pachomius,' *Studia Patristica*, V, *TU* 80. Berlin, 1962. Pp. 266-269.

_____ . 'Pachomian Sources once more,' *Studia Patristica*, X. Berlin, 1970. Pp. 54-64.

Crum, W.E. *Theological Texts from Coptic Papyri edited with an Appendix upon the Arabic and Coptic Versions of the Life of Pachomius, Anecdota Oxoniensia, Semitic series* 12). Oxford, 1913.

_____ . *Der Papyruscodex saec. VI-VII der Phillipsbibliothek in Cheltenham. Koptische theologische Schriften. Mit einem Beitrag von A. Ehrhard. Schriften der Wissenschaftlichen Gesellschaft in Strassburg* 18. Strasbourg, 1915.

De Clercq, D. 'L'influence de la Règle de saint Pachôme en Occi-
dent,' *Mélanges d'Histoire du Moyen Age dédiés à la mémoire
de Louis Halphen.* Paris, 1951. Pp. 169-176.

Delhougne, H. 'Autorité et participation chez les Pères du cénobitisme,' *RAM* 45 (1969) 369-394; 46 (1970) 3-32.

Deseille, P. *L'esprit du monachisme pachômien, suivi de la traduction française des Pachomiana latina par les moines de
Solesmes, Spiritualité orientale* 2. Bellefontaine, 1968.

Draguet, R. 'Le chapitre de HL sur les Tabennésiotes dérive-t-il
d'une source copte?' *Muséon* 57 (1944) 53-145; 58 (1945) 15-95.

Ehrhard, A. 'Zur literarhistorischen und theologischen Würdigung der Texte,' W.E. Crum, *Der Papyruscodex....* Pp.
129-171. [Concerns the letter of Theophilos to Horsiesios].

Gindele, C. 'Die Schriftlesung im Pachomiuskloster,' *EuA*, 41
(1965) 114-122.

Gnolfo, P. 'Pedagogia Pacomiana,' *Sal* 10 (1948) 569-596.

Gribomont, J. 'Pachomios der Ältere,' *LTK* 7² (1962) Col. 1330-
1331.

Grützmacher, O. *Pachomios und das älteste Klosterleben.* Freiburg, 1896.

Halkin, F. 'Les Vies grecques de S. Pacôme.' *AnBoll* 47 (1929)
376-388.

_____ . 'L'Histoire Lausiaque et les Vies grecques de S. Pacôme,' *AnBoll* 48 (1930) 257-301.

Hedrick, C.W., 'Gnostic Proclivities in the Greek *Life of Pachomius* and the *Sitz im Leben* of the Nag Hammadi Library,'
Novum Testamentum 22 (1980) 78-94.

Hengstenberg, W. 'Pachomiana (mit einem Anhang über die Li-
turgie von Alexandrien),' in A.M. Königer, *Beiträge zur
Geschichte des christlichen Altertums und der Byzantinischen
Literatur. Festgabe Albert Ehrhard.* Bonn and Leipzig, 1922.
Pp. 228-252.

Heussi, K. 'Pachomios,' in Pauly-Wissowa, *Realencyklopädie der
classischen Altertumswissenschaft,* 18 (1942) Col. 2070 ff.

Ladeuze, P. 'Les diverses recensions de la vie de S. Pakhôme et
leurs dépendances mutuelles,' *Muséon* (1897) 148-171; (1898)
145-168; 269-286; 378-395.

_____ . *Etude sur le cénobitisme pakhômien pendant le IVe*

siècle et la première moitié du Ve. Louvain and Paris, 1898; rpt. 1962.

Leclercq, H. 'Pachôme, in *DACL* XIII/1 (1937) Col. 499-510.

Lefort, L.T. 'Théodore de Tabennêsi et la lettre pascale de S. Athanase sur le canon de la Bible,' *Muséon* 29 (1910) 205-216.

_____ . 'Un texte original de la règle de saint Pachôme,' *Comptes rendus de l'Académie des Inscriptions et Belles-Lettres*, 1919. Pp. 341-348.

_____ . 'La Règle de S. Pachôme (étude d'approche),' *Muséon* 34 (1921) 61-70.

_____ . 'La Règle de S. Pachôme (2ᵉ étude d'approche),' *Muséon* 37 (1924) 1-28.

_____ . 'La Règle de S. Pachôme (Nouveaux documents),' *Muséon* 40 (1927) 31-64.

_____ . 'S. Pachôme et Amen-em-ope,' *Muséon* 49 (1927) 65-74.

_____ . 'Littérature bohaïrique,' *Muséon* 44 (1931) 115-135.

_____ . 'S. Athanase écrivain copte,' *Muséon* 46 (1933) 1-33.

_____ . 'La Règle de S. Pachôme (nouveaux fragments coptes),' *Muséon* 48 (1935) 75-80.

_____ . 'Les premiers monastères pachômiens. Exploration topographique,' *Muséon* 52 (1939) 379-408.

_____ . 'Les sources coptes pachômiennes,' *Muséon* 67 (1954) 217-229.

Lehmann, K. 'Die Entstehung der Freiheitsstrafe in den Klöstern des heiligen Pachomius,' *Z. d. Savigny-Stift. f. Rechtsgesch., Kan. Abt.* 37 (1951). Pp. 1-94.

Leipoldt, J. 'Pachom,' *Bulletin de la Société de l'Archéologie Copte* 16 (1961-62) 191-229.

_____ . 'Pachom,' *Koptologische Studien in der DDR. Wissenschaftliche Zeitschrift der Martin-Luther-Universität Halle-Wittenberg.* Sonderheft 1965, 236-249.

Levis, A. 'Koinonia e comunidade no monacato pacomiano,' *Claretianum* 15 (1975) 269-327.

Lozano, J.M. 'La comunità pacomiana: dalla comunione all'istituzione,' *Claretianum* 15 (1975) 237-267.

Monachino, V. 'Pacomio,' *Enciclopedia Cattolica* 9 (1952) Col. 511-514.

Morson, J. 'The sixteenth Centenary of St. Pachomius.' *Pax* 38 (1948) 65-74

Orlandi, T. 'Nuovi Testi copti pacomiani,' *Commandements du Seigneur et Libération évangélique, SA* 70. Rome, 1977. Pp. 241-243.

Peeters, P. 'A propos de la Vie sahidique de S. Pacôme.' *AnBoll* 52 (1934) 286-320.

_____. 'L'édition critique des Vies coptes de S. Pacôme par le Prof. Lefort,' *Muséon* 59 (1946) 17-34.

_____. 'Le dossier copte de S. Pacôme et ses rapports avec la tradition grecque,' *AnBoll* 64 (1946) 258-277.

_____. 'L'oeuvre de L.T. Lefort,' *Muséon* 59 (1946) 41-62.

_____. 'Un feuillet d'une Vie arabe de saint Pacôme,' *Muséon* 59 (1946) 399-412.

Pietschmann, R. 'Theodorus Tabennesiota und die sahidische Übersetzung des Osterfestbriefs des Athanasius vom Jahre 367,; *NGG* (1889) I, 87-104.

Quecke, H. 'Ein Pachomiuszitat bei Schenute,' *Probleme der koptischen Literatur. Wissenschaftliche Beiträge der Univ. Halle-Wittenberg.* 1968. Pp. 155-171.

_____. 'Briefe Pachoms in koptischer Sprache. Neue deutsche Übersetzung,' *Zetesis (Festschrift E. de Strycker).* Antwerp and Utrecht, 1973. Pp. 655-664.

_____. 'Ein neues Fragment der Pachombriefe in koptischer Sprache,' *Orientalia* 43 (1974) 66-82.

_____. 'Die Briefe Pachoms,' *ZDMG*, Supp. II (1974) 96-108.

_____. 'Die griechische Übersetzung der Pachombriefe,' *Studia Papyrologica* 15 (1976) 153-159.

_____. 'Eine Handvoll Pachomianischer Texte,' *ZDMG*, Supp. III, 1 (1977) 221-229.

Revillout, E. 'Funérailles des moines égyptiens au temps de Saint Antoine et de Saint Pacome,' *Académie Delphinale*, Bull. s. 2,1 (1856-60) 374-386.

Řežáč, I. 'De forma unionis monasteriorum Sancti Pachomii,' *OCP* 23 (1957) 381-414.

Ruppert, F. *Das Pachomianische Mönchtum und die Anfänge klösterlichen Gehorsams. Münsterschwarzacher Studien* 20. Münsterschwarzach, 1971.

_____ . 'Arbeit und geistliches Leben im pachomianischen Mönchtum,' *OstKSt* 24 (1975) 3-14.

Samir, K. 'Témoins arabes de la catéchèse de Pachôme "A propos d'un moine rancunier". (CPG 2354.1),' *OCP* 42 (1976) 494-508.

Schiwietz, S. 'Geschichte und Organisation der pachomianischen Klöster im vierten Jahrhundert,' *Archiv für kathol. Kirchenrecht* 81 (1901) 461-490; 630-649.

Steidle, B. '"Der Zweite" im Pachomiuskloster,' *BM* 24 (1948) 97-104; 174-179.

_____ , and O. Schuler, 'Der "Obern-Spiegel" im "Testament" des Abtes Horsiesi († nach 387),' *EuA* 43 (1967) 22-38.

Steidle, B. 'Der Osterbrief unseres Vaters Theodor an alle Klöster. Zur 1600. Wiederkehr des Todesjahres (368-1968),' *EuA* 44 (1968) 104-119.

_____ . 'Der heilige Abt. Theodor von Tabennesi. Zur 1600. Wiederkehr des Todesjahres (368-1968),' *EuA* 44 (1968) 91-103.

Tamburrino, P. 'Koinonia. Die Beziehung "Monasterium"-"Kirche" im frühen pachomianischen Mönchtum,' *EuA* 43 (1967) 5-21.

_____ . 'Bibbia e vita spirituale negli scritti di Orsiesi,' in C. Vagaggini, ed., *Bibbia e spiritualità, Biblioteca di cultura religiosa* 79. Rome, 1967. Pp. 85-119.

_____ . 'Les saints de l'Ancien Testament dans la Ière catéchèse de saint Pachôme,' *Melto* 4 (1968) 33-44.

_____ . 'Die Heiligen des Alten Testaments in der 1. Katechese des heiligen Pachomius,' *EuA* 45 (1969) 50-56.

Van Cranenburgh, H. 'La "Regula Angeli" dans la Vie latine de saint Pachôme,' *Muséon* 76 (1963) 165-194.

_____ . 'Nieuw licht op de oudste kloostercongregatie van de christenheid: de instelling van Sint-Pachomius,' *TGL* 19 (1963) 581-605; 665-690; and 20 (1964) 41-54.

_____ . 'Actualiteitswaarde van het pachomiaanse kloosterleven,' *TGL* 24 (1968) 233-257.

_____ . 'Valeur actuelle de la vie religieuse pachômienne,' *VS* 120 (1969) 400-422.

_____ . 'Etude comparative des récits anciens de la vocation de saint Pachôme,' *RBén* 82 (1972) 280-308.

_____ . 'Les noms de Dieu dans la prière de Pachôme et de ses frères,' *RHS* 52 (1976) 193-212.

Van Molle, M.M. 'Essai de classement chronologique des premières règles de vie commune en chrétienté,' *VS Supplément* 84 (1968) 108-127.

_____ . "Confrontation entre les Règles et la littérature pachômienne postérieure,' *VS Supplément* 86 (1968) 394-424.

_____ . 'Aux origines de la vie communautaire chrétienne, quelques équivoques déterminantes pour l'avenir,' *VS Supplément* 88 (1969) 101-121.

_____ . 'Vie commune et obéissance d'après les intuitions premières de Pachôme et Basile,' *VS Supplément* 93 (1970) 196-225.

Van Rijen, A. 'Een regel van Pachomius,' *Ons geestelijk leven* 48 (1971) 334-344.

Veilleux, A. 'Le problème des Vies de Saint Pachôme,' *RAM* 42 (1966) 287-305.

_____ . *La liturgie dans le cénobitisme pachômien au quatrième siècle*, SA 57. Rome, 1968.

_____ . 'San Pacomio, abate di Tabennesi,' *Bibliotheca Sanctorum*, Vol. X (1968) Col. 10-20.

_____ . 'Pacomio il Giovane,' *Ibidem*, Col. 9-10.

_____ . 'Teodoro di Tabennesi,' *Ibidem* Vol. XII (1969) Col. 270-272.

_____ . 'Holy Scripture in the Pachomian Koinonia,' *Monastic Studies* 10 (1974) 143-153.

Vergote, J. 'L'oeuvre de L.T. Lefort,' *Muséon* 59 (1946) 41-62.

_____ . 'En lisant "Les Vies de saint Pakhôme",' *ChE* 22 (1947) 389-415.

_____ . 'La valeur des Vies grecques et coptes de S. Pakhôme,' *Orientalia Lovaniensia Periodica* 8 (1977) 175-186.

Vogüé, A. de. 'Points de contact du chapitre XXXII de l'Histoire Lausiaque avec les écrits d'Horsièse,' *StMon* 13 (1971) 291-294.

_____ . 'Les pièces latines du dossier pachômien,' *RHE* 67 (1972) 26-67.

_____ . 'L'Anecdote pachômienne du "Vaticanus graecus" 2091. Son origine et ses sources,' *RSH* 49 (1973) 401-419.

_____ . 'Le nom du Supérieur de monastère dans la Règle pachômienne. A propos d'un ouvrage récent,' *StMon* 15 (1973) 17-22.

_____ . 'La vie arabe de saint Pachôme et ses deux sources présumées,' *AnBoll* 91 (1973) 379-390.

_____ . 'Saint Pachôme et son oeuvre d'après plusieurs études récentes,' *RHE* 69 (1974) 425-453.

_____ . 'Sur la terminologie de la pénitence dans la Règle de saint Pachôme', *StMon* 17 (1975) 7-12.

_____ . 'Les noms de la porte et du portier dans la Règle de Pachôme,' *StMon* 17 (1975) 233-235.

Wirszycka, E. 'Les terres de la congrégation pachômienne dans une liste de payements pour les apora,' *Le monde grec. Pensée, littérature, histoire, documents. Hommage à Claire Préaux.* Brussels, 1975. Pp. 625-636.

Zananiri, G. 'Saint Pacôme et le monachisme.' *Revue Confér. Franc. Or.* Cairo, 1948, 178-185.

* * * *Pachomiana. Commémoration du XVIème Centenaire de St Pacôme l'Egyptien* (348-1948). (*Publications du Centre d'Etudes Orientales de la Custodie Franciscaine de Terre-Sainte, Coptica 3*). Cairo, 1955.

SOURCES
Editions and Translations

A: *EDITIONS*

Coptic

Lefort, L.T. *S. Pachomii vita bohairice scripta, CSCO* 89. Louvain, 1925; rpt. 1953.

——————. *S. Pachomii vitae sahidice scriptae, CSCO* 99/100. Louvain, 1933/34; rpt. 1952.

——————. 'Glanures pachômiennes,' *Muséon* 54 (1941) 111-138. [S[19], S[20], and fragments of S[3], S[3c], and S[4]].

——————. 'Vies de S. Pachôme (Nouveaux fragments),' *Muséon* 49 (1936) 219-230. [Fragments of S[2]].

——————. *Oeuvres de s. Pachôme et de ses disciples, CSCO* 159. Louvain, 1956.

Quecke, Hans. *Die Briefe Pachoms. Griechischer Text der Handschrift W. 145 der Chester Beatty Library eingeleitet und herausgegeben von Hans Quecke. Anhang: Die koptischen Fragmente und Zitate der Pachombriefe. Textus Patristici et Liturgici* 11. Regensburg, 1975. [Coptic texts: pp. 111-118].

——————. 'Ein Brief von einem Nachfolger Pachoms,' *Orientalia* 44 (1975) 426-433.

Greek

Halkin, F. *Sancti Pachomii Vitae Graecae, Subsidia hagiographica* 19. Brussels, 1932.

——————. 'La vie abrégée de saint Pachôme dans le ménologe impérial (BHG 1401b),' *AnBoll* 96 (1978) 367-381.

——————. 'Une vie inédite de saint Pachôme,' *AnBoll* 97 (1979) 5-55; 241-287.

Bousquet, J., and F. Nau. *Histoire de saint Pacôme (Une rédaction inédite des Ascetica) Texte grec des manuscrits Paris 881 et Chartres 1754 avec une traduction de la version syriaque et une analyse du manuscrit de Paris Suppl. grec. 480, PO* IV, 5. Paris, 1907.

Lefort, L.T. 'La Règle de S. Pachôme (2ᵉ étude d'approche),' *Muséon* 37 (1924) 1-28. [Text of the Greek *Excerpta* of the Rule of Pachomius. Rpt. in A. Boon, *Pachomiana latina...*, *p. 169-182*].

Draguet, R. 'Un morceau grec inédit des Vies de Pachôme apparié à un texte   d'Evagre en partie inconnu,' *Muséon* 70 (1957) 267-306.

_____ . 'Un Paralipomenon pachômien inconnu dans le Karakallou 251,' *Mélanges Eugène Tisserant*, Vol. II, *ST* 232. Vatican City, 1964. Pp. 55-61.

Quecke, Hans. *Die Briefe Pachoms. Griechischer Text der Handschrift W. 145 der Chester Beatty Library eingeleitet und herausgegeben von Hans Quecke. Anhang: Die koptischen Fragmente und Zitate der Pachombriefe, Textus Patristici et Liturgici* 11. Regensburg, 1975.

Latin

Boon, A. *Pachomiana latina. Règle et épîtres de s. Pachôme, épître de s. Théodore et 'Liber' de s. Orsiesius. Texte latin de s. Jérôme, Bibliothèque de la Revue d'histoire ecclésiastique* 7. Louvain, 1932.

Van Cranenburg, H. *La vie latine de saint Pachôme traduite du grec par Denys le Petit, édition critique, Subsidia hagiographica* 46. Brussels, 1969.

Arabic

Amélineau, A. *Monuments pour servir à l'histoire de l'Egypte chrétienne au IVe siècle.—Histoire de Saint Pakhôme et de ses communautés. Documents coptes et arabe inédits, publiés et traduits par E. Amélineau, ADMG* 17, 2 Vol. Paris 1889. [Arabic text: Vol. II, pp. 337-711].

Syriac

Budge, E.A.W. *The Book of Paradise*. London, 1904. [Syriac version of the *Paralipomena*, which Budge erroneously calls the Rule of Pachomius].

Ethiopic

Dillmann, A. *Chrestomatia Aethiopica*. Leipzig, 1866; 1941[2], pp. 57-69. [Ethiopic version of the Rules of Pachomius].

Löfgren, O. 'Zur Textkritik der äthiopischen Pachomiusregeln I, II,' *Le Monde Oriental* 30 (1936) 171-187. [Critical *apparatus* to be added to Dillman's edition].

Arras, V. *Collectio Monastica*, CSCO 238. Louvain, 1963. Pp.
141-143. [Ethiopic translation of the Greek *Excerpta* of the
Rule of Pachomius].

B: *TRANSLATIONS*

From Coptic

Lefort, L.T. *Sancti Pachomii vita bohairice scripta*, CSCO
107. Louvain, 1936. [Latin translation].

_____ . *Les Vies coptes de Saint Pachôme et de ses premiers
successeurs, Bibliothèque du Muséon* 16. Louvain 1943; rpt.
1966.

_____ . *Oeuvres de s. Pachôme et de ses disciples*, CSCO
160. Louvain 1956.

Draguet, R. *Les Pères du désert*. Paris, 1949. Pp. 87-126.
[French translation of a Life of Pachomius reconstructed
from the Coptic fragments].

Quecke, H. 'Briefe Pachoms in koptischer Sprache. Neue
deutsche Übersetzung,' *Zetesis. Festschrift E. de Strycker.*
Antwerp/Utrecht, 1973. Pp. 655-664.

Vögué, A. de. 'Epîtres inédites d'Horsièse et de Théodore,'
Commandements du Seigneur et Libération évangélique, SA
70. Rome, 1977. Pp. 244-257.

From Greek

Athanassakis, A.N. *The Life of Pachomius (Vita Prima Graeca). Translated by Apostolos N. Athanassakis. Introduction
by Birger A. Pearson.* Missoula, MT, 1975.

Festugière, A.-J. *Les Moines d'Orient, T. IV/2: La première
Vie grecque de saint Pachôme. Introduction critique et traduction.* Paris, 1965.

Mertel, H. *Leben des hl. Pachomius, BKV* 31. Kempten, 1917.
[German translation of the second Greek Life and of a few
fragments of the fourth Greek Life].

From Latin

D'Andilly, A. *Les Vies des Saints Pères des Déserts*, Lyon, 1663.
Pp. 175-276. [French translation of the Latin Life].

Bacht, H. *Das Vermächtnis des Ursprungs, Studien zum Frühen Mönchtum* I. Würzburg, 1972. [German translation of the *Liber Orsiesii*].

De Elizalde, M. *Libro de nuestro Padre San Orsisio. Introducción, traducción y notas de Martín de Elizalde. Cuadernos monásticos*, Nos. 4-5 (1967) 173-244.

Steidle, B. and O. Schuler. 'Der "Obern-Spiegel" im "Testament" des Abtes Horsiesi († nach 387),' *EuA* 43 (1967) 5-21. [German translation of the chapters 7-18 and 39-40 of the *Liber Orsiesii*].

From Arabic

Amélineau, E. *Monuments pour servir.* . . . [French translation under the Arabic text].

From Syriac

Budge, E.A.W. *The Book of Paradise.* London, 1904. [English translation of the Syriac version of the *Paralipomena*]. Rpt. in *The Paradise or Garden of the Holy Fathers.* London, 1907, Vol. 1, pp. 283-315; and again in *Stories of the Holy Fathers*, Oxford, 1934, pp. 373-416.

Nau, F., in Bousquet J. and F. Nau, *Histoire de saint Pacôme* (Cited above). [A French translation of the Syriac version of the *Paralipomena* is given in front of the text of the sixth Greek Life].

From Ethiopic

Arras, V. *Collectio Monastica, CSCO* 239. Louvain, 1963. Pp. 104-105. [Latin translation of the Ethiopic version of the Greek Excerpta of the Rule.].

Basset, R. *Les apocryphes éthiopiens traduits en français*, fasc. 8. Paris, 1896. Pp. 28-40. [Translation of the Ethiopic Rules].

König, E. 'Die Regeln des Pachomius', *TSK* 51 (1878) 328-332.

Löfgren, O. 'Pakomius' etiopiska klosterregler. I svensk tokning.' *Kyrkohistorisk Årsskrift* 48 (1948) 163-184. [Swedish translation].

Schodde, G.H. 'The Rules of Pachomius translated from the Ethiopic,' *Presbyterian Review* 6 (1885) 678-689.

SIGLA

Ag	Arabic Life in Göttingen Ms.116.
Am	Arabic Life published by E. Amélineau.
Am. Letter	Letter of Bishop Ammon (*Epistula Ammonis*).
Apoph.	*Apophthegmata Patrum.*
Av	Arabic Life in Vatican Ms. 172.
Bo	Bohairic Life.
Den.	Latin Life translated by Denys (*Dionysius Exiguus*).
Draguet Fragm.	Fragment published by R. Draguet.
G^1, G^2, etc.	First Greek Life, Second Greek Life, etc.
H.L.	Lausiac History of Palladius (*Historia Lausiaca*).
H.M.A.	History of the Monks in Egypt (*Historia monachorum in Aegypto*).
Hors. Fragm.	Fragments from Horsiesios.
Hors. Instr.	Instruction of Horsiesios.
Hors. Letter	Letter of Horsiesios.
Hors. Reg.	Regulations of Horsiesios.
Hors. Test.	Testament of Horsiesios (*Liber Orsiesii*).
Inst.	Institutes (*Praecepta et Instituta*).
Jer. Pref.	Jerome's Preface to the *Pachomiana Latina.*
Jud.	Judgements (*Praecepta atque Judicia*).
Leg.	Laws (*Praecepta ac Leges*).
Pach. Fragm.	Fragments from Pachomius.
Pach. Instr.	Instruction of Pachomius.
Pach. Letter	Letter of Pachomius.
Paral.	*Paralipomena*

Pr.	Precepts (*Praecepta*).
S¹, S², etc.	First Sahidic Life, Second Sahidic Life, etc.
SBo	Recension of the Life represented by the group Bo, Av, S⁴, S⁵, S⁶, S⁷, etc.
Theod. Fragm.	Fragments from Theodore.
Theod. Instr.	Instruction of Theodore.
Theod. Letter	Letter of Theodore.
VB	L.-T. Lefort, S. *Pachomii vita bohairice scripta.*
VC	L.-T. Lefort, *Les vies coptes de saint Pachôme et de ses premiers successeurs.*
Vit. Ant.	Life of Antony by Athanasius (*Vita Antonii*).
VS	L.-T. Lefort, S. *Pachomii vitae sahidice scriptae.*